A Rainbow Book

WorldTrek

A Family Odyssey

RUSSELL AND CARLA FISHER

Rainbow Books, Inc.
FLORIDA

Library of Congress Cataloging-in-Publication Data

Fisher, Russell, 1950-
  Worldtrek : a family odyssey / Russell and Carla Fisher. — 1st ed.
      p. cm.
  Includes index.
  ISBN 1-56825-104-1 (trade softcover : alk. paper)
1. Fisher, Russell, 1950—Travel. 2. Fisher, Carla, 1950—Travel. 3. Fisher family—
Travel. 4. Voyages around the world. I. Fisher, Carla, 1950- II. Title.
  G440.F543F57 2006
  910.4'1—dc22
  [B]

                                                                          2006026143

WorldTrek — A Family Odyssey © 2007 by Russell and Carla Fisher
ISBN-10: 1-56825-104-1
ISBN-13: 978-1-56825-104-2

Published by
Rainbow Books, Inc., P. O. Box 430, Highland City, FL 33846-0430

Editorial Offices and Wholesale/Distributor Orders
Telephone: (863) 648-4420 • Email: RBIbooks@aol.com
www.RainbowBooksInc.com

Authors' Website: www.WorldTrekOnline.com

Individuals' Orders
Toll-free Telephone (800) 431-1579 • www.AllBookStores.com

Ⓨ The paper used in this publication meets the minimum requirements of the
American National Standard for Information Sciences—Permanence of Paper
for Printed Library Materials, ANSI Z39.48-1984.

First Edition 2007
13 12 11 10 09 08 07   7 6 5 4 3 2 1

Printed in the United States of America.

Dedication

First and foremost to our daughters, Lesley and Andrea, travel-wise beyond their years.

Also to our parents, Norma and Lloyd Houston, Jane and Stephen Fisher, and all the intrepid travelers who regularly load the family station wagon and set out to educate their children by sharing in the discovery of unfamiliar places and cultures, both near and far.

And finally to Tom, Mary and Rebecca Nesbitt, the crew of the *Carpe Diem*, who showed us that our beliefs could be turned into action.

Contents

Acknowledgments

We would like to acknowledge the efforts of Diane Byrne, Linda Harrington, Stephanie Wiegand, Cheryl Frey, Kim Harden, and Jay Potter; they read and critiqued the manuscript for this book. Their helpful suggestions made our work easier.

Making the Pitch

LOOKING BACK FROM THE VANTAGE POINT of having returned home from our around-the-world trek, I remember with clarity how it all began on a rainy Sunday morning well over a year before our departure. My wife Carla and I were sitting in bed, reading and having a cup of coffee. The house was quiet. Our two girls were asleep, trying to recover from the ravages of a Friday night sleepover.

I said to Carla, "You know we've often talked about taking a big trip some day, something truly life changing, something the girls will carry with them for the rest of their lives."

Carla sipped her coffee and waited for me to go on. She could tell that the caffeine had begun to take effect and my slightly squirmy demeanor meant I was about to hatch some scheme.

"Do you remember when we were in college? We wanted to do something different with our lives? Like all 22-year-olds, we honestly believed the only thing that held people back was the unwillingness to imagine, to put conventional commitments aside for a year and experience life. I've been thinking about taking a truly big trip, something worthy of a lifetime — like going around the world. And honestly, Carla, I can't come up with a good reason not to. The girls are at the perfect age, old enough to remember it but still young enough to tolerate being stuck with us for a whole year."

I paused for a minute, ready to make my last point and let the subject drop for a week or two. "I've always wanted to see the world. We could wait until the girls are out of school, but then they'll have their own lives to lead. Besides," I concluded, "I can't imagine who I would rather share a truly great adventure with than you and the girls."

So there it was. The seeds were planted. Now, like any good steward, I would see how the germination process went. I didn't think it would require any real selling of the idea to Carla. I figured she would leave on a moments notice. In reality, I was actually looking for her input.

Carla nodded and said, "It's a thought, Russ," and continued reading the morning newspaper.

We let things drift along for a couple of weeks, discussing it on and off, but she didn't express any serious reservations. It seemed the moment had arrived to bring it up to the girls. So, at the dinner table one Sunday evening, I said, "Girls, what would you think if we packed everything up and spent a year traveling around the world?"

Looking up from her plate, Andrea asked, "What would we do about school? Would we just miss a grade, lose a year? I want to stay up with my friends." With that, she went back to sawing her pork chop into small cubes.

"Well, that would be sort of up to you two," I said. "If you decided you wanted to take the time to study, we could get home school materials to do on the trip. It would take a fair amount of discipline, but I'm sure you could do it."

Lesley, who was completely absorbed in sculpting her mashed potatoes, paused and said, "What will we do with the house and all of our stuff? And what about your job?"

"Those are all just things we would have to deal with," I admitted. "We won't be able to leave any loose ends. So everything we do in our daily lives will have to be put in some kind of order. Sort of like pushing the PAUSE button on the VCR."

Silence ensued. Lesley went back to her artistic endeavors. Not entirely satisfied with her creation, she gave passing consideration to actually eating the potatoes. Andrea, with no apparent emotion, put her knife down, lifted her fork and started clearing her plate of all things edible.

"Mom and I are actually serious about this," I said, trying to get some dialog going. "We want you to ask whatever questions you have, voice your feelings and concerns. We need to talk about it every week or so as ideas develop. If something comes up where we just can't do it, well, we will simply have to put the idea to rest and go on with our lives. But I think we should make a serious run at it. Also, there is a fun side you need to think about. Let's start by each making a list of the places you feel you just absolutely must see on the trip.

"Personally," I offered, "ever since I first took geography in the fourth grade, I have wanted to see the Coliseum in Rome and one of the famous aqueducts. And I can still see in my mind's eye those images from a *National Geographic* article on Pompeii back in the 1960s."

We talked about Mt. Vesuvius and Pompeii for a few minutes, the ghostly remains and plaster casts of the people who were entombed in the hot volcanic ash.

"I think I want to see Big Ben in London, and the pyramids and the sphinx." Here was the first sign that Lesley had actually taken in enough of the idea to begin to work with it.

"How about the Taj Mahal?" I asked. "You just couldn't go around the world and not see the Taj Mahal."

Carla cast a vote in favor of more northern destinations. "I want to see the fjords in Norway and cross the Arctic Circle. We ought to go to Moscow. Our relationship with Russia has come so far in the last ten years and their culture is so rich but still so foreign to us."

"Maybe we could take the Trans-Siberian railroad," I suggested. "I've always liked the name Vladivostok, Russia's most important Pacific port."

"How about China, the Great Wall?" Andrea now suggested. "My science teacher said the Great Wall of China is one of the few man-made things the astronauts could see from the Space Shuttle. We've got to see the Great Wall."

And so it went, flights of imagination punctuated by doses of reality. We encouraged the girls to voice their fears and concerns. There was, however, an element of inevitability.

Lesley succinctly aired her feelings, saying, "So, if you guys decide to go, then we are going to go. Nothing Andrea or I say would change that."

"Well, that's not entirely true," I responded, "but it would have to be something big to make us decide not to do it. Let's just keep talking about it every week or so or whenever you have something you want to say, and we'll see how it develops."

That's how it all began. Each of us went about his or her daily life and began to fancy places we wanted to go while mulling over the risks and challenges we would be facing.

We weren't rank novices when it came to traveling. Carla and I had taken a month off in 1984 and traveled around England, Scotland and Ireland. Other destinations since the advent of children were Mexico, Costa Rica, Hawaii, Puerto Rico, Spain, and in the United States —

from the Everglades to the Boundary Waters, from the Great Smoky Mountains to the Canyonlands. Traveling was something with which we were all familiar. But a year of trekking around the world was a different kettle of fish.

The next year involved great introspection. No, this wasn't a mid-life crisis or anything urgent; neither was I feeling particularly morose, worrying about growing old or dying any time soon. I felt I was only dealing with the facts; time was not standing still, the girls were growing up, and Carla and I would begin to face the inevitable challenges of being fifty and hopefully even older than that.

Taking a Year Off

No matter what high-minded justifications we might give for severing ties with everything familiar, the primary reason to take the trip was simple. It was an adventure!

As people go through life they tend to accumulate either things or experiences. Carla and I knew on which end of that scale we fell. That being the case, we could conceive of no greater gift to our children than the experience of a trip around the world.

Sitting on the sidelines of the soccer field on a Saturday morning with the other parents, you probably couldn't pick us out of the crowd. Our life style would probably be described as modest by American standards. While we are not hermits or ascetics, we avoided rolling credit card debt and too many electronic gadgets. Like other households with two kids, we had our TV and VCR, a computer and two cars, and even a cat. The fact is, we didn't actually choose the cat. He sort of moved in on us.

Our two children were entering their teenage years and that was the deciding factor for the timing of the trip. As parents, there was the desire to give them something unique. Education has the longest lasting effect. In a single sentence, professor and author Joseph Novak captured it best:

"Education should lead to a constructive change in a person's ability to cope with experience." (Novak, 1998)[1]

---

[1]Joseph D. Novak, *Learning, Creating and Using Knowledge*, Lawrence Erlbaum Associates, Inc., Mahwah, New Jersey, 1998 (ISBN 0-8058-2626-2)

And we hoped the trip would do just that.

Our family odyssey lasted 376 days, departing Houston, Texas, on June 12, 2001, and returning on June 22, 2002. During that time we covered over 50,500 miles and visited 20 countries. For much of the trip we used public transportation — trains, buses and ferries. In a few places we rented a car, relying on commercial airlines for the big leaps. Our two daughters Andrea and Lesley were 12 and 13 when we departed, and with the aid of some excellent prepackaged math and English language curricula, they received the year's education on the road.

We had two audiences in mind when we first conceived this book. The first and probably largest are those people who want to know what it is like to travel around the world as a family. The second are those who think they might actually like to do something similar to what we did. For them we provide some planning and budgeting details in the two appendices at the end of the book, information we would have liked before starting out.

The Characters

Traveling is not just about trains and boats, plans and budgets. It is about people and experiences.

Andrea, fifteen months junior to Lesley, is our sports enthusiast. Soccer, roller blading, running and general socializing are her passions in life. She is disposed to action and is less likely to spend an afternoon in her room reading. Harry Potter only captured her attention for the first installment. She had played the piano since she was four and a half.

Lesley, as is true with both her parents, is slightly built. She is a quiet young lady with a musical laugh and a gentle demeanor. Most of her first six or seven years were spent up in the mimosa tree in our front yard. She has a passion for all things living and has inherited Carla's powers of observation. It doesn't take much encouragement to get her to read a book as long as it has something to do with dragons, wizards or an occasional Agatha Christie mystery. Lesley plays trumpet in the school band.

Carla tends to take a more considered, less verbal approach to life. She will stay up well into the night reading travel guides as though they were the latest best-selling thriller. Fortunately, for everyone else, she has an innate sense of direction that is almost infallible. During our journey, this gift was put to the test on a daily basis.

Finally, I am the primary voice of this book — Russ. I am the extrovert of the confederation and would prefer sharing a conversation over a cup of coffee to reading a novel. Slim build, physically active, gregarious, I am better at driving than navigating and will always stop to ask directions — it is, after all, an opportunity to talk with someone!

As a family, we have, within limits, encouraged an open communication and free exchange of ideas with our children. That style of family communication is not universally accepted throughout the world and needs to be tempered in some of the social settings that have more rigidly defined roles. Generally, the girls were pretty good at sensing when Western teenage behavior was inappropriate.

What We Hoped to Accomplish

The primary objective of the trip was to go around the world, crossing all 360 lines of longitude and the equator. In large measure the idea that the trip was an educational experience for all of us gave purpose and helped sustain us for the duration. The three essential qualities we hoped to develop in our girls were self-reliance, compassion and persistence. Acting as parents, traveling companions, teachers and mentors, we hoped for a family bond built on a year of shared experience.

We sincerely enjoyed writing this book. Each time a section was added, edited or revised, it was an opportunity for us to relive the experiences we had and firmly fix them in our memories. However, we will gain the ultimate satisfaction, if just one family is inspired by our book to take the trip of a lifetime, a trip that can change lives for the better.

Getting Our Ducks in a Row

As the idea took root, Carla became a regular in the travel section of the local library, bringing home armloads of dog-eared guidebooks on every country that had potential and was not in the midst of civil war, famine or plague. Travel classics filled Carla's office and flowed onto the dining room table. I studied Norway, Germany, and Greece, while Carla took on Russia, France and the Baltic countries. Then, there were Italy, India, Egypt and China with which to contend. Lesley and Andrea remained pretty much focused on school, sports, music lessons and being kids.

Planning was one thing Carla and I were not afraid to do. The list of details to be resolved was mind numbing — everything from figuring out what to do with our cat to our credit cards, insurance, and a leasing agent for our house. We used project management software to input all the tasks and organize them in time relative to each other, making sure no details fell through the cracks. We assigned tasks to each other and periodically updated the list. By printing out the task lists every few weeks, we felt the trip grow nearer, as we understood what had been accomplished and what still needed to be done.

Bi-weekly meetings around the dining room table on Sunday nights gave us all a chance to exchange ideas, ask questions and update everyone as to the things we had accomplished in the previous two weeks. Carla and I tried to respond to any questions from the girls but found that we just didn't have answers to all the questions about where we would stay, what kinds of food we would eat or how we would get around. The more we learned and planned, the more apparent it became that there was going to be uncertainty along the way, since much of the trip would have to be planned on the fly.

Reading everything we could get our hands on, we realized some of our fantasies were probably not practical. But we also began to get an idea of how we wanted to travel and the time factor involved. With all that we wanted to do, a year seemed barely enough; we resolved to spend a month in each country and plan as many one-week stays in cottages and apartments as possible to avoid travel fatigue.

Mindful of the changing landscape on the international front, the *Economist* became a regular read for us as we went on with our planning. The slightly different slant and coverage of international news felt increasingly relevant. It was important to keep abreast of developments in the countries and regions we planned to visit. In September 2000 things seemed to be heating up in the Middle East. We just hoped the political situation would hold together. Our plans to visit friends in Jakarta, Indonesia, started to look increasingly tenuous as time for departure approached, but later in the trip a final decision could be made.

In the fall of 2000 it was time to get serious about planning. We got our wall map with all the pins in it and the laminated twelve-month planner, then spread them out on the living room floor. With a marker I made the first broad sweeps across Ireland, England, up into Scandinavia over to St. Petersburg, then Moscow. Carla took it through Prague, then to Germany, France and Italy. We drew time bars for each country on the planner and started negotiating among ourselves over times, distances and sites each person wanted to see. We knew one thing for sure: We wanted to be headed in a southerly direction by September

By November 2000 Carla had chosen an airline ticket consolidator out of San Francisco with whom she felt comfortable. A consolidator will arrange very low cost tickets for a given itinerary using any number or combination of airlines, most of them not U.S. based. Using a consolidator requires some flexibility on departure dates and arrival times. We usually gave him a window of a week or so to get us from one place to another. He would look at all the options and within a couple of weeks get back to us with a proposed schedule. Planning to set out in June, we were in the position of only being able to secure tickets through the end of the year. This boiled down to two flights, one from Houston to London and the other from Moscow to Prague. The rest of the arrangements we would have to make while on the trip. By early January 2001, Carla was spending twelve hours a day at the computer, getting information and working out the details

A Matter of Personal Preference

To put things in their proper perspective a word about traveling-style is in order. Clearly every individual, and more so every family, develops a style of travel. Traveling style has to do with expectations that are part of the decision-making process when you look for accommodations or a place to eat. The kinds of activities you hope to engage in and the types of places you hope to see begin to define your traveling style.

To a great degree it depends on what you are accustomed to and what you choose to compare it to. As a family, we had spent a fair amount of time camping. Anyone who has ever attempted to take a shower in a state park after sleeping on hard, rocky ground would be well equipped for the vagaries of long term family travel. Actually, our accommodations were never quite that primitive, but on our global adventure I tried to relax my standards, especially since we were on a budget.

Travel style also relates to planning. How much do you want to "wing it?" Winging it is more thrilling and requires many quick decisions. So, if you are an adrenaline addict, maybe you can just skim the sections on planning. Taking that approach, more of the time on your trip will be spent working out basic details of where you are going to stay and how you are going to get to your next destination. As you read through these pages, you will begin to understand our travel style as a starting point for gauging your own.

Languages

There is no better way to connect with people in another country than to make even the most elementary attempt at communicating in their language. If you happen to come from an English-speaking country, you are lucky. Thanks to the broad appeal of our movies and the influence of the Internet, English is spoken just about everywhere. The negative side of this coin is that you as an English speaker might be content to just drift from one country to the next without attempting to make even simple greetings in the local tongue. This is a big mistake — a missed opportunity

Along with all the planning we decided to start some language practice with the girls; language was one of the areas we wanted to emphasize on the trip. It is difficult to get genuine practice and maintain any kind of fluency, even in something as close to home as Spanish, but leaving the U.S. and having to get by on our own would change all that. The girls seemed to agree.

Starting with French and German, we purchased the cassette tape children's versions and then some more advanced courses for use as we gained proficiency. Part of the idea was that each of us should come away with at least the capabilities of understanding and using basic greetings and asking directions in a second or third language. I worked through the songs and jingles of the children's German course with Andrea, while Carla did the same with Lesley in French. We all had some good times sitting on the bed singing the silly little songs together. This kind of activity helped to engage the girls' imaginations and brought home the reality of the trip.

Irreversibility — How to Quit Your Job

Many of the decisions we had to make and tasks we had to accomplish after the initial, more or less tentative decision to go forward were small steps. However, a few big ones entered into the realm of irreversibility. I always stress to the girls that there are some things in life that are, for all practical purposes, irreversible, such as getting a tattoo or having kids or driving your car into a brick wall.

Sitting in my office at work I felt a sense of anticipation, of something that couldn't be taken back, as I pulled a brown interoffice mail envelope from the pile on my desk. It had the soft, wrinkled feel of a real veteran. On it names and dates, cancelled by hastily drawn lines like battle ribbons, gave evidence of its many short, anonymous trips through the mail room.

Standing on the threshold of a world outside the realm of interoffice memos, I was gaining a deeper appreciation for the word "irreversible." I slipped my plain white envelope, with the hand written "Personal and Confidential" on the front of it, inside and wound the string around the little red paper posts. Everyone around me was going about his or her normal daily routine as I placed the envelope in the plastic "Outgoing" box suspended from the office partition. I walked back down the hall, sat behind my desk, let the goose bumps subside, pulse rate return to near normal and tried my best to get back to work with the same single-minded dedication I had for the last 16 years.

Putting Words into Action

My letter of resignation did not go into any great detail about my plans. The company was in the process of reinventing itself, and I wanted a change of scene. They were quite gracious. To my relief, security guards did not immediately appear at my office door, demand I gather all personal effects and escort me from the building. While my letter moved around from one desk to another and people tried to decide if I was serious, we began to make the first tangible steps toward our goal. Two or three boxes at a time were packed and loaded into my old Buick. Each morning on my way to work, I stopped to carry the boxes into the storage unit we had rented. A feeling of momentum was gradually building each day. Packing was something we could accomplish very deliberately.

The satisfaction I got from watching the bare walls of the storage unit disappear made real the feeling of change and excitement, knowing each box brought us a little closer to our goal.

As my three months notice drew to an end at the office, I remembered childhood and that last balmy spring day when school finally let out for the summer — all sins forgiven. I just wished I had that old hand-me-down Schwinn bike, so I could go rocketing from the parking lot like a crazed monkey escaping from the circus. Barely able to contain myself, I took the elevator down, walked up to the third level of the parking garage where my trusty 11-year-old Buick sat with its self-assured expression and worn Velour seats. Carefully extracting it from the narrow canyon created by two shiny new SUVs, I inserted my favorite CD, turned up the volume, opened the windows and drove home in the thick, humid Houston air.

I expected there would be some difficulty for a man my age returning to work after a year of travel, but I felt it was time, and I was prepared to take the risk. For a moment I envisioned Carla and the girls walking through a steamy foreign marketplace, taking in sights, odors and sounds. The value of a gift, I thought to myself, is in some part measured by the level of sacrifice or risk borne by the giver.

Health, Safety and Physical Conditioning

Immunizations for everyone had to be brought up to date. We wrestled with the issue of which malaria medication to take during Asian travel. Looming ahead was the dreaded day when we would show up at the physician's office and receive five or six shots in rapid-fire succession. It came and went. The girls stood in front of the elevator, rubbing their arms and grumbling. There wasn't much point in trying to put a positive spin on it, but Carla and I had the satisfaction of knowing we had at least taken the basic precautions to protect our health.

Looking after our girls' health while traveling was probably the single biggest concern for us. As it worked out, we all had the usual winter colds, an occasional dose of the flu and an incident or two of intestinal distress. Finding professional advice is not difficult. There are very good doctors in most countries, and they generally speak English. Also, we carried a particularly good reference book. (It is listed in Appendix A.) With some care and caution you can usually treat most of the problems that come along with medications available over the counter. Any prescription medicines, of course, must be taken with you or sent to points along the way.

Irrespective of your traveling-style, should you choose to take an extended trip, I recommend getting in the best physical shape time allows prior to setting out. The better shape you are in, the better you will feel. Further, you've just made yourself more capable of hauling your luggage on and off of buses and trains. Even better still, you will be inclined to spend more time walking — in our opinion the best way to see the world.

Afoot

Most significant events in our neighborhood were given prominence by a block party. So Carla and I threw a going-away block party in our cul-de-sac. Friends and neighbors were all kind enough to keep their feelings about our apparent madness to themselves and wished us the best of luck.

The next step was checking into one of those "suites" hotels. The family who leased our house moved in on the first of June; our departure was not scheduled until the twelfth.

Carefully negotiating the piles of clothing carelessly thrown on the industrial grade carpeting of our hotel room, I glance at Lesley and Andrea sleeping peacefully on the foldout couch. I am a morning person and tend to be up well before the sun. In search of a cup of coffee, I snuck out of the room, quietly closing the heavy door behind me.

It was another summer dawn in Houston — about 78 degrees, 100 percent humidity. Trying to burn its way through the shroud of gray misty fog that forms every morning as the temperature drops through the dew point, the sun appeared as an orange disk just above the horizon. Even at that low angle I could feel its rays shinning almost horizontally, warming a side of my face. It was going to be another hot one.

I glanced across the parking lot, eyes searching for my faithful old Buick. It was not there. I had kept that old thing running until the last. Gone now was that familiar feeling of worn Velour upholstery, the odor of countless cups of spilled coffee, creaky electric windows that struggled to complete one more cycle and the arm rest with a depression from my elbow. Carla's car would be spared the auction block and stored for our return.

The parking lot was quiet. I was a man without a car, truly afoot, no longer separated from the basic elements around me. I had a decent pair of shoes and renewed enthusiasm for meeting people eye to eye and on my own terms. I had a sense of liberation I hadn't enjoyed in years.

I felt the hair stand up on my arms as I continued through the parking lot and headed for the thoroughfare. For 16 years I had known these streets, yet the soles of my shoes had never touched them. It was as though I was discovering them for the first time.

The only other walkers in the sultry morning air were a group of ladies of Central American origin probably. They had been dropped off out on the access road and were finishing the last quarter mile to their jobs at one of the other hotels along the street. They spoke to each other softly in Spanish as we passed. I couldn't resist the opportunity to smile and offer, "*Buenos dias.*" Polite to a fault, they reciprocated in almost perfect unison; then like school girls, they laughed at themselves as they moved on.

I admired their courage; they got up every day in a semi-hospitable country to do the jobs that no one else wanted. They were out of their comfort zone — or were they? Maybe they had just expanded their comfort zones to include a larger part of the world. I would be subjecting myself and my family to something similar, but we weren't taking the same risks. We had a safety net — the insurance coverage, the U.S. passports, the ATM card. As we would learn in the days ahead, the larger percentage of the human race is without a safety net and on foot.

I almost felt closer to those ladies I had passed than the circle of friends I had enjoyed dinner with the night before. There is a certain simple purity about being afoot and one of those nameless people beside the road. I just wanted to walk, get a little more in touch with the ground beneath my shoes and enjoy a renewed awareness of the passage of time. Free of my possessions, I began to take heart in one of the memorable bits of wisdom my father had passed along: "You don't own things; they own you."

That morning I ended up at the local library, using their Internet connection to check my e-mail. We still had arrangements to make and details to take care of, but for all practical purposes we were free. If a tornado had come along and wiped out all of our possessions, it just wouldn't have mattered to me.

The anonymity of the situation was appealing as well. We had watched all the travel shows, the remote and exotic destinations. It was usually some famous travel figure or movie star having all those culturally enriching experiences. The difference was that they had a film crew following them around, someone to make arrangements, look after finances and take care of details. But when we walked down the street, we would just be part of the crowd — anonymous.

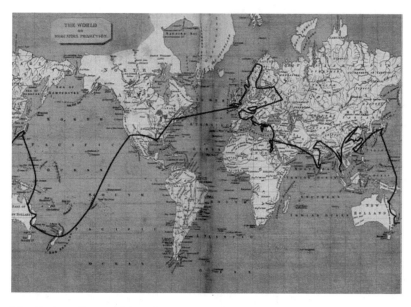

The Trek on Paper. Driven by a sense of adventure, curiosity and childhood fantasy, the WorldTrek route followed no straight lines.

Chapter 1 _____

Getting Started –
Great Britain and Ireland

SHARING THE AIRWAVES WITH SEVERAL layers of arrival and departure announcements, plus a yipping robotic dog that had lost its way added to the minor chaos of the departure area. Headed into the newsstand, I dodged the miniature airplanes circling over a fishbowl with the bobbing plastic submarine and wondered who in the world bought this stuff. I was in need of something to read on the flight to London; I found my way to the back of the store and picked through the magazines. The cover of *The Economist* proclaimed, "Mr. Bush goes to Europe."

"Yeah, me too!" I said quietly.

Taking an issue off the rack, I moved back toward the register through the bright maze of ceramic cowboy boots with thermometers imbedded in the smudgy glaze and beer glasses with maps of Texas. Out of habit, I reached for a candy bar. PayDay season usually begins in May in South Texas. I had spent enough time as a geologist in the field to know that you always go out prepared. I thought about buying three or four but held myself back.

I rejoined the family and sat down to see what Mr. Bush was up to on his first trip to Europe. I slid the PayDay candy bar into a spare Ziploc bag, squeezed out the air, sealed it and tucked it into in my daypack.

"Why did you buy that candy bar?" Lesley demanded.

"Just in case," I told her.

"In case of what?" she persisted in her 13-year-old way.

"I don't know. Someone might get hungry along the way."

The boarding area was all too familiar. I had been flying out of this airport for more years than I cared to remember. No briefcase, no laptop; neither were we headed out on a two week vacation. There's simply no way to describe the feeling of the beginning of a major adventure except for the relief that the trip is finally underway. While we waited to board the flight, I was aware of the fact that I really had no idea how this was all going to turn out, but if everything went well, we would not be back for an entire year!

The night before had been anything but relaxing. We had rented a unit in a boat and vehicle storage yard for Carla's car. Our canoe was balanced on the car's roof. All of our lawn furniture and garden tools were stored along the walls. In an effort to maximize floor space, we had tied the bicycles to the roof rafters. It was about 9:30 at night. The temperature was 88 degrees. Humidity was approaching the dew point. Stretched out on the concrete floor of the storage unit, I was about to perform my last official act as a resident of The Woodlands, Texas.

I positioned the jack under the axle of the car, raised the tire off the ground, slid a jackstand in next to it, let some of the air out of the tire, lowered the jack and crawled on to the next one. It was hot, and I was dirty. The combination of sweat and repellant were a magnet for dirt and dust from the undercarriage of the car. Heat still radiated from the engine and exhaust system, but I was savoring the feeling of closure. Oddly, I didn't hurry. A small part of me didn't want it to end.

Our good friend Linda had followed us to the storage yard to drive us back to our motel. She and Carla stood there, a couple of silhouettes in the failing light, swatting mosquitoes and offering tidbits of humorous commentary, while I crawled around on the floor.

"You must be running on pure adrenaline." Linda observed.

I guess we were, but I had visualized this exact scene so many times over the past year, I just wanted to rub around in the grit and sweat a little more to make sure I was actually registering the true feeling of the moment.

This was it.

I poured a small can of stabilizer into the gas tank, squeezed by the cardboard barrel full of rakes, shovels and yard tools, lifted the hood and disconnected the battery cable. I will never forget swinging those big old doors shut and putting the lock through the bolt.

"Free at last," I announced.

Back at the motel, the lobby was quiet. The evening manager, a young lady with a bubbly disposition, asked if we were ready to set out on our big trip. We acknowledged that we were. Dirty, tired and a little self-conscious about the way I looked, I was not in a frame of mind to keep up my end of a conversation. Undaunted, she went on to tell us how lucky we were to be able to take this trip and repeated it several times. I wanted to say, "Lady, if there is anything that was not involved in the last twelve months of planning, packing, negotiating and just plain grunt labor, it was luck!"

Now at the airport, as I sat in the departure lounge with my insurance policy of one PayDay candy bar safely tucked away, scraping a last stain of grease from beneath my nails with a pocket knife, I took a deep breath and thought: We're actually about to do it . . .

Meanwhile, Carla was writing in her journal:

06/12/01 — Carla

Sitting here, gazing out at the clouds, it is difficult to believe our trip has begun. With an intermediate stop in Toronto, we will be in London before noon, and a new reality will take over. The last year of planning has been fun. I have felt the excitement and learned the patience required to put this together. Now, after the intense two months of moving and final arrangements, it feels awfully good to sit and reflect a little.

Yes, I'm excited by all we will encounter. Now it's time to relax and enjoy the year together and create a wealth of memories.

Great Britain

Stepping across the threshold into London's Heathrow Airport, Lesley observed, "We now have an accent."

Kids do surprise you every so often with their comments. I shouldn't have been too surprised; kids are always changing. Adults are the ones who often stop changing or growing.

The first in a long line of customs and passport control agents heralded our formal admission to the United Kingdom and the European Union in a drum roll of resounding thumps as the official rubber stamp came down firmly on the largely vacant pages of our passports. We were novices, truly green horns. Gathering our gear, we found an ATM, then located a bus to the city, where an American woman, judging from her accent, asked if we were on vacation.

Being new at the game, I replied quietly, "No, yearlong trip around the world."

She began to exclaim at full volume and ask a seri[...] for the benefit of everyone in shouting distance. At that [...]ntly decided that in the future, we would just say, "Yes, we're [...]onday."

For a yearlong trip, it could be said we were traveling light. Each of us had a roll-on backpack. They were the kind with wheels and telescoping handle but also had backpack straps concealed in a compartment. Traveling light is all a matter of opinion. My pack, the largest roll-on travel pack we could find, weighed close to forty-five pounds. After wrestling it on and off a few buses and trains, and up a few flights of stairs in a bed and breakfast, I felt differently about whether I was in fact traveling light. In addition, we had small daypacks for cameras, snacks, raingear, et cetera. In all we had six pieces when we set out, four travel packs and two daypacks. I also carried a messenger's pouch (which could be called a man's purse, but we won't go into that) as I had given myself a couple of reading assignments and needed to tote them around. Getting on and off of trains and buses was always an effort, but it was something that we eventually mastered with the help of Andrea and Lesley — after about ten months of travel!

The London underground is a wonderful system geared for commuters — not people with luggage. Fortunately, we were a little ahead of peak morning rush hour. Londoners are like morning commuters around the world. The small part of the brain that is actually switched on and operating is fully engaged in guiding the body along the familiar route to work. The remaining part is struggling to accept the arrival of another day of work and what challenges it may pose. A bunch of inexperienced tourists with large pieces of luggage, trying to negotiate a turnstile, might be entertaining at another time of day but not on your way to work.

Ever mindful of our need to stay on a budget, we decided to take public transportation in England. Train and bus transport are so reliable that renting a car didn't make sense. We always enjoy train travel and have even been supporters of Amtrak over the years. Public transportation forces you to interact in stations, in trains and at destinations. It is impossible to remain isolated when sharing a coach with several dozen other people. A special feeling comes from being entirely free and on your own, prepared to deal in real time with whatever comes your way.

Our hotel in London was not a fancy place. An old row house in the Russell Square area, it had been ingeniously fitted with a few extra bathrooms along with a kitchen and eating area in the cellar. The walls, door moldings and windowsills all had a sort of rounded look. Detail and sharpness had been softened by countless coats of paint. In fact, the original dimensions of our room might actually have been slightly larger if the paint had been stripped away. For all I knew, the paint might be the only thing holding the place together.

The hotel was operated by a Pakistani man who spent most of his time sleeping on a cot behind the desk, waking only to eye Lesley and Andrea suspiciously every time they went by. He was a friendly enough guy, if you worked on him a bit, but getting a smile out of him took some effort.

We had one longish room with four squeaky beds that sagged even without an occupant. There was scarcely enough room to stow our gear and still have a path to walk. Windows, opening out onto the street, allowed us to appreciate the after midnight singing of those who had recently closed the local pub.

The bathrooms were down the hall. One little room had a toilet; the other had a bathtub that essentially filled the entire room from wall-to-wall except for about two square feet of floor space where a person could stand.

Hoping to stay in reasonable shape for the duration, we resolved to keep up our regular jogging schedule. Our mornings in London began with a run through the drizzly morning air. There is no better way to see a city and no better way to keep mind and body connected for the long haul.

Breakfast, included in the price of the room, was an adequate affair of flakes, yogurt and white bread toast. Lesley and Andrea derived the greatest enjoyment from the jar of transparent orange gelatin labeled Value Point Marmalade. Suspended in each jar were one or possibly two gossamer filaments of orange peel thus technically fulfilling the minimum requirements for the product as labeled.

All of this could be endured because of the fortuitous location of a small coffee/espresso shop at the end of the block. Each morning I would get a cup, sit on the front step and watch a cross section of London go by.

Our plan was to spend a few days in London, visit the pilgrimage sites, then make our way west to Bristol to catch a ferry to the port of Rosslare on the east coast of Ireland. We had planned most of our accommodations for the first few weeks through Ireland and back into the Yorkshire dales. After that, we would pretty much be making arrangements on the fly — until we arrived in St. Petersburg.

Pilgrimage Sites, Tourists and Tours

The high profile tourist sites or pilgrimage sites, as I call them, are the places where I often felt I should tag base in order to validate my tourist status. England is loaded with them — the Tower of London, St. Paul's Cathedral, Westminster Abbey, the British Museum and a sampling of real English pubs. In other parts of the world, Blarney Castle in Ireland, the Eiffel Tower in Paris, the Coliseum in Rome, the Parthenon in Athens, Ayasofya in Istanbul, the pyramids at Giza and the Taj Mahal should appear on any self-respecting tourist's list.

Pilgrimage sites put you in the category of being a "tourist." The word tourist is often spoken by other tourists with some rancor. There is this contradiction people engage in when they are tourists. They profess to not want to go to the places all the tourists go. Accepting that you are a tourist is humbling. The best one can hope for is to not stand out or fall into those behaviors associated with foreigners — like wearing shorts, goofy hats and Hawaiian shirts when visiting a holy shrine. Except in very hot countries, such as Thailand, almost no one wears shorts. In Europe most people wear darker colors.

Packaged tours are another way of seeing a country. They tend to receive the largest share of scorn for herding tourists around, but it is important to remember that someone who books a fully scheduled tour has done something that most people haven't — that is, dropped the TV remote control, disengaged from the La-Z-Boy lounge chair and departed for new sights and sounds.

While everyone has a different traveling style, the depth of your experience is up to you; this comes from learning as much as you can about the history, the culture and a bit of the language of each country you visit. With every trip away from home, a traveler gains more confidence and tends to venture out more on his or her own. The important thing is to go and not worry so much about exactly how you do it.

We visited as many pilgrimage sites as our feet would allow. We are walkers — it is our preferred way to see a city. We may jump on the underground to get to an area of the city, but upon arriving, often spend several hours walking. In fact, we may end up walking all the way back to our starting point. The first day in a new city we like to ride the city buses. A bus is inexpensive, and you get to rub up against the locals and experience a slice of culture. Carry a map with you and try to trace the course. Later you can come back on your own, if you have the time or desire.

Each of us had his or her own favorite places to visit in London. Mine was Westminster Abbey. Somewhere between a cathedral and a museum, Westminster was mostly constructed between about 1220 A.D. and 1270 A.D. It still offers regular services in addition to state functions such as coronations and the like. As is the English tradition, famous people are buried in Westminster Abbey. A moving experience is to stand at the stone marking the death and burial of Charles Darwin, Geoffrey Chaucer, Sir Isaac Newton or Charles Dickens. Having read their works, it is difficult to step across those worn inscriptions — polished by the soles of thousands of visitors — and not feel humble. The vast cavernous space enclosed by Westminster is also hard to grasp.

Stumbling out through Westminster's ancient doors and into the light of day, we set out walking back across Westminster Bridge, worked our way over to Buckingham Palace and up the Mall to Trafalgar Square. The sky was threatening, and a few drops of rain began to fall. Arriving at the foot of Lord Nelson's Pillar, we were all running low on energy; we opted for a snack at the nearby Spar Market. Our budget shot the night before on a delicious meal at a Bangladeshi restaurant around the corner from our hotel, lunch amounted to four containers of yogurt and a couple of packages of sandwiches (baguettes). At that point, however, the rain started to come down in earnest. Carla and I were feeling pretty seasoned and road worthy. After all, we had been out four whole days. We decided to sit along the edge of the sidewalk with the other street people and have our lunch. It took some adjustment for me to shed years of upscale conditioning. I wasn't entirely without reservations. After all, I was a business executive. I ate in nice restaurants — or at least I used to. On the other hand, I was also accustomed to operating a business on a budget. I knew what our budget was. Now the thought arose:

Budgets are nice on paper, but can we really live by one for whole year?

Finally the rain subsided. With renewed vigor, the girls set out to feed the pigeons in Trafalgar Square. They were still children, enjoying the pleasures of childhood, and being engulfed by pigeons was one of them. Meanwhile, I had a great time taking a few photos. Some of the least costly events are among the most memorable.

Trafalgar Square. Huge bronze lions at the foot of Nelson's Column were the starting point of WorldTrek. Lesley and Andrea, veterans at this point of only four days travel, are filled with anticipation. (Russ)

We saw more than our fair share of museums in the twelve months, but even the girls, whose capacity for museums was not all that great, admitted that the British Museum in London was one of the most memorable. The antiquities displayed there from Mesopotamia, Eastern Mediterranean and Egypt stirred the imagination as we came to the realization of how sophisticated artwork was at the time they'd been created. The granite and andacite used as media for works of sculpture, like the giant Bulls of Nineveh, are very hard rocks and a challenge to even modern tungsten carbide tools. Taking into account the state of metallurgical development and the tools available 4,500 years ago, mostly impure copper and bronze, the task of sculpting such precise and refined masterpieces seemed impossible. Even the girls were impressed. They proclaimed these works, "Awesome!"

We are seldom good for more than a few days in any large city, and soon bade farewell to our Pakistani host. In single file, packs rolling along behind us, we made our way through the London underground and on to St. Pancras Station. At Lesley's request we stopped at Kings Cross Station to verify that Harry Potter's Platform 9-3/4 was nowhere to be found. We were off to the west through Bristol for a couple of days, then on to Cardiff and the port of Fishgard. On the way we stopped for a visit at Stonehenge, a true pilgrimage site.

When Carla and I visited England in 1984 we had come away with the impression, primarily from the natives, that the temple of early Druid culture was very small, overrun by tourists and generally a great disappointment that wasn't worthy of a side trip. This time, however, it was decided among the four of us, especially Lesley and Andrea, that we just couldn't neglect this cultural icon.

Contrary to what we had been told, the archaic, jumbled ring of stones was still a magnificent structure. Yes, it was roped off; and no one could climb around it. True enough, we were not the only ones there. But it was worth every minute of the long bus trip from Bristol. And all four of us came away pleased that we had made the effort.

In Bristol we enjoyed our first taste of International Youth Hostelling. The hostel was a sturdy, converted old warehouse along the riverfront. It was clean, friendly and a busload of school kids just added to the atmosphere. After a stroll around the lively waterfront and a fisherman's platter at the Ostrich Inn, the squeaky bunk beds felt pretty good.

Rising early the next morning, we set out for Cardiff after enjoying breakfast on a park bench in front of the Bristol Cathedral; we were furthering our image as street people. Lesley and Andrea fed pieces of their Cornish pastries to the pigeons and drank milk from the carton. Carla and I enjoyed one of our last cups of Starbucks before we set out for the train station.

Ireland

Carla had arranged for two one-week stays in cottages, one down on the extreme southwest coast of Ireland and the second in County Tipperary, where some relatives from my mother's side of the family lived.

Disembarking from the high-speed ferry in Rosslare on the east coast of Ireland, we picked up a car and headed west to County Kerry.

Our first week's stay was in the tiny village of Castlecove on the rocky southwest coast, looking out onto the cold North Atlantic. On the drive across southern Ireland we stopped to kiss the Blarney Stone. This was a pilgrimage pretty much required of all U.S. tourists; even the most tenuous claim to Irish ancestry demanded it. Realizing by this time what we had undertaken, I was going to cover all my bets with a second kissing of the Blarney Stone. I figured the effects from my previous visit some thirty-five years earlier had worn off.

Castlecove consisted of a small combination gas station and store run by everyone's fairytale Irish grandmother, Mrs. O'Leary, who leaned on the counter and passed the time of day with anyone who had a minute to share. A few yards down the lane were a post office, a pub and a couple of other buildings. I would have guessed the population was less than one hundred.

About half a mile up a dirt road into the foothills, we found our cottage nestled into the rocky slope across the valley from the rugged peak of Eagle Hill. The front yard of the cottage was apparently within the domain of a shaggy old ram that gave every indication he was determined to hold his ground. He eventually stepped aside as we negotiated our way through the front gate but looked on contentiously while we extracted our gear from the too small trunk of the car. Getting everything packed into the small car had seemed such a miracle that it pained me a little to have to take everything out when we arrived at our destination.

The cottage was a delight. Heat consisted of a small fireplace; it was fueled by a bag of coal I was not very good at keeping lit. That, in combination with a few pieces of peat I picked up along the road, lay to rest the old adage that claims, "Where there is smoke there is fire." Happily the weather was comfortably warm, and we just wore more clothes inside.

In a moment of genius, Carla struck a bargain with Lesley and Andrea that they should plan, purchase ingredients for and prepare one evening meal each week during the trip. It was always an adventure. While the girls argued about who was to peel the potatoes, Carla and I sat reading in the tiny living room. The discourse in the kitchen finally subsided, and it seemed likely dinner would result. Mince and taties was the featured item on the menu for the evening meal.

Dinner turned out to be a culinary masterpiece, enjoyed as we all huddled around the miniature dinette looking out over the gray north Atlantic. The sun had dipped behind gathering clouds.

"How are you girls feeling about being away from all your friends?" I asked as we ate.

"I don't know. I think we have been so busy that we just haven't thought about it," replied Lesley.

Andrea said, "Will we still be able to visit Ashley and Whitley in Indonesia when we are there?" A couple of Andrea's friends had moved to Jakarta, Indonesia, several months before we left. Their father had accepted a two-year assignment for a major oil company there.

"Dad and I would really love to go there — but things there seem chancy right now," Carla offered. "There's unrest, even around the capital of Jakarta."

"Well, I really want to go," Andrea asserted.

"So do we," I countered, "but we will just have to wait and see how things develop. "

The young lady who owned our cottage in Castlecove also ran a small hotel, restaurant and pub a couple of miles away. Unlikely as it seemed, the cook, I should say chef, created some truly outstanding dishes that went well beyond anything we expected for rural Irish cooking. The folks in the pub looked on, a little uncertain as to the motives of an anomalous American family hiding out in southwestern Ireland. Occasionally, the owner Sheila, also the bartender, fixed her penetrating gaze in my direction, almost as if I wasn't there; she might've been trying to resolve a spot on the wall. The Guinness had a way of breaking through all that. As we traveled we always had the best times when we made the effort to strike up a conversation. I may have come off a little garrulous, but that's expected of people from Texas.

Skellig Michael

Wednesday morning found us up early, headed up the coast to the village of Portmagee to catch a tour boat to a craggy little piece of rock jutting out of the ocean. For centuries the rock had been called Skellig Michael. We had seen a postcard picture and wanted to get a closer look.

It was about an hour's ride in a small boat that carried ten passengers. The sky was undecided, but clear enough to make the trip worthwhile. The Skellig rocks are two small, irregular spires of barren rock that, for lack of a better word, are called islands. Skellig Michael's notoriety comes

Skellig Michael. Isolation and hardship were the tenets of daily life in the sixth century monastery. The unforgettable view was worth the trip. (photographer unknown)

from the ruins of a monastic community that had established itself and eked out an existence for approximately 600 years starting around 588 A.D.

With full rain gear we bounced along over the waves on a course set for two mountain peaks standing defiantly against the gray sky. It was a cool day, and we were all sitting close together to stay warm, ducking the occasional spray of seawater over the bow. I tried to imagine what it might have been like back in 800 A.D. for a young man, maybe only 16 years old, making his first and perhaps last crossing out to that desperate piece of rock. It couldn't have been easy for him.

Our boat slammed into a cresting wave, jarring me back from the ninth century with a dash of cold spray. The girls were struggling to contain their laughter as they fixed upon the oversized rain pants slowly slipping from around the waist of a skinny old Scotsman, who was himself fixed on the task of photographing the approaching monoliths while we bounded over the waves.

Meanwhile, I couldn't imagine the conditions that prevailed on the mainland to drive people to such an extreme refuge. Given its improbable location, this was definitely not a pilgrimage site. Still, it was so unique that it was certainly worth the trip.

The trail from the modern-day dock ascended almost straight up the barren rock cliffs. Andrea and Lesley shot ahead of us and up the trail. Five hundred and fifty-eight narrow steps to climb, according to Andrea's count, each one cut into the rock, presumably by the hands of early residents. The last fifty steps, climbed at nearly sixty degrees, were wide enough for only one person. Eventually we arrived at a more or less horizontal shelf several hundred feet above the sea. The few meager structures — little domes of rock — allowed a space of no more than a dozen feet between any two walls. There, clinging to a rising slope, was a cluster of stone beehive structures, the core of the monastic community. This was really more a collection of small dwellings with a common meeting place.

Lesley and Andrea were captivated by the thousands of puffins living in every little space between two rocks. Their call is somewhere between the sound of a creaking door and someone's stomach grumbling for lack of food. Equally absurd is their leap of faith each time they dive from the edge and wait to open their wings until they have reached sufficient velocity to generate lift. For us — without the aid of wings — descending was more unnerving than the climb up; we were forced to look back down the rocky track that stays unnervingly close to the edge and a vertical drop to the water below.

The cruise back to the mainland allowed us time to internalize the sheer drama and harshness of Skellig Michael. The reoccurring thought of having to extract a means of survival from those cold stones is epic in proportion and a testimonial to human determination.

Our time at Castlecove was like something out of a storybook. Lesley and Andrea spent afternoons exploring the rugged coast with its hidden beaches and an occasional playful dog. A tired old pony that lived on an acre of rock connected to the mainland by a tiny isthmus came to meet them each afternoon when they brought handfuls of fresh grass from across the way. At their ages they were still young enough to enjoy the unstructured freedom of a day kicking around the rocks but old enough that we didn't feel concerned about leaving them to their own devices.

On the days it rained Carla continued her efforts to master some basic phrases in Norwegian. I resumed my self-imposed reading assignments, struggled with the Russian alphabet and tried equally hard to keep the fire of peat and coal going in the fireplace. If there was anything I had hoped to do on our trip it was to capture a few moments like these. The Russian alphabet eventually worked its way into my brain. The peat fire would just have to wait until our next visit.

As the week came to a close, we packed our things and headed off to County Tipperary. I had written some relatives telling them of our plans. No reply had come before we left the U.S. I would just have to sort it out when we got there.

Carla had booked a cottage on a working farm run by a retired large animal veterinarian John Harold-Barry and his charming wife Dinky. Lesley was reading *All Creatures Great and Small* by John Harriott at the time. Andrea was working her way through *Oliver Twist*. Not Irish, but certainly in keeping with our plan to read relevant literature along the way.

Tipperary Town, to distinguish it from the county, is a true slice of southern Ireland. Primarily a farming community, one can count on finding at least one large tractor or piece of farm equipment plying the narrow main street at any time of day. You won't find many tourists, but plenty of things of interest are in reach of a short drive. The Galty Mountains afforded some great hiking through heather and bog.

The Rock of Cashel, the seat of power for the medieval kings of Munster, is about 15 kilometers from Tipperary. It derived its name from Caiseal Mumhan, meaning the stone fort of Munster. Rising above the broad valley, known locally as the Golden Vale, the solitary limestone outcrop was established as a point of defense as far back as fourth century A.D. when Conall Corc built the first stone fort. Cashel remained the primary residence of the kings of Munster until around 1100.

From the Cathedral of St. Patrick, built on the site in 1169, the bishop could look down on the Dominican Friary, built in 1243, and the Cistercian Abbey, built in 1266. Ruins of both abbeys are in a moderate state of preservation and well worth the trip to see them.

Legend has it that St. Patrick came to the Rock around 450 A.D. to baptize Aengus MacNatfraich, then King of Munster. During the ceremony, Patrick raised his staff in exaltation. Bringing it down with great force, he inadvertently drove the spiked end through the brave old king's foot. Assuming it to be part of the ceremony and a test of his faith, the king remained silent. His fervor unmitigated, Christianity then spread throughout Ireland.

Wednesday evening in Tipperary town was sing-along night at the

Kickham Public House on the main street. Musicians began showing up, instruments in hand, around seven o'clock in the evening. By eight o'clock, they were coming into form and continued practically nonstop until closing time. This was accompanied by singing, clapping and an all around good time.

Fortunately, we got there early. The regular patrons didn't seem to mind too much that we had taken four of the prime seats. Soon we were surrounded by the gleeful, windburned faces of farmers and their wives enjoying each others company in the lively atmosphere. I got the impression they didn't get many visitors from the U.S., and they seemed happy to have us. Naturally, Guinness was the draft of choice. As teenagers, Lesley and Andrea thoroughly enjoyed the Irish entertainment.

We said farewell on the seventh day to our hosts in Tipperary. Intent on making connection with our Irish roots, we eventually located relatives who had moved up from Clonmel to Dublin and adjacent communities. My second cousin Theresa and her husband Arthur received us warmly at their new home in Newbridge. For a couple of nights we moved into the bedrooms of their grown and departed daughters.

Dinner the first evening had been arranged at Arthur's golf club, situated in the most exquisite pastoral setting of flowing green hills dotted with puffy white sheep. Conversation was going along well enough, but as I ordered a pint of Guinness, I could detect in Arthur a certain warming of our relationship. When it came to ordering a second, he shot a glance at Theresa who seemed to give it the OK, with some reservation.

An impromptu family reunion came together the following day. We had the pleasure of sharing an afternoon with a good portion of our living relatives in the Emerald Isle. A walk around the local park and castle included a stop at the local Gaelic Athletic Association for another Guinness sampling. When we arrived back at the house on Texas Lane the whole family, Liam and Kay, their children John and Sinead and granddaughter, Theresa, Arthur and daughter Louise, Donal and Anne, Michael and his fiancé, were all in attendance. It was the evening of a lifetime. I knew we had earned some small consideration among the members of the clan when the bottle of Potchine made its appearance, and Kay brought out the prized port she had been saving for a special occasion. The real treats, however, were the stories and family sing-alongs of old Irish favorites.

The next day we said our farewells and headed off to the Dublin Ferry docks. After the 2:00 A.M. bedtime, we all felt a little impaired but happy we had made the effort to connect with this Irish side of our family. We dropped the car, caught a taxi to the docks and boarded a ferry to Hollyhead in northwestern Wales. Then we caught a train to Chester and a city bus to the tourist information office. They were in the process of closing for the day as we came through the door. Despite the time and without hesitation the young lady behind the desk quickly located a bed and breakfast just outside the fortified walls of the old city. We finished our trek that day by pulling our bags through the medieval streets of Chester. We had traveled a long way in a single day but found enough reserve energy to climb the long flight of stairs to our rooms. Shedding packs in our proper and well-appointed rooms, we stumbled down the street to the first pub we could find for dinner.

At first the girls were hesitant about eating in a pub, but in many towns pubs were the only places to eat a reasonably priced evening meal. There's almost always a family section, the food is reliably good, and the people are reliably entertaining. Besides, pubs are an essential part of English culture; it would have been a shame to miss the experience.

Chester and York, farther along our route, are two enchanting medieval cities complete with encircling city walls, narrow streets and Gothic cathedrals. Not widely appreciated is that both cities date back to Roman times, around A.D. 50, when they served as the legionary forts of Deva and Eboracum.

Working our way across northern England, we stopped for a week of hiking in the Yorkshire Dales. Settle, a small village in the

Exploring York, the Shambles district. Lesley follows Andrea down Swinegate and they imagine life in medieval days, walking these narrow streets as children. (Carla)

valley of the tumbling Ribble River, was home for our last cottage stay in England. Only a block off the tiny town square, it was well positioned for getting about. An excellent bakery with quite passable coffee was scarcely 200 feet away. Our days were spent wandering the trails and back roads of the Yorkshire Dales, through the chain of rolling hills, the Pennines, and checkerboard pastures divided by ancient lichen-encrusted stone walls.

Tuesday in Settle was market day. That meant at about 6:30 in the morning vendors pulling trailers from town to town set up in the cobblestone square to sell their wares. This was our first market day, and we were excited. Looking back and comparing it to markets in Genoa, Alexandria or Bangalore in India, it was quite tame. The most exotic purveyor of things foreign that we came upon in Settle was an Indian guy selling jeans.

Sorting through the offerings of meat, cheese, vegetables, arts, crafts and clothing in the cool English mist, Lesley and Andrea began gathering supplies for their weekly dinner. On the way back across the square, I stopped to buy some kippers (smoked herring). I asked the fish vendor to explain the differences between the varieties of kipper. I listened carefully to make out the reply in his Northumbrian accent.

He handed my change and kippers across the counter and added with a grin, "From the sound of it, you've come a long way for these kippers."

We had, in fact, been waiting for weeks to have some good kippers, and the "aroma" of kippers filled the house at breakfast the next few mornings.

Having passed the gauntlet of the market place and put together another meal, the girls began to imagine themselves traveling through Europe with their friends when they got to college. Carla pointed out that learning how to prepare meals while traveling was an important training exercise. Traveling on a student's budget would probably not allow for too many expensive restaurant meals.

North of Rome

We left the Yorkshire Dales and caught a train north from the town of Tipton, changing at Carlisle for the Northumbrian town of Haltwhistle and the hostel at Once Brewed. The train rocked along through the largely treeless hills of Cumbria and into the County of Northumberland. Off to our left outcrops of yellow sandstone beds, pushed up to the north, were partially obscured by low clouds. The contours of the ridgeline were fringed by a 70-mile-long masonry structure known as Hadrian's Wall. The wall swells at regular intervals to encompass crumbling settlements and fortifications. These ruins marked the northern most limit of the Roman Empire until about 400 A.D. Named for the Emperor Hadrian, the wall originally stood about ten feet in elevation and reached from the Irish Sea west of Carlisle to Newcastle on the North Sea coast of England.

This monumental construction project was begun in 122 A.D. by Emperor Trajan and connected a series of fortresses begun along an earlier road called the Stanegate. Some of the fortresses, like Vindolanda that archeologists have excavated near Haltwhistle, were large enough to garrison a thousand infantrymen. The wall served as a defensive barrier to protect against raids perpetrated by the Picts. Built wide enough for centurions to march three abreast along most of its length, it also served as a communications thoroughfare with turrets every mile and fortresses every three miles.

Hadrian's Wall was a stirring reminder of the enormous range of influence established by Rome, a single city-state more than 1,100 miles to the south. At that time, the administrative and logistical range of its empire stretched from Carlisle to the first cataract of the Nile — over 2,800 miles away. At its peak there were somewhere in the neighborhood of 40 million people under its control.

Near sunset we donned our sweaters and strolled to the north of the wall. Looking toward the Roman frontier, the land falls away and rolls out onto vast open plains of tall grass, appearing almost desolate. From a vantage point on the wall, a Roman sentry, perhaps of Syrian birth, literate, educated and accustomed to the warm Mediterranean climate, could see in the distance the approach of fierce bands of Celtic tribesmen wearing little more than face paint. Our family's ancestors, it seems, numbered among those who the Romans were determined to keep out.

Continuing east along the boundary of ancient Rome, we arrived at Newcastle, our jumping off point from England and ferry departure port for Norway. Separating from one of the last ties to our previous life, we enjoyed our final cup of Starbucks in Newcastle before catching a bus for the docks. I only hoped that they knew how to make good coffee in Norway. Just to be sure, I started carrying half a kilo of ground coffee with me for those occasions when I could find water and a pot to boil it in.

As was generally the case, we got off the bus at the wrong stop, well over a mile from the correct dock. Guessing which way to go in order to arrive where the boat appeared to be, we trundled along hauling our bags behind us. It is always best to leave some extra time to get lost. Getting lost is inevitable, but if you maintain the right frame of mind, it is all just part of the fun and part of the memories.

Boarding the ferry for Kristiansand on July 23 was the beginning of about six weeks of almost continuous travel. We had some prearranged times to be in Russia and a car to pickup in Frankfurt on September 4th. The village of Settle was the last cottage stay for a while.

Chapter 2

Scandinavia and Estonia

On Tuesday, July 24, 2001, six weeks out, we awoke to the steady harmonic drone of the DFDS Scandinavian Princess' diesel engines. In search of an early morning cup of coffee, I made my way to the upper deck, passing the cook as he finished the job of pressing brass buttons through holes in his starched white waistcoat. He looked as though he had that same need for a caffeine jump-start.

Leaning on the railing as the sun began to come through the clouds, I wrapped my hands around the warm cup of Norwegian coffee that was going to make the grade. The hour was 6:30 A.M. Greenwich Time, and we were about two and a half hours from the port of Kristiansand, Norway. Looking out across the glassy surface of the North Sea, I had to remind myself that this remote corner of the Atlantic had a reputation that had earned it the respect of those who plied its waters. Fortunately, July was one of the North Sea's calmest months.

The first day's destination was Preikestolen (the name translates to Pulpit Rock). Some hiking was to be found there as well as a youth hostel set on the rocky shores of a mountain lake.

Norway

Arriving in port, things were pretty sleepy in Kristiansand for the height of the tourist season. I glanced at my watch and realized it was still early in the day and most of the shops were not even open. We found breakfast in a hole-in-the-wall bakery with sidewalk tables. The sun hadn't quite made it over the tops of the buildings. Norwegians and most Europeans sit outside to eat, wearing sweaters and stocking caps, reveling in whatever meager beams of solar radiation may penetrate the clouds. My thin Texas blood had me up and walking as soon as I finished the rolls and coffee.

It wasn't long before we were rocking along on the train, taking in our first glimpses of the extraordinarily rugged fjord country between Kristiansand and Stavanger. Only about 85 miles up the coast, Stavanger is one of Norway's main ports and the home of its oil drilling industry.

Jumping off at Stavanger, we pulled our packs across town to the regional ferry dock where we boarded a smaller ferry to the village of Tau. By now, the afternoon was more than half spent. The weather had been uncertain all day. But clouds were beginning to gather and yield an occasional sprinkle. We clambered up the narrow stairway with our packs, once again begging the indulgence of the regular commuters, and plunked them down inside the steamy cabin to find a table near the snack bar.

Everything aboard this commuter ferryboat had a slightly used appearance, giving it a comforting and homey feel. By that time, experience had taught us to watch the locals and do whatever they did. In almost all cases getting a seat is a priority. Two or three fairly determined commuters hastily set their belongings down, snatched up a tray and headed into the food line among the urns of coffee and racks of potato chips in the cluttered little snack bar.

We couldn't imagine anyone being so eager to eat in a ferryboat snack bar. These folks appeared in a rush to get something that was served in a Styrofoam cereal bowl, the top of which stood up above the rim of the bowl and appeared to be a large white hemisphere. The breakfast back in Kristiansand had long since worn off. Carla went off to investigate the odor of food.

A few minutes later she returned with our very own Styrofoam bowl with a large white hemisphere settled into a sauce of what looked to be melted butter with a few tiny cubes of ham swimming around in it. Without any prompting or conversation we set about sectioning this thing into equal pieces. Plastic forks in hand we sopped up every drop of the buttery sauce with pieces of the starchy elastic dough. The treasure inside was a one-inch-cube of ham that Carla carefully portioned out. Soon we were all fighting to keep our eyes open as the warm humid air of the cabin and gentle rocking conspired with an overload of greasy starch to induce sleep.

The only escape from a sound nap was out on deck in the cool air to watch the jumble of rocky tree-covered islets drift by against a backdrop of pine-blanketed mountains. Many of the islets were just a few square meters with a solitary pine tree clinging to the barren rock surface. The water was dark and clear, and perfectly smooth except for the occasional wake created by other ferryboats of various sizes headed off in all directions. Norway's rocky, jagged coast makes ferry travel the most convenient form of transportation — and most small towns, such as Tau, are served by ferries. From Tau, we caught a bus that we hoped would take us up to the hostel at Preikestolen.

From Tau by Bus to Jorpland

Once we had established our bearings and had become committed to Norway, the climate began to show some of its true nature. We found ourselves standing in a light rain in the village of Jorpland, an unplanned stop. Earlier in the day, the driver explained that the bus would go all the way to the Preikestolhytta (the youth hostel and lodge). But after 3:00 P.M. the bus only went as far as Jorpland. The driver volunteered to call a cab for us on his cell phone (for a small fee); and we covered the last few kilometers by taxi.

This was one of the many instances where connecting with someone on a personal level, bus driver, newsstand attendant or desk clerk made a difference. We found that treating other human beings with respect and dignity always paid off. The bus driver could see we were stuck and volunteered his help, since it was obvious that we were clueless.

Two ferries, a train, a bus and a taxi were all in a day's travel. As we first glimpsed the Preikestolhytta, the simple rectangular box of a lodge looked like a great brown bear sleeping beside a lake with its riotous sod covered roof sporting a profusion of grasses and wild flowers. All they needed was a goat on the roof to keep the grass in check, and the scene would have been complete. We wrestled our stuff into a narrow room; it was no bigger than the ferry cabin of the night before, leaving very little space to stand or turn around.

We had finally left the security of the British Isles and stepped out into our first nominally non-English speaking country. Carla had been cramming the previous few weeks with her Norwegian and did what she could to get our needs across. But, as it so happened, almost everyone in Norway spoke perfect English.

Our hike out to Preikestolen the next morning was fueled by a true Scandinavian breakfast — by U.S. standards, more like lunch. The dining hall was attended by a couple of pretty, college age Norwegian girls, the kind with blond hair, blue eyes and big smiles. As one of the servers hustled out more loaves of fresh hot bread and paused to recapture a lock of hair falling from behind her red bandana, I asked if she was familiar with the ball of dough we had eaten the day before. Her eyes rolled back, a dreamy smile came over her face and she said, "Ah, *sorland kompe*, those are my favorite." With the climate being what it is, it seemed that everyone had to load up on carbohydrates to stay warm. Not so surprisingly, very few Norwegians would be considered overweight.

Andrea sat down next to Carla with a huge not-so-skillfully-cut piece of bread, a couple of slices of salami and some cheese on a small plate.

"I'm not sure I like eating lunch for breakfast," she muttered.

In her other hand she carried a bowl of coarse-grained muesli with a thick white slightly lumpy liquid that looked like yogurt on top. I had been watching her pick her way through the various offerings in the milk cartons.

"I wanted some milk for my cereal," she said, "and I'm not sure what I got. Once I started to pour, it was too late to stop. It looks gross."

To a girl of 12, most things were either acceptable or gross.

"Andrea, it's a cultured milk, kind of like a liquid yogurt. You like yogurt. Give it a try," Carla offered.

Carefully applying a uniform coating of butter to her bread she was determined to leave no corner uncovered. Eyeing her cereal bowl with suspicion she complained, "I just wanted milk. I don't want people to think I'm some picky American kid, but it looks gross."

"Just watch what the other people are doing," Carla prompted. "They are using the same carton for their cereal. What are they putting on top of theirs?"

"It looks like strawberry jelly," Andrea said.

"I think that's probably what it is. Why don't you try it?"

Andrea took another bite of the bread, stood up and got in line with the others. A minute later she returned with what looked more like an ice cream sundae. It was, in fact, a more acceptable cherry jelly.

"We are going to take a pretty long hike today," I reminded everyone. "Make sure you load up with carbs. We'll carry a light lunch, but let's start out fully fueled." When it comes to eating you have to be an opportunist.

Eyes began to roll. I didn't pursue the subject any further.

Preikestolen (Pulpit Rock) Lysefjord, east of Stavanger, Norway. Lesley (right) testing the breeze while looking down 2000 feet over the edge of Preikestolen. No safety rail or warning signs here . . . only nerve! (Carla)

Preikestolen

If you have ever seen two travel posters for Norway, one of them was probably Preikestolen. It is a little sliver of rock that juts out from a sheer cliff overlooking Lysefjorden about 25 miles inland from Stavanger. The hike from the hostel was about two hours, a steady climb over a well-marked and well-traveled trail. It is also the pilgrimage site in south-western Norway. A walk up the trail is like a trip through the U.N. — every European nationality is represented from the Mediterranean on up with some Japanese thrown in for good measure. It was a lively crowd on the trail. Everyone moved at his or her own speed, young and old, some in street shoes, others with more appropriate footwear.

Lysefjorden is a vast, half submerged canyon chiseled out by the slow and relentless movement of a long-since-melted river of ice. The highland trail comes abruptly to the edge of the fjord where we were confronted by an alpine vista of snow-capped peaks on the opposite side. The trail then picks its way through the rocks and boulders along the edge, which plunges straight down a couple of thousand feet to the placid inky water below. Luckily we had a perfectly clear day; visibility was unlimited. Walking out onto the rock platform — about seventy-five feet square — you step across a couple of deep cracks, reminders that nothing lasts forever and some day gravity will finish its work on Preikestolen. In some ways the place was terrifying, just a small platform surrounded on three sides by a sheer drop of almost 2,000 feet (604 m). We watched as most people approached the edge on hands and knees, laid flat on their stomachs and peered over the edge. Not a single warning sign was in sight.

It is one spectacular place to eat lunch and gaze at the raw, unparalleled beauty of the fjord country. Preikestolen is truly a world-class pilgrimage site. It is worth the hike, no matter what kind of shoes you are wearing. Everyone brings his or her own lunch. All wrappers and papers brought there are packed out again.

Looking out across the snowy peaks and down to the water below, it was easy to understand why the Vikings had set out upon the open sea to find their fortune. There is little in the way of arable land in Norway and the growing season is short. As fishers, seafarers and all around marauders, they became adept at taking what they needed during the summer months from the British Isles and the northern European mainland.

The two nights we were lucky enough to spend at the Preikestolen lodge were just a hint of the adventure and beauty of Norway, barely enough time to grasp the stark ruggedness of rock and water with a few trees sprinkled across the landscape for color.

Port of Call: Bergen

Heading back out to the coast, we worked our way by bus and ferry to the postcard-perfect city of Bergen. Reaching the International Youth Hostel was another ten-minute ride on a city bus; the hostel sat part way up the mountainside that overlooked the city. We walked the last quarter mile, pulling our packs up the steep residential street as the weather began to darken and a few drops of drizzle fell against our faces. A middle-aged German lady with a small backpack, exited the bus and walked along with us. I had actually found someone with whom I could practice my elementary German. As was often the case, vocabulary slipped back into some lost corner of my brain when the time to use it arrived.

The atmosphere in the reception area was a slice of Europe with people from everywhere. Excitement was in the air, and everyone seemed in a hurry to get out and connect with whatever was going on. The afternoon brightened as we checked into our room and set out for the corner grocery store to purchase food for dinner.

The next morning we hiked up to the top of the mountain against which the hostel was located. Sitting on the observation deck below the tramway and looking out with binoculars, I could see down to the port of Bergen. Along the waterfront were a couple of majestic old square-rigger sailing ships. This was something worth seeing. As I moved my focus along the inner harbor it seemed there was one enormous sailing ship after another. Handing the binoculars to Carla for a second look, we couldn't imagine what had brought them all to this little city so far to the north.

Dumb luck was more than our occasional companion. We had inadvertently stumbled into town the same day that the Cutty Sark International Tall Ships Race also called on the port of Bergen. Over 100 ships from every corner of the globe take part in the annual race, sponsored by Cutty Sark since 1956. Cadets from Moscow to Mexico have a chance to sail their historical tall ships, exchange greetings and capture memories of something about which most of us can only fantasize.

A short time later we stepped down from the lumbering city bus and hurried to the quay; it was lined by brightly painted clapboard shops and warmed by the afternoon sun. The forest of towering masts, and the jungle of ropes and sails were like stepping back in time. We began to understand why the hostel seemed so electrified the night before. It was something we had never imagined we would see.

The afternoon and well into the evening was spent touring the ships, listening to sea chanteys sung by the Berlevag sailor's chorus, walking among the crowds and the sidewalk vendors. They may not have had much to show in the way of home grown tomatoes, but there was an incomparable selection of fresh seafood. We eventually packed a pound of fresh shrimp and a huge slab of peppered salmon into my daypack before boarding the bus for the climb back up to the hostel.

Upon arrival there, I headed down to the kitchen, hidden in the basement at the end of a long, institutional-looking hallway. The atmosphere inside was quite a different story. A shabbily dressed collection of weary hikers, travelers and family vacationers vied for elbow-room at one of the several cooking stoves. Determination was a necessary ingredient in the mix, and after staking out an area to prepare food, I found I had to make a trip back up to the reception desk to check out each and every pot, pan or kitchen utensil. To my disappointment I found that tokens were required for the little meter on the wall that controlled the flow of electricity, also conveniently available back at the reception desk, staffed by affable but slightly overcommitted young college kids. I arranged for a spatula, skillet and some tokens as a crop of new arrivals was checking in for the evening.

Back in the kitchen, I began to get things going while Carla and the girls set a place at a picnic table outside. To my left was a young Italian couple who had driven a VW bug up from Naples. They were beginning to show signs of caffeine withdrawal as they reverently set their espresso pot to heating. The shrimp were doing okay, but I didn't have anything to add to the skillet for the salmon. Fortunately one of a group of middle-aged men at the stove on my right had a large bottle of cooking oil. The men were from the Czech Republic. I struck up a conversation with them and ultimately begged an ounce or two of cooking oil. Bringing the temperature of the skillet up quickly, the hefty filet of salmon sizzled loudly when I placed it skin side down in the thin layer of oil. Several heads turned at the sound. A cloud of steam rose as I placed a lid on the pan.

One of the Czechs glanced over at me with a curious and doubtful expression. He seemed to view my salmon cooking technique with some skepticism. In a few minutes, I managed to turn the slab of salmon with the limited tools at my disposal, bolstering the illusion that I knew what I was doing. The Czech, now with arms folded, continued to look on. I drained the shrimp, turned the hot salmon onto a brown paper shopping bag and quickly scrubbed my pot and pans. With a nod and wink to my Czech friend I headed triumphantly back into the hallway, up the stairs and out to the yard that overlooked the city a thousand feet below. Lesley and Andrea had found a patch of wild blueberries and generously made their contribution to the feast. The evening was cool, the bread was fresh, and the butter was in ample supply. It just didn't get any better than that.

Deep Into Fjord Country

The village of Balestrand, the next stop on our northbound trek, is located on Europe's longest fjord, the Sognefjord. The great ice-cut canyon stretches 150 miles into the heart of southern Norway and is confined by sheer rock walls that fall without pause 2,000 feet into icy blue water. More than three miles wide in some places, Balestrand appears as a fleck of white on the northern shore. The youth hostel was a grand, old wood frame hotel with floors that creaked and wooden door-frames that showed their age. With a view out onto the glassy waters, it was a perfectly comfortable place to spend a few nights.

Balestrand is only a few miles south and a little to the west of Jostedal Glacier National Park. Jostedalen is a vast elevated plateau of permanent ice fields that rises to over 6,800 feet above sea level. The remaining glacier, Jostedalsbreen, is a remnant of the last Ice Age and dates back some 18,000 years; it still covers about 190 square miles of the central plateau. A real jewel was the Breamuseum, as was the bus ride to the glacier's tip. Lesley and Andrea nonchalantly collected stones from the melt stream below where the shotgun-like cracking of the glacier was a reminder that this mega flow of ice was still on the move. Jostedalen is an area worthy of at least a week of dedicated hiking and camping, a place to revisit.

Andrea, our cookie maker, experienced her first big success with shortbread at Balestrand. Along the way she had picked up a discarded girl's magazine and found in it a recipe for shortbread. It was pretty simple; butter, flour and sugar. After a couple of experiments, she could turn out a batch in a few minutes and bake it in whatever oven and in whatever kind of pan was available. The odor of baking shortbread was always irresistible, and everyone in the hostel was drawn into the kitchen to discover its origin. Many friends were made over a piece of freshly baked shortbread, still warm and soft. Even the most standoffish newcomer would brighten as Andrea and Lesley offered the product of their labor. As time went on, the two of them experimented with cinnamon and sugar or a liberal dusting of Nestlé's chocolate drink mix. Shortbread was a dependable icebreaker.

The idea that youth hostels are limited to young people is something of a misnomer. More than half the residents were over forty years old, and families were welcome in most. Many travel books warn about the potential for crime in hostels, particularly where dormitory sleeping arrangements prevail. Traveling as a group of four, we could always get a family room and didn't have to worry about someone going through our stuff while we were out. I don't know if it is much of a problem — once the common sense precautions are taken to secure your things. It is strongly suggested and probably wise to bring your own combination lock. The irony was that I carried a heavy bicycle lock and cable all the way around the world and never found a need to use either one of them.

Above the Arctic Circle

From Balestrand we continued north, arriving in Trondheim on a rainy Sunday morning before the town awoke. All but shut down on the day of rest, we had to scrounge around town to find something to eat. Checking into the hostel we decided on a swim and hiked over to an indoor water sports arena overlooking the fjord. Pelted by cold rain and wind, we walked in silence along railroad tracks in our rain gear and enjoyed the feeling of the vagabonds we had become.

Carla had quietly held to her goal of getting us up across the Arctic Circle. We kept on the move until we arrived at Bodø, a small port city just above the Arctic Circle at about sixty-seven degrees north latitude. It lies on the northern shore of Saltfjorden, a broad embayment that runs some 20 miles inland.

Bodø's hostel is conveniently located in the train station. It didn't take long to get to know the layout of the town. We did our morning jog along the railroad tracks and spent a few carefree afternoons hiking in the nearby mountains, investigating the town on bicycles and taking bus excursions into rugged glacially sculpted countryside. Unforgettable was the Maelestrom, where tidewater rushes through a narrow strait between fjords. Perched on a rock jutting out into the channel, we shared a lunch of reindeer salami, cheese and hard tack. Below us spiraling whirlpools capable of swallowing a small boat rushed by in the current.

Pressing north along the west coast of Norway to Narvik, about 135 miles above the Arctic Circle, we had unequivocally checked the Arctic Circle box on Carla's list of things to do. At Narvik we turned east across the backbone of the peninsula and into Sweden. From our landing in Kristiansand our northerly migration had taken us well over 700 miles along the dramatic western coast of Norway.

Stopping for a night in the pleasantly dreary mining town of Gällivare, we found the hostel over the railroad track and down a roughly paved little path near an abandoned schoolhouse. It was a little shabby but clean nonetheless, and I thought it appropriate for a mining town. In the height of the summer tourist season, there was only one other guest in the hostel, a girl from Germany. Searching to find a place to eat, we finally relented in our quest for something of local origin. The only place open for dinner was a bright little Chinese restaurant that served mostly pizza.

The following day, as we found our compartment on the train to Stockholm, we noticed it had a decidedly local aroma. Still, we couldn't put a finger on it. The compartment warmed and our noses were inured to it, except when one of us stepped out into the passage and came back in. Pulling into Stockholm station the next morning, we made our last check under the seats for anything that might have fallen through the cracks. Andrea reached way to the back and brought out a partially consumed jar of pickled herring in garlic. Lesley offered that it was probably a Norwegian air freshener.

Sweden

Stockholm was a bright, enthusiastic city. Throngs of young tourists milled about in the pedestrian mall captivated by spray paint artists and the gentle strains of a violin and cello duet that rode upon the evening breeze. The weather was everything we could have hoped for in the month of August, bright days and warm, humid evenings. The underground system is known as the T-Bahn, and on it we found our way to all parts of the city. Carla and I drew a feeling of satisfaction as Lesley and Andrea raced ahead of us along a street to the local T-Bahn station and disappeared down the stairs. They were perfectly at ease. Looking occasionally over their shoulders to check directions, they found their places on the platform.

During the course of our trip we visited our fair share of museums and exhibits of historical artifacts. None, in my estimation, were comparable to the Vasa Museum. The Vasa was a seventeenth century sailing vessel, a heavily armed fighting ship and an unprecedented work of baroque shipbuilding art. Launched with great pomp and ceremony on Sunday, August 10, 1628, it left its slip in Stockholm harbor, moved into

Folk Museum in Gällivare, Sweden. Just ouside Stockholm, where primitive dwellings were on display. If the hostel had been full, we could have been quite comfortable here. (Carla)

the center of the channel and fired a salute. Within minutes it began to list, righting itself once. Beginning to roll again, water rushed in through the gun ports. Standing helplessly along the quay, dignitaries and the proud residents of Stockholm, not to mention the Dutch shipbuilder, looked on as Vasa promptly sank.

Settled into the soft cold mud of the harbor for over 330 years, the Vasa was recovered from its murky resting site in 1961 and carefully preserved with a specially formulated solution of ethylene glycol. Permanently ensconced in its berth on the island of Djurgården, it is a memorable and slightly eerie exhibit. Truly a ghost ship — somewhere between thirty and fifty men went down with her. I would recommend a trip to the Vasa Museum for anyone who is lucky enough to find himself in Stockholm.

In mid-August, on Lesley's birthday, we concluded our time in Scandinavia, boarded a ship and headed for one of the former satellites of the great northern empire — the Soviet Union of Russia. My diary reads:

08/14/01 — Russ

7:00 Sitting at an empty table in front of a Stockholm café waiting for the Internet bar to open next door. The temperature is about 70 degrees F., a light drizzle and gray skies. People pass by, cast a glance our way and go on. We are sort of digital street people, moving from place to place, sometimes wet, sometimes cold, usually well fed, always dropping into smoky cafés and coffee shops with Internet connections in the basement. Studying maps, asking directions, always strangers, always at home.

16:00 Silja Liner Terminal: I think our trip is just now beginning as we take another step away from the familiar.

Are we there yet?

"Just where did you say we were going?" Lesley inquired cautiously.

"A country called Estonia," Carla replied. "It used to be part of the Soviet Union. What they called a satellite state."

"Yeah, I know. We studied about those in history," Lesley said.

"When are we going to be there?" Andrea put in.

"Don't kids ever get tired of that question?" I asked.

Carla decided to head off that line of dialog and started looking through her purse. "I'm not really sure. Let's take a look at the tickets here and see if it is printed on them what time we arrive. If not, we can ask up at the concierge desk."

Lesley persisted, "Does it say how far it is? Are we going to have to wake up early again?"

"Well, I doubt the ticket will say how far it is, but if you want, we can estimate the distance by looking at the map. All we need are the latitude and longitude, and we can figure the distance." I seized the opportunity to work in a little math practice. Home schooling wouldn't formally start until September, but it never hurts to keep the gears in working order.

"No, thanks, I wasn't really that interested." Lesley was hoping to repair the damage as she tried in vain to head off another wave of geographic trivia.

"Dad, why don't you just measure the distance on the map?" she submitted hastily.

"I don't have a ruler long enough, and I don't think we have a single map that spans the distance," I said. "Let me ask you something. Do you know what the shortest distance between two points is?"

"A straight line. We learned that pre-algebra class." Lesley just couldn't resist getting drawn into the discussion.

"That's only true if you are a mining engineer or a gopher," I replied. "We live on the surface of a sphere. So the answer is the arc of a great circle. If you are standing at a point on the equator, for example, and you walk half way around the earth — "

"Which you couldn't do, because you'd have to swim across the ocean," Andrea put in.

I reached into the food pack and pulled out an orange. "Think about this for a second, and I promise I'll quit. We get used to looking at maps that are printed on flat and rectangular pieces of paper." I drew a facsimile of the continents on the orange with a marker. "Now go ahead and eat the orange, but as you peel it, try to lay the pieces of peel down so that they make a flat, rectangular map and you will see the problem map makers have wrestled with for centuries."

"Can we go now?"

"Okay, go ahead. You've suffered enough."

The girls beat a hasty exit into the corridor to do some more exploring lest they be subjected to another geography lesson. Carla and I stayed behind to wrap the few minor gifts and candy bars we had purchased to commemorate Lesley's fourteenth birthday. Obsolete maps of England and Scandinavia proved to be an expedient substitute for wrapping paper.

The huge ferryboats that sail in northern waters are very well appointed with comfortable, modern cabins. Restaurants are targeted at any price level with very high standards of service. Andrea and Lesley enjoyed having the freedom of the ship on those occasions. They could always go up on deck to burn off excess energy accumulated from riding on buses and trains.

Returning from their explorations and as discretely as the confines of the ferry cabin would allow, Lesley and Andrea approached Carla in hushed tones. Anticipation was palpable as they disappeared into the passageway. They had discovered some eye shadow in the gift shop and wanted help picking out the best shade. Fully aware that I had nothing to offer on this subject, I stayed behind to study Russian for a few minutes. Experimentation had begun as their minds and bodies moved from unfettered, uncomplicated days of childhood, and this was their moment.

The next morning our stop in Helsinki, Finland, was only long enough to walk a quarter of a mile into the city center, fumble with the local currency for a few minutes, then get back on the ship to Tallinn, Estonia. None of us had even the most rudimentary mental picture of what our destination would be like.

Estonia

The *CIA World Factbook*, a reliable source of geographic information, tells us that Estonia, known to its citizens as *Eesti Vabariik*, has a population of just over a million people who live in a country about the size of New Hampshire and Vermont combined. Literacy rate is 99.8 percent and life expectancy is 71.4 years. Estonian natural resources include oil shale, peat, phosphorite, clay, limestone, sand, dolomite, arable land and sea mud. The last of these, despite a career as a geologist, I had never come across before. We have plenty of sea mud in Texas. Maybe, I thought, there was an untapped market I could investigate when I got back home and found myself jobless.

We stepped off the boat at the port with a fairly light crowd of other tourists and business travelers. When Carla was planning our passage into Russia, she had selected this intermediate stop for some reason unknown to me. She had booked reservations in a hostel in the old town district. It was a converted hotel that was given pretty high marks for a hostel, based mostly on its proximity to the old town square. In most of the travel books there was, however, this mention of an "erotic" nightclub downstairs, which seemed to share a common entrance. Neither Carla nor I were too hot on the idea of dragging our daughters through an erotic night spot each evening on the way to bed, but the travel books downplayed the issue, and they had been pretty reliable to that point. We looked at each other, shrugged, and decided to go for it.

The old town district was closed to certain types of vehicular traffic, especially taxis. The taxi driver who brought us from the landing was required to drop us off a couple of blocks from the address we had jotted down on a slip of paper and put in his hands back at the ferry dock. He was good natured, and his English was pretty good, which was great with us, since we had not taken time to familiarize ourselves with elements of the Finno-Ugric language group to which Estonian belongs. I was still preoccupied with sounding out Russian words and attaching the correct sounds to the backwards R that represents the syllable *yah*, and the X sound that is best made with a little phlegm in the back of the throat. The driver's English vocabulary was short some of the adverbs, and his declaration that he was prohibited from driving in the historic district sounded a little like we were being evicted from his back seat. Language can be a funny thing.

We settled up and started off into a shadowy medieval alley. It was only for three nights, we thought, and we could always change if the erotic side spilled over into the hostel. Pulling our packs over the rough cobblestone streets and narrow sidewalks, we found our way through the maze of lanes running off at odd angles and disappearing around bends. It took a couple of passes up and down the sidewalk to find the hostel entrance tucked into an archway that led into a dark courtyard. No sign of the erotic night spot here. It was only a few minutes before we were carrying our gear up the sweeping marble staircase that arched its way to the first floor or the first level above the street. I think the U.S. is the only place where the first floor is at street level. Happily, we had to travel only one major flight of stairs to get to our room.

The hostel was a little used looking and reminded me of some of the older dormitories I had stayed in during college. This was after all Eastern Europe, and we were in the medieval part of town. The young lady at the desk was very pleasant, and the sheets were clean. There was a reasonably well-equipped kitchen with essentials. I had my half-kilo of Swedish Gevalia coffee, so I was all set. Without a doubt this was one of the best coffees I had on the entire trip.

Tallinn was a delight. It had more of an old-world feel than had been evident in Scandinavia. No remnants of that stodgy Soviet-block dreariness were apparent in the city center. The Estonians view the period under Soviet rule as an occupation. Their hearts and economies are firmly linked to the Finnish, with whom they share a similar language and culture. Over a span of four years Estonians succeeded in winning their freedom from the Soviet Union by staging massive nonviolent singing demonstrations. In 1991 Estonia was the first of the Baltic Republics to declare its independence in what has come to be known as the Singing Revolution. A country with a population of barely a million that boasts 133,000 folk songs has certainly got its heart in the right place. It was impossible not to feel a bit of excitement as we walked the streets of Tallinn.

The people seem anxious to get on with things and to enjoy life. Capitalism had taken root in the decade since Soviet rule. Most of the winding streets eventually spill into the old town plaza, a two-acre area of open space paved in brick, lined with outdoor cafés and a sprinkling of gift shops. Streets with sweet-smelling bakeries, arts, crafts, fashion and souvenir emporiums meander off in no particular pattern. It is one of those old towns you have to learn by Braille — feeling your way out from the familiar. Theme restaurants were popular; we chose one of the Medieval Feast places for Lesley's official birthday meal. It was a big open hall with rough cut wooden tables and a huge open-fire grill. They offered an assortment of grilled specialties and fresh vegetables, served with a mound of sauerkraut and coarse-grain bread, washed down with a half liter of local brew, Fanta for the girls. I think it was a memorable evening as Lesley completed her fourteenth year in Tallinn, Estonia.

The castle on the hill topped off the medieval appearance of the city. The view from the promontory, the classic view of Tallinn, is one of steep cone-shaped caps of red tile on nearly smooth walled cylindrical towers of stone. Sidewalk artist have immortalized this view in postcard-sized paintings and photos suspended on wire racks and frames along the winding cobblestone lanes and passageways.

We found Tallinn a very comfortable city and would recommend it without hesitation; and we never did figure out exactly where the "erotic" night club was.

Part of traveling as a family means that rules and discipline, and all that child rearing stuff must continue in spite of changing surroundings. Much to my parental pleasure the northern European view of things is this: If something is designed as a seat, then it is sat upon — no feet propped up on it, no lounging like a sack of potatoes in it. It is that ole "sit up straight and put your feet down" thing about which parents always harp at their kids. I had about run out of steam while we were waiting in the Tallinn station.

There really weren't enough places to sit. So Andrea, feeling a little at odds with things, chose to sit by herself on the sill of the window with feet up. When the mood overtook her she had the ability to flow across a surface as though there were no connective tissues joining the structural elements that give the human body its characteristic upright form. I didn't think this was going to go over very well with the locals, but I was tired of harassing her. She and Lesley were convinced that I was making the whole thing up anyway. Within only a few minutes of her getting settled into a very petulant slouch, a uniformed, rifle toting security guard appeared at her side and grunted a syllable or two. None of it made any sense to her, but the message was clear enough — seats were for sitting and sills were for whatever, maybe for collecting dust, but certainly not for lounging. Duly admonished, she gathered her miscellaneous parts, transformed them back into something recognizable as a 12-year-old girl and sheepishly looked for a proper place to sit.

I have to admit to a certain amount of parental "I told you so" and thought seriously about going over and shaking his hand. A High-Five seemed a bit overstated. But when the guard walked by, I just caught his eye and offered the shadow of a smile and a little nod. He reciprocated.

Heading East

From inside the station Track No. 1 was hidden from view. As we waited for the train to appear, Carla finally realized it was apart from the others, off to one side of the station. Gathering up our belongings, we rolled out onto the platform. Not exactly what we had become accustomed to in Scandinavia, I thought, but it was clean and looked like it would get us to St. Petersburg. The evening was warm and the crowd light as we moved toward the train, not in any big-city hurry. Before climbing aboard I glanced up and down the platform, imagining I might catch a glimpse of agent 007 picking up a newspaper or a handful of flowers for his traveling companion.

Chapter 3

Russia and The Czech Republic

To Andrea and Lesley Russia was just another country, and they absolutely loved it. Carla and I did, as well, but unlike our daughters our perceptions came from another point of reference. Saturated as we had been with Cold War images and old James Bond movies featuring hefty matrons concealing cyanide injectors in the soles of their shoes, I hated to admit it, but I still had some mental baggage when it came to Russia. The idea that we were actually going behind the old Iron Curtain engendered a sense of risk and danger.

The overnight train into Russia from Tallinn, Estonia, was everything my 1964 mental scrapbook would have predicted, minus the sharp edge of the real Cold War days. I half expected Sean Connery to pass through our car at any moment in his perfectly pressed light-gray suit with a thin leather brief case chained to his wrist. He must, I reasoned, have been in first class; 007 would never travel coach.

The train departed Tallinn around 10:00 P.M. We had booked a four-berth sleeping compartment, and once we figured out where the train was waiting, we had no trouble finding our places. Other passengers were moving about in the narrow passage with their luggage and checking compartment numbers against their tickets.

Our compartment was adequate, but four adult-sized people, four substantial packs and about ten square feet of floor space ended up like an old Three Stooges movie. Eventually it all fit in the tublike storage bins beneath the two lower berths. The banter that ensued between the four of us in English earned us a few stares. As it was, we provided some portion of the evening's entertainment for people in adjacent compartments. They would walk by and cast cautious glances at us to see the kinds of strange rituals in which Americans engaged. When they saw us hacking away at a lump of cheese and a piece of salami wrapped in oily butcher paper, they no doubt muttered, "Hmm, normal after all."

The train was old; it looked to be of 1960s vintage, but it was clean and surprisingly well maintained. The air conditioning, while not essential at 59 degrees north latitude, didn't seem to be working. I drew down one of the windows out in the passageway. It was a pleasant evening, probably about 70 degrees.

At last, the train pulled out of the station, and before we knew it we heard a knock on the compartment door. Our car steward wanted something; it didn't take any time to determine it was money for sheets and pillowcases — about 100 rubles. The exchange rate at that time was 29 rubles per U.S. dollar. I could tell from this encounter that communication was going to be a challenge. He shook his head as he realized that we didn't speak any Russian beyond the polite greetings.

So, we rocked through the lowlands along the route from Tallinn to St. Petersburg in the warm evening air, swatting an occasional Estonian mosquito and working over the two big pieces of salami we had purchased several days earlier in Bodø. That's the great thing about hard salami; it keeps forever and packs a lot of calories. The car was quiet. All the tales we had heard of harassment on Russian trains were finding no support from our experience. We drifted off to sleep.

Russia

Somewhere around three o'clock in the morning, the train glided to a halt, brakes squealing, luggage shifting slightly forward. We didn't make any effort to stir. There is a certain quality of sleep that can only be had on a train with the rhythmic sway and the regular clatter of wheels at each joint in the track. I lay there with the door open a couple of inches, trying to encourage any movement of air to make itself evident in our compartment. Silence always seems so absolute after the clatter of a moving train. I drifted off again.

I regained consciousness to another rhythm. This was a series of four resounding metallic "ka-thunks," each separated by a few seconds. It sounded like something slamming against the door of a compartment at one end of the car. A muffled conversation followed. It didn't seem as though there was any effort being made to keep from disturbing other passengers. A few minutes later, the sound of a compartment door sliding open, some conversation, then the same four ka-thunks.

Having been through enough customs and passport control offices, I surmised we had been boarded by Russian immigration agents. If they had to work at three o'clock in the morning, then everyone was going to know it. For about half an hour I listened to the familiar sequence of sounds. Not a word of English was spoken. From what I could tell there were four people in each compartment; four people, four passports, four ka-thunks, and there were four compartments between the end of the car and ours. Slowly, methodically my quintessential image of a robust uniformed Russian immigration agent presented herself as a silhouette looming in our door. She tried a few words of Russian, realized the futility of that and, with a slightly disdainful demeanor, went through her prescribed ritual. I kept my eye on the soles of her shoes and didn't try to engage in any unnecessary dialog, not that it was a possibility.

About the time we got resettled, another knock came at the compartment door. A young man in fatigues with a tired looking carbine gestured to us, indicating he wanted to look around our compartment. I think his enthusiasm was diminished when he saw that we were a family, and two of us were young girls. He went about his search in a perfunctory way and left almost apologetically.

For a while I listened to the progression of ka-thunks, realizing no one had yet come to look at our declaration form. No point in trying to go back to sleep. In a few minutes, along he came with his own rubber stamp. I had passed the time before leaving the station back in Tallinn trying to figure out how to complete the form in Russian. It required that each denomination of currency we carried be listed, while spelling the quantities alphabetically. The chore had kept me occupied for almost an hour. Surprisingly this had more impact than I could have imagined, and he was almost cordial.

The immigration agent, inspector and customs agent worked their way through the car. Fully awake after the Russian welcome wagon, I got up to gaze out the half open window and get some fresh air. A couple of tracks over sat a huge silent locomotive. In the orange haze of the sodium vapor lights, it appeared to have been a product of the same design team that conceived the 1949 Ford. One great headlamp and two tiny eye slit-like portals and a couple of blunt fins broke the otherwise smooth aerodynamic surface. The skin looked as if it were made of half-inch armor plate but still gave the impression of forward motion, even as it sat there in a serenade of crickets and frogs. It was a museum piece, the stuff of evocative Communist Party posters of the 1960s. I still wonder if it was in use or just standing there on a siding year after year. I thought about the awe it must have inspired when it rolled into Leningrad Station back in 1965 with surging diesels and hissing airbrakes and an aura of raw power.

Anticipation and a little tension at the uncertainty of our situation had us up early. We would be taking one more step from our familiar world. Unlike the other countries we had visited where English was either the first language or had been adopted as a strong second, Russians are quite satisfied with their own language. It might not be all that easy to get along. Carla and I were both noticeably on edge as we entered Russia. Most of that melted away in a matter of days, though, as we enjoyed the people and their take-life-as-it-comes attitude.

Part of the mystique of visiting Russia comes from the requirement that a person needs to have an invitation from a sponsor. That was easy enough to do as any hotel or tourist organization was anxious to cooperate in any way it could. There are still some contradictions firmly rooted from the days of Communist Party domination.

St. Petersburg

We rolled into Moscow Station in St. Petersburg just about on time. Our host Dimitri, a slight young man in his early thirties, was there to meet us. I'm pretty sure we were the only Americans on the train. As a result, there was not much confusion on Dimitri's part in deciding which group of four American tourists he was to meet. Dimitri's family, his father and mother, had gone off to their country *dacha* on holiday. We would be staying at their apartment in the heart of the city.

Carla had arranged our stay in St. Petersburg through the Host Families Association or HOFA. We planned four nights in St. Petersburg with Dimitri and three nights with a family in the medieval city of Novgorod. All that being prearranged, we just had to make sure we were at the right stations at the correct times. Our hosts took care of getting us to and from the stations and also purchased any additional bus and train tickets for us. These services were offered at a small additional fee.

After we had loaded our things into Dimitri's trunk he set a course for the center of old St. Petersburg. Edging his car out into the traffic, he began an interesting, if somewhat monotone recitation of the names of the cathedrals and palaces as they drifted by — Gostny Dvor, an eighteenth century bazaar and the sweeping colonnade of the Kazan Cathedral, burial place of Field Marshal Kutusov. The city looked like any other classical European city, maybe a little dingy, but with the look of a place people work, live and call home.

Passing by the Griboyedov Canal, Dimitri directed our eyes to the right for a glimpse of the Church of the Savior on the Blood, its colorful onion-shaped domes marking the spot where Tsar Alexander II was mortally wounded in 1881.

The Church of The Savior on the Blood, St. Petersburg, Russia. A beautifully ornate Russian Orthodox church that marks the spot where Czar Alexander II was mortally wounded (hence "the Blood"). (Russ)

For a moment the sky appeared to brighten as buildings dropped back from the busy avenue and our impromptu tour brushed by the vast openness of Dvortsovaya Plaza (Palace Square). Trimmed in white baroque scrolls against pea green stucco, Peter's great Winter Palace — it also houses the huge Hermitage Art Museum — looked out over cobblestone parade grounds.

Continuing down Nevsky Prospekt to the Dvortsovy Most (Dvortsovy Bridge) the old custom house sat on an island in the broad River Neva. Dimitri carried on with his fairly dry but continuous monolog. We proceeded across another bridge, the Birzhevoy Most, and on to his apartment located on the north side of the river almost directly across from the Winter Palace. The Peter and Paul Fortress, built in 1703, birthplace of St. Petersburg and a burial place of Russian Tsars, was only a couple hundred yards away. During the 20-minute drive from the station, we realized we'd not allowed enough time for St. Petersburg.

We bounced across tram tracks in need of a few spikes. They flopped chaotically up and down with each passing trolley. A narrow opening in the block-long apartment building revealed a drive-through into the dim light of an inner courtyard. Dimitri muttered as he carefully picked his way through the potholes and mud puddles, maneuvering around the trash containers and a desperate looking tree, crying out for just a few minutes of direct sunlight, plus a half dozen or so cars here and there. He tried to avoid blocking in someone else but failed.

The setting was gray; the sky, the building, the ground, and even the poor old tree were gray. We were all taken aback momentarily. But this was Russia, kind of what we had expected, a little gray, a little dingy, but with the soul of a people who had learned to keep their expectations in line with reality. I detected an attitude of optimistic resignation — things had been bad under Soviet rule, but now things were different, not necessarily better but less bureaucratic and perhaps with more opportunity.

Dimitri was an accommodating young man. He had the week off, and as was customary, he prepared breakfast for us each morning. We asked questions about Russia, and despite the fact that he had answered the same dumb questions many times before, he patiently responded in his careful Russian manner with a few subtle pauses and hints of inflection that showed his personal complexity and dry sense of humor. Measuring his words and never restating the obvious, I got the feeling that there was more to Dimitri than years of Soviet conditioning would allow him to reveal. He related a story about the days in the early nineties when Russia was undergoing political change — change that most of us in the West were unable to fathom.

A group of Russians were standing in line waiting for their daily purchase of bread. After some time one of two men who had engaged in a friendly bit of conversation finally said in exasperation, "I can't take this any more, all this change, all this upheaval. Everything we have known, now it is different, except for this bread line. I am going to go down to the Kremlin and shoot Gorbechav."

His newly found acquaintance nodded and they parted company. Inch by inch the one who remained moved closer to the front and finally after a couple of hours was rewarded with the opportunity to exchange his crumpled notes for two loaves of crusty white bread. As he turned to leave and was walking back to his apartment he met the man he had talked to in line earlier in the day. He was returning from the direction of the Kremlin.

He smiled and asked, "Well, did you shoot Gorbechav?"

"No" he admitted, "When I got to Red Square the line to shoot Gorbechav was longer than the bread line. So now I have neither bread nor satisfaction."

We laughed about change, and Dimitri explained that waiting in a Soviet bread line had become a defining part of Russian society. There had developed, over the years, a "Culture of the Line" that was now beginning to disappear. It had been based on the fact that people standing in close proximity to each other were eventually driven to make conversation with those within speaking distance. Friendships, ephemeral as they might be, were made and fragments of the daily experience shared. Dimitri expressed some small sense of loss.

St. Petersburg is a wonderful city to cover on foot, and we had a great time doing it. A surprising number of people spoke English and were more than happy to offer assistance when we looked in need. Russians do have a well-developed sense of humor, and we provided our share of grist for that mill.

We were truly in another country and a different culture, out of the English zone. This was made even clearer by signs on the stores and shops in alphabetical characters that were foreign to us. I had only digested enough Russian in the previous two months to be able to sound out words and ask for a few basic necessities. Language is an endless source of entertainment

We took our place in the line leading to the Hermitage Art Museum early one morning, probably an hour before opening. The line already stretched along the front and around the west side of the building. Drawn by curiosity, I had become addicted to the Russian alphabet. I stood there idly sounding out words and advertisements in all direction. My gaze momentarily arrested by a street vendor's cart, I began to work through the letters.

Let's see, I thought. "X" was a kind of guttural "h" sound.

I gathered some moisture in the back of my throat and gave it a little breath. This is not a sound that a native English speaker is adept at making. Next letter, the "o" more of an "aw" than an "oh" sound. I put the two together and came up with a sort of guttural "haw" and added what I recognized as the Greek "t" or tau. Concentrating on the sounds and resigned to the fact that meaning was well beyond my scope, I tried "hawt," "hawt." A Cyrillic "d," and another "o," that "aw" sound again. That gamma-looking thing on the end has "geh" sound. I stood there working it over in my mind, trying to put the sounds together. "Let's see now, hawt dawg, hawt dawg."

It didn't take too many repetitions for my mind to seize upon the familiar phonetic construction. "Ah, yes, I get it. Hot dog!" I laughed out loud. The line advanced a few paces. The people behind me edged forward, anticipating that I would close the space that had developed. I turned around to catch up. Bridging the cultural gap, I thought, as we walked across the great cobble stone plaza of Tsars and revolutionaries. We'd come a long way to find a hot dog stand.

The Hermitage Museum

The Hermitage Art Museum, occupying a large portion of Peter the Great's Winter Palace, was constructed by Catherine II; it is home to an unimaginable collection of world-class artistic masterpieces — a cultural icon and truly a St. Petersburg pilgrimage site.

Catherine, it seems, took it upon herself to build a small annex to the Winter Palace where she could get away from it all. The small annex was called The Hermitage. She was also determined to bring European culture to Russia and set her agents out on a quest to purchase collections of art. The resulting collection ranged from ancient gold work dating as far back as 400 B.C., artifacts, sculpture and paintings through contemporary masters. Soon the small annex was enlarged. Her avocation was further pursued by subsequent Romanov royalty until the Revolution of 1917. The state then took the opportunity to nationalize collections held by many aristocratic Russian families and added to the treasures of the Hermitage.

Two paintings by Leonardo Da Vinci and an incomplete sculpture by Michelangelo are among the famous Italian works. The mastery of light, detail and the tenderness of the renderings of Rembrandt, such as the "Portrait of an Old Jew" completed in 1654, held me for some minutes. It is sad to note that two years later in 1656 Rembrandt was judged bankrupt. His paintings and all his possessions were set on the block for auction.

A visit to the Hermitage is an all day event, similar to the British

Museum in London. It was an overwhelming maze of rooms and passageways. Without the aid of a detailed guidebook it would be impossible to navigate. We decided to plot a course and not wander around. I have to admit that my navigating skills are not the best, and I had us thoroughly lost within about the first ten minutes. Carla patiently came to the rescue and got us back on course.

Exhausted from hours on our feet, we stepped out into a beautiful afternoon in the vast open space of Dvortsovaya Plaza to find throngs of people milling about in a somewhat excited state. The atmosphere was almost festive with a sea of people standing on any elevated point to get a clearer view. What, we asked ourselves, had they all come to see? We dove into the crowd of mostly young people, wearing more color than we had come to expect in northern European dress, and found ourselves in the midst of a Russian motorcycle festival. The bikes were mostly modified bombs of the pseudo-chopper genre — a random collection of hardware, an odd assortment of two- and four-cycle creations with unlikely bits of chrome here and there, and some improvisational elements supported by the Russian equivalent of baling wire. Whatever the reason, the sun was bright, the afternoon warm and everyone was having fun.

We fully enjoyed every encounter with the Russian people. Securing meals was often our biggest challenge. Most of the smaller restaurants didn't have English menus, so we frequently had to wing it. Depending on how much pity the wait staff was willing to indulge, we were usually able to get ourselves fed, but it was always an adventure.

On one occasion we settled into a brightly lit coffee shop/restaurant with what appeared to be a family clientele. We had my limited knowledge of Russian, not a real asset, but something. We had our menu translator foldout card from one of our language books and a Russian phrase book. It was questionable just how much of this we were going to be able to cope with when hungry. We found that the clear and precise categories in the foldout menu translators seldom lined up with those items on the menu. We could kind of figure out the main categories, but the adjectives they used were well beyond our resources. Every word was an effort since we were dealing with a different alphabet.

The waitress was patient, but standing there with her pencil poised over her pad intensified the situation and created a sense of urgency that was not conducive to the process. After begging a couple of time extensions, we concluded the more expensive items were main entrées. So pretty much at random we chose a couple. We pointed to what a few other customers were eating, baguettes (sandwiches), and indicated we would take two of those, then went on to work our way through drinks. A half hour later we stepped back out onto the busy sidewalk feeling a great sense of accomplishment.

Perhaps the most memorable meal in Russia was at a little place that claimed to serve authentic country dishes. The waiter had a great sense of humor and a desire to practice English. I ended up ordering what turned out to be a three-inch-by-three-inch cake that was an inch thick of pure white pork lard. It had been carefully sliced into two layers and liberally filled with fresh garlic and chopped onion, then sliced vertically to almost resemble bacon without any lean. The recommended accompaniment was at least fifty grams of vodka.

Not wanting to appear too judgmental or critical of the customs of our host country, I accepted the waiter's recommendation. I think I could become accustomed to the vodka part, and I could appreciate that the Russian climate tended to encourage a higher caloric intake. The bite of the onion and sharpness of the garlic added flavor and some texture that was otherwise in short supply. Not much chewing was required, and, as might be expected, it melted in my mouth.

Lesley and Andrea, conditioned to a complete aversion to fat, looked on in awe. I don't think it would become a regular item in my diet, but I wanted to make a point. You just have to try something truly outrageous every so often. As I ate my slices of fat, they dunked pieces of coarsely grained bread into bowls of borscht and washed it down with glasses of cold kvass, a drink somehow made from black bread, which ferments over night. It is a dark murky liquid with a surprisingly fresh taste.

That scene, in one way or another, was to play itself out in many countries. We eventually lost any feelings of self-consciousness and sometimes were reduced to moos, snorts, and clucks to indicate beef, pork, or chicken. I am a firm advocate of learning languages, but there's only so much you can do.

We left St. Petersburg with one regret. We chickened out on the Metro. One afternoon, after walking for about six hours, we directed Lesley and Andrea back to the apartment, while Carla and I went in search of some train tickets that had been arranged for us and then sent to a hostel a mile or so from our lodgings at Dimitri's. We had very little reservation about sending the girls off on their own, since we jogged the route together early each morning.

Carla and I decided we would try the underground. We walked up Nevsky Prospekt to the station. It occurred to us later that we had shown up at the wrong time of day — rush hour. The place was an absolute zoo, and adding to the chaos, a major street renovation and building facelift were going on outside the station. Hordes of people were pressing through the turnstiles, some climbing over, some climbing under, and some squeezed through the exit. Carla and I stood there for a few minutes, trying to figure out where the entrance was and where the tickets were sold. This was not a place for beginners or those who intended to execute anything more than the exchange of money for tickets. We caught each other's eye, headed back into the street and started walking in the direction of our destination. I suppose we could have taken a taxi, but we didn't know exactly where the hostel was and thought getting a taxi driver in the middle of it wouldn't help if his English was anything like our Russian.

On the appointed day, Dimitri got us off to the bus station, and we headed south toward Moscow with a planned stop in Novgorod. Novgorod was the ancient capital of Russia, long before Moscow. Novgorod the Great, as its residents are fond of calling it, gave us an opportunity to glimpse day-to-day Russian life. It was also endowed with a couple of historical cathedrals, an old Kremlin area and an interesting Friday market.

Bus travel is really an excellent way to get around in Russia, especially for trips of a few hours. We enjoyed passing through the countryside. The short stretch between St. Petersburg and Novgorod was lush farming country. Clusters of steeply roofed houses with rough-cut plank exteriors were huddled together into villages. From the window of a bus, they did not appear too different from the little farming communities you might come across in the Upper Great Lakes region of the U.S. The unpaved lanes streaming off from the main highway exposed the heavy organic soil. Each house was adjoined by a fenced in garden with temporary trellises straining under a load of string beans and glistening tomatoes. Freshness filled the air. There were very few private cars, mostly just tractors moving from field to field. Occasionally the tractors carried ladies in floral print babushkas clutching shopping bags while seated on the sheet metal fenders as they hitched a ride to town.

Rumbling south along the two-lane blacktop, Lesley and Andrea gazed out the window and occasionally mustered enough discipline to complete another paragraph from their assigned reading. Entering each new country, one of the first things on our list was to locate an English bookstore where we might find something relevant for the girls to read. Carla was usually successful in locating at least one book that told a story about the country or had been written by native authors. In this instance she had found an autobiographical sketch of Maxim Gorky's childhood and a collection of short stories by Anton Checkov. Reading assignments were pretty much continuous. Some were engaging and could catch a young reader's imagination. With others, they labored over each page.

Around midday we rolled into the Novgorod bus station. Extracting ourselves from the confinement of our narrow seats, we stretched, made a perfunctory attempt to pull the wrinkles out of our clothes and brushed off the litter of crumbs. Gathering our stuff from the overhead rack and with a quick inventory of daypacks, purses and book bags, we stepped down into the warm afternoon sun.

Novgorod

The bus stop was just a curbed area in the parking lot of the train station. People milled about, either waiting for an arriving bus or fumbling to organize their luggage. The driver dislodged suitcases and boxes from the compartment in the belly of the bus and stood them on the sidewalk. Our modern travel packs were not typical of the lot and were easy to spot. Most everyone seemed absorbed in his or her own thoughts, and remarkably no clutch of vendors waved trinkets in our faces. We scanned the crowd for our contact. A soft-spoken, slender young lady offered her hand to Carla and introduced herself as Olga.

The Russian people are as warm a group of human beings as you will find anywhere in the world. It does not take much to elicit a smile, but in their faces certain seriousness prevails that seems to be a product of many years of hardship and uncertainty. No better example was this pretty young lady named Olga; she shared her apartment in Novgorod with us for a couple of nights while we explored the city and surroundings. With a friend and her young daughter, they lived in a massive self-sufficient apartment block located a few miles from the center of Novgorod. It was surrounded by agricultural fields, small manufacturers and warehouses.

Olga had come to Novgorod from the Ukraine. People of the ex-Soviet satellite had continued to suffer under a rather repressive government that had not relaxed their adherence to hard line Communist doctrine. With a degree in computer science she could not earn enough to feed her daughter, so she had migrated to Russia. At that time it was a veritable land of opportunity.

As a trade and administrative center, the city of Novgorod was established around A.D. 860 by the Swedish brand of the Vikings. It seems the Norse and Danes headed south and west in the first half of the ninth century to pillage and plunder the British Isles. An eastbound contingent, historians call the Varangians, took control of the village at Novgorod and developed it as a trade center among the North Slavic people. They soon established trade routes ranging as far south as Constantinople. The Republic of Novgorod was absorbed by the Principality of Moscow late in the fifteenth century

Fully enclosed in its well-preserved deep red walls is the area known as the Ditenets or Kremlin. As it turned out, the word Kremlin applies to an old town and its fortifications. Any medieval town may have a Kremlin area, contrary to the idea that there was only one Kremlin, and it was in Moscow. The Novgorod Kremlin rises on a sandy hill above the broad, fertile flood plane of the River Volkhov. The Volkhov is a slowly meandering, lowland river with muddy brown water that lazily delivers its cargo of silt to the Gulf of Finland.

Five of the onion shaped domes that have come to symbolize the orthodox churches of eastern Europe rise from the St. Sophia Cathedral, which we found tucked up against the Kremlin walls. Built in the years 1045–1050, it is one of the few medieval churches constructed of stone and, hence, still standing. Major construction projects in medieval times often lasted at least a decade, sometimes over a century. In fact, construction and improvements at St. Sophia continued well into the thirteenth century. It is amazing enough that it was built at all and still more remarkable that it was in a condition that permitted regular use.

Carla and the girls were required to wear babushkas to enter the Three Babs of the cathedral. Makeshift skirts were available at the front door for those females inappropriately dressed. Andrea, wearing full-length pants that almost covered her socks, was not in the eyes of the monk appropriately feminine and was required to wear a skirt. This was a small price to pay for the opportunity to view beautifully gilded walls and icon paintings within the historic Orthodox Church.

Novgorod Monastery, The Three Babs. Babuskas are considered appropriate attire for ladies entering the twelfth century cathedral of St. George near Novgorod. (Russ)

On the opposite side of the river from the kremlin is a settlement that includes a jumble of shops, historic churches and chapels in various stages of repair. They were built by wealthy Russian merchant families in the years between the eleventh and fifteenth centuries when Novgorod was still an independent principality. With the rise of capitalism a lively farmers' market has now blossomed on that side of the river.

I often took the video camera along on days we went to markets. No doubt the supermarket is a more efficient means of delivering fresh, high quality meats and produce to its customer base, but it is obvious why many cultures hold on to their traditional markets and regular market days. It is free enterprise at its most basic, the direct exchange of goods for currency between the two people to whom the outcome is most important, the producer and the end user.

For whatever reason, the gene that controls development of visual perception, especially that of young men in uniform with brass buttons, awoke and found full expression in Andrea somewhere along the way. She took more than a passing notice of these young men and was consumed with the idea of joining the military when age finally permitted. We neither encouraged nor discouraged this, but conversation often turned in that direction, especially if uniformed young men were in the vicinity.

The afternoon sun warmed our backs as we walked along the banks of the Volkhov. Andrea was pressing me for details about the Russian military, a source that was quickly exhausted after the first couple of questions. All I could do was draw some comparisons to what little I knew of our own military. Making our way up the slope from the river's edge to the main Kremlin gate, I began to explain to her how the Russian military uniforms we had seen back in St. Petersburg seemed to have a less finished look. They do not tuck their shirts into their trousers but have a narrow belt of fabric with a single prominent button. It does have its advantages, I allowed, since as officers develop a middle-aged profile, the actual location of the waist becomes a matter of some debate. Making our way up to the bridge in front of the historic city gate, a group of uniformed military officers stepped out through the heavy wooden doors.

"What branch of the service do you think those men coming out of the gate are in? Do you think they're Russian?"

"Well Andrea, I don't know, but since we're in Russia, it is a good chance they're Russian, and looking at the blue uniforms, I'd cast my vote for Air Force. The uniforms are not too different from those you might see back in the U.S., except the Russians don't tuck in their shirts but have that little button affair."

"I kind of like it." Andrea said, quickly coming to their defense.

"I don't think it looks as sharp as our guys' uniforms," I countered. Pausing, I said, "Some of them have their shirts tucked in, and I just think it looks a little neater. In fact, those men with their shirts tucked in may not be Russian."

As we approached the small contingent of about a dozen or so people mostly in blue uniform, it became more apparent that we were seeing a mixed group of military officers, probably some kind of exchange program. About half the men in uniform were from the U.S. Air Force. That conveniently emphasized my point about uniforms.

We drew off to one side and watched them mill about for a minute. They seemed to be on some sort of tour being conducted by a couple of Chamber of Commerce types. They were, for the moment, looking as though they had all heard enough Russian history. One of the Americans, a fit looking officer in his early forties, shirt tucked-in, was idly looking down at a pamphlet of some kind. He was separated from the group by a few feet.

I just couldn't pass up the opportunity. I took in a little extra air, cleared my throat, and let loose, "Where yah from?" adding just the right amount of Texas intonation to differentiate it from the brand of English that was barely capturing his attention.

The officer had just begun to take the first step in the direction of his party when my message arrived, ploughed its way through the haze of travel fatigue and lodged in his consciousness.

Lesley, who had just walked up, saw his reaction.

He turned his head to the left to face us and lifted his right foot, now trying to change directions toward the origin of the more familiar sound. The result was a rather exaggerated, almost theatrical double-take. "Dallas. How 'bout you?" he said.

"Houston," I replied.

His expression brightened. He walked over, and we shook hands. He motioned to one of his traveling companions and said, "He's from Dalhart." Pointing to still another, he added, "And he's from Amarillo."

Soon we were engaged in a joyous mini-reunion, exchanging a few y'alls and howdys in true Texas style. They were astonished to find a family from the U.S. wandering around unescorted in Russia, in Novgorod, no less. He asked just what in the world we were doing there and went on to say they had been gone from home almost a week.

I told him we had been in Russia only a few days ourselves but didn't bother to mention we had been away from home for over two months. It was only a matter of a minute or two before their hosts realized they no longer had the undivided attention of the U.S. men, and they were politely asked to rejoin their group. We shook hands and parted. We stepped through the gates of the old city and went our separate ways.

Up until that point we had not been seeking opportunities to meet folks from back home. But I have to admit — I truly enjoyed seeing them.

On the afternoon of the third day, Lesley and Andrea sadly wished their new, young friends at the apartment goodbye as Olga rounded up a taxi for us. After a few minutes of pushing and shoving luggage into the trunk, the six of us, including the driver, piled in along with some portion of our luggage and headed back to Novgorod station. The ample portions of coarse-grained bread we had devoured for lunch, along with fresh tomatoes and cucumbers, were taking their toll in the afternoon sun, and our attempts to keep the conversation flowing were strained at best. Olga, determined to see to our well being up until the last, stood with us on the platform until we were safely and securely situated on the train for Moscow. As the train began to move slowly along the platform, she waved and smiled. She had a gentle, pretty smile, especially for someone who had experienced more of the serious side of life than we were ever likely to know.

Moscow

We arrived in Moscow at about four o'clock in the morning. Arrangements had been made through our hostel to be met and transported. Our contact, a young lady in her twenties, tried to act as though she was happy to see us. But she appeared as sleepy as we were. She probably had a day job and a family waiting for breakfast somewhere.

A light rain had covered the streets in the vicinity of the train station, and the brightly illuminated advertisements and neon lights made wavy reflections on the wet paving bricks. It wasn't at all the dreary shell of the post Soviet era, but a lively looking district even before sunrise.

Leaving the center of the city, we sailed through the still-sleeping streets of Moscow. Only a few maintenance workers and street cleaners were going about their duties tidying up in advance of the imminent flood of humanity and the associated debris brought on by another day in the city. The only sound was the car's squeaky suspension as we dodged an occasional pothole. The backdrop to the broad, tree lined avenues was a mosaic of high-rise apartments buildings, the spaces between packed with hastily built shops and magazine stands wearing their night dress of worn plywood sheets and blue tarps.

The car pulled up to what appeared to be a towering hotel in a relatively nice neighborhood. We slipped past the vacant reception counter. The concierge was sleeping at his metal desk. Two security guards were doing their best to remain conscious by playing a game of cards, while a television in the corner of the lobby was idly offering up reruns of what looked like Russian soap opera — the only sound at 4:30 A.M.

The elevators were a bit creaky and made it known they were doing us a favor to draw us up to the tenth floor, the location of the hostel; it seems the hotel rented out a floor or two to a hostelling organization. The rooms were a bit dingy with stained wallpaper and hastily swept floors. Bed sheets seemed to be clean, but the maintenance budget was probably a bit short of what might have been necessary to meet standards we had experienced in Norway or Sweden. The young college age staff were friendly, spoke very good English and were happy to be of service in any way possible.

We caught a couple hours of sleep and prepared to go out for some exploring. Breakfast, included in the price of the room, consisted of a container of yogurt, a single slice of individually wrapped lightly colored cheese, the type you might put on a sandwich, and all the hot water you could use to make coffee or tea. I was still well supplied with the coffee I'd picked up in Norway plus the remainder of our Norwegian reindeer salami.

Sipping my coffee, I asked the young man behind the desk if there were facilities to do laundry in the hostel or even a coin operated laundry close by. His expression gave some evidence of how absurd he thought the question was. He seemed amused and said not just "no," but "certainly not." He suggested we rinse what we needed in the shower or bathroom sink.

I will always remember the last part of our visit to Russia as my "blue period"; I wore the same blue shirt and navy blue pants for several days running. The girls learned to plan ahead for what they hoped to wear in succeeding days. We strung our tenement line from the window frame to the bathroom door. It sagged under the weight of damp socks and undergarments creating a kind of partition.

Setting off to see if we could figure out the subway or Metro system in Moscow, we found a station a few yards from the hostel. We were surprised to find traveling around Moscow very easy. For a mere 140 rubles (about US$4.80), we could buy a ten-ride pass. The computerized turnstile automatically debited the pass each time it was put through. If a person attempted to walk through without a pass, a pair of knee high iron curtains shot out and brought instant misery to the delinquent commuter; it was best to make sure the pass went through the reader correctly.

Maps of the system were easy to come by, and the stations were well marked — but only in Russian. We found that it was not difficult to recognize Russian alphabet characters. In addition, each car had a system map posted; we could also count our stops.

Moscow's underground stations are reputed to be works of art, and they lived up to that notion. Each one was slightly different with elaborate tile and paintings on all surfaces. Every stop increased our anticipation for the next marvel of the Russian metro artists — from abstract designs to depictions of communes and steely proletarian workers. Everything about the system was clean, well marked and a pleasure to use. Moscovites on their way to and from work did their fair share of staring but were pleasant and polite during our occasional interactions. Self-conscious as 12- and 14-year-olds are, Andrea and Lesley garnered plenty of appraisals from their Russian contemporaries. It might not have been obvious that we were American, but it was clear that we were not natives.

Carrying commuters into the system are what seemed to be the world's longest and steepest escalators. Leading down into the labyrinth below the city, at times it was impossible to see the other end. Recent converts to capitalism, their transportation authorities had learned to take advantage of a captive audience and had added posters along the inclined passageways extolling the benefits of Coca Cola and the next action flick from the U.S.

The biggest hit with the girls was Red Square. It had a certain magnetic quality, and it seemed we had to touch base there each day we were in Moscow. Carla and I still remembered newsreels with Nikita Khrushchev reviewing the goose-stepping troops and ICBMs rolling by on somber green transports during May Day celebrations. The atmosphere we found was almost festive, and it was hard to see much of the old Communist

St. Basil's, Red Square, Moscow. Built by order of Czar Ivan the Terrible in 1561, St. Basil's Cathedral is the world-renown symbol of Moscow and Red Square. (Carla)

presence except for the solitary Soviet Star or two topping the gate towers of the Moscow Kremlin. This was the Kremlin we all had come to know.

Along one side of Red Square, still lying in state, is the preserved corpse of Vladimir Ilyich Lenin. We, of course, made the circuit down into the almost pitch dark mausoleum that was well beneath the ground level of the square. There, in the center of an illuminated glass case in the otherwise solemn darkness, were the remains of the man who engineered the great cruel experiment from which the Russian people have been trying to extract themselves for the past decade or more. There is a measure of poetic justice in that Mr. Lenin has to face the enormous GUM center, a crowded commercial center on the opposite side of Red Square with all its capitalist trappings from Armani and Luis Vuitton to Russian fast food.

We found the streets of Moscow as vibrant and exciting as any large European city. They were filled with street performers, trinket and souvenir vendors, and every kind of shop and eatery. It was hard to see a vestige of the Soviet era. A few places still have the feel of the old system, and one of our most enjoyable afternoons was spent at the Museum of the Revolution. On display were the great hammers and sickles from government buildings and an incredible collection of World War II paraphernalia. Authentic propaganda posters of the People's Revolution from the past eighty years were arranged in a very thought provoking way. There were enough three dimensional displays and large-scale exhibits to keep Andrea and Lesley fascinated. Each exhibit hall had an elderly person seated at the door, hopeless boredom etched into the lines of their faces. Most would brighten with a simple, "*Zdrastvuytye*," especially if it came from the mouth of a Western tourist. Some of them looked as if, after many years, they had been released and finally walked off the pages of one of Ian Fleming's novels to tend the relics of a glorious past.

Stepping out into the Russia of the twenty-first century, we were confronted by another bit of irony in red-and-white stripes. Illuminated in the afternoon sun, a TGI Fridays sat immediately across the street. It bustled with Moscovites eager to indulge in a taco salad or probably a bacon-cheddar burger. We went down the block to a Mongolian hibachi fast food place for some grilled beef and vegetables.

Equally engaging were the Russian Military Museum, an incredible performance of the Russian circus and an evening at the ballet. Of those, the circus, a form of entertainment of which I'd never been too fond, was spectacular. Executed entirely on ice, each act developed a feeling of anticipation as they accomplished increasingly more difficult, almost outlandish feats. They were all within the expected realm of circus acts — jugglers, acrobats, dancing bears and troops of clowns — but they had gone far beyond what seemed humanly possible. Even better, the acts were announced in both Russian and English.

Our time in Moscow was truly an enjoyable adventure. Transportation was easy. Food was plentiful and reasonably priced. Ordering was occasionally a challenge, but the local waiters were willing to go the extra distance to make us feel comfortable.

The afternoon of our last day in Moscow we spent searching the Arbat, a pedestrian mall, for the perfect Matryoshka doll. As daylight began to fade, at the girl's insistence, we made one last pass through Red Square, and, of course, we had to put our foot on the brass marker that symbolizes the center of Russia one more time. Our final meal was in a little restaurant in the GUM center, topped off with 50 grams of vodka (for adults only).

We had come to know and enjoy Moscow, and I think we were all a bit sad to be leaving. Although I felt I was actually going to miss our old adversary, an adversary we had always respected as a peer, I believe Carla and I had finally shed the remaining cold war baggage.

The Czech Republic

Carla and I both felt a little tension melt away as we got off the plane in Prague. Looking back on it, this doesn't seem all that remarkable. Jumping into a cab, the Imperial Hotel in downtown Prague was our destination. A private hostel, meaning it is not affiliated with the Hostelling International organization, it's really just an old hotel that rents rooms at half the walk-in price, if you make reservations through an agent or online. Built in 1914, it is not ancient by European standards, but it is a landmark. The restaurant is unique; the walls and ceiling are covered with ornately sculpted ceramic tile, qualifying it for historical building designation. A brightly lit and noisy place, the walls tend to amplify the normal restaurant clatter and conversation.

Our room for four overlooked Na Porici Street and a main trolley line. It seemed airy, since the ceiling was a good 12 feet overhead. The creaky beds had a homey feel, and we spent a couple of rainy afternoons catching up on reading assignments, writing in our journals and generally relaxing. Since leaving Settle back in the Yorkshire Dales, it had taken us forty days to work our way from the southern tip of Norway, up across the Arctic Circle, down through Sweden, over to Estonia and then into Russia. The longest we had stayed in any one place was four nights. Our plan had been to cover the northern latitudes while summer temperatures still prevailed, and that we had done. Prague was a time to regroup, prepare for our entry into Germany and then on through Europe.

Mornings we started with a run through the old town district, then across the stone bridge to the base of rising cliffs on the other side of the River Vltava. Prague Castle, a thirteenth century stronghold, commanded the horizon above us. In the chilly morning air we went on past clusters of commuters waiting at their regular bus stop and finished our circuit at a little bakery that had become an instant favorite with the girls. The odor of warm pastries rose temptingly from the white paper bag as we enjoyed a leisurely pace back to the Imperial Hotel.

Making the hike up to the castle one bright afternoon along the winding cobblestone streets, it was impossible not to feel as though we had truly arrived in the heart of Old Europe. Rising in the midst of the castle courtyard was St. Vitus Cathedral; it was built on the site of the original tenth century Rotunda of St. Wensaslas. Construction had begun in the year 1230 and continued on and off for well over 200 years. The girls derived no end of pleasure from the gargoyles, saints and demons sprouting from every parapet and arch. Finally, climbing the musty spiral steps to the top of the bell tower, the modern city of Prague rolled out to the low hills in the distance.

Below the ridge and bounded on two sides by the Vltava and its seven bridges, Prague's old town was a perfect place to stroll away a week. Buildings were an absolute riot of baroque sculpture, and florid archways were embellished in every conceivable manner. Many a young sculptor made a living practicing his trade in Prague.

Evenings found us enjoying a Budweiser (the original), schnitzel and noodles, and wasting time in the souvenir shops looking at the puppets and other unique creations. The famous Karluv Most (Charles Bridge), dating back to 1357, could be counted on for an entertaining retinue of street performers and sidewalk artists.

An art form we especially enjoyed and popular in Prague involved stage performances utilizing a variety of highly imaginative puppets, props and costumes responsive to the use of black light (UV). Modern adaptations of Faust and several other classical works are offered in cramped little theaters in the old town district. Quite acceptable and entertaining to all four of us, it had upbeat and quickly paced music. We sampled the performing arts in many cities along the way, but the black light theater in Prague was truly unique.

09/03/01 — Russ

I have been reduced to hanging out in train stations, truly a homeless person. There are no seats in the tiny hotel lobby. The girls are still asleep, Carla is in the shower, and I want to write. The train station is about two blocks from the hotel, a quiet place to sit: a Dunkin' Donut shop. Table rent — one coffee, one donut.

The first signs of comfortable familiarity began to creep into our bones at the end of seven days. It was a defining symptom — time to pack up and prepare for the next leg of the journey.

Chapter 4 _____

Germany, France and Italy

ANOTHER 4:30 A.M. WAKE-UP TO MAKE A 6:25 A.M. train. Conversation was limited. Only the sounds of zippers being pulled and plastic buckles snapping into place broke the silence as we finished packing and collected our gear at the door for a final inventory.

The sidewalks of Prague were empty. On through the darkened pathways of the Vrchlickeho Sady, the city park surrounding the main train station; we hurried along in a brief predawn rain shower. Waking birds in the trees overhead and the clattering wheels of our packs on the rough concrete followed us. An occasional trolley rumbled soberly by with lights inside ablaze — an aquarium tank on wheels, the passengers absorbed in newspapers or blindly staring at the advertisements posted above the windows. The sounds that had lulled us to sleep each night in our room now seemed comforting, drawing us back to the assurance of things known. Again we shed the entanglements of our brief love affair with Prague.

From the damp serenity and darkness outside we passed into the warmth of the main train station, Hlavni Nadrazi. The inside perimeter was lined with ticket sellers, money exchangers and snack vendors. A sprinkling of people lounged in the few available seats. The rest were huddled into little clumps here and there. The young ones leaned against their brightly colored backpacks made of high tech material, while others with worn suitcases had equally worn expressions on their faces at 5:00 A.M.

The brightly lit signboard displaying train numbers, platforms and departure times, alternating from Czech to English, was suspended from the ceiling and shone down on everyone. Pausing at a battered plywood vendor stand, I grabbed a cup of coffee and our final Czech snacks for the trip into Germany.

We needed to cover a little over 200 miles, not much time to leaf through our books and travel information to see what lay ahead. The destination for the day was Gunzenhausen, a town about a hundred miles into the heart of southern Germany, in the Free State of Bavaria, as Bavarians like to say. This preoccupation with being a free state is not too different from the idea many Texans cling to, believing that on any day they can just pull out and go their own way.

Comfortably settled-in, the girls ate their breakfasts of fresh pastries and milk as the train departed the station. I rummaged through my daypack searching for a crinkled Ziploc bag with remnants of the three week old Norwegian salami. As I cut the remaining little hemisphere into pieces and passed them around, I reckoned my trusty Leatherman Multitool would not be in need of lubrication any time soon. We finished off with a couple of juice packets, and all was well.

While in Prague, Carla had located a hostel in Gunzenhausen on the Internet, and that was about all we knew of the place. Finding ourselves on another strange platform in mid-afternoon was becoming routine. But it was now time to exercise my year's worth of German study in hopes of getting directions from the ticket agent.

Germany

When it comes to basic communications, you use everything that is at your disposal, and if it hadn't been for some serious hand waving and gestures, we might not have found the footpath to our destination. About a mile from the station, we turned up at the door of the hostel, where a prominent sign announced that the reception area would not open until 5:00 p.m., a common schedule in European hostels. With a couple of hours to wait, we stowed our bags in the foyer of their very clean and modern dormitory and sent the girls out onto the street to scope the place out. Carla went off in a separate direction. Sufficiently humbled by my first encounter, I chose to work on my German vocabulary. Led by their instincts and noses, Lesley and Andrea discovered a bright deli/bakery about a hundred feet from our hostel and came back beaming with a few items to carry us until dinner.

Genzenhausen was one of those well-scrubbed little German towns; from the looks of it, I suspected it had been mostly rebuilt after World War II. The polite forty-ish hostel administrator, who opened the desk promptly at 5:00, supplied us with sheets and a copy of the hostel rules and regulations. I nodded to Andrea, hoping for some support, and tried again with my German, but when he came back with understandable English, I caved in and fell like a backsliding novitiate into my more comfortable native tongue. Andrea, who had been my German study partner, was too shy to give it a try. I was disappointed at my lack of facility with German. It was almost as though our visit to Russia had intervened and wiped out my year's efforts to speak some German. Nevertheless, we had a place to sleep for a couple of nights.

There were very few locations where we didn't try to check our e-mail. Internet cafés were located in most towns. The words Internet café or bar have pretty broad connotations, meaning they have between one and twenty-five computers. The café part means anything from an espresso machine and a cooler of soft drinks to a full bar and restaurant. Such places were often located in a basement or some remote corner and were usually run by a variety of entrepreneurial thirty-somethings with geeky hair and nicotine stained fingers.

We finally found the Internet café in Gunzenhausen, but it didn't open until 5:45 in the afternoon. Later that evening, leaving the girls at the hostel to do some reading, we walked the mile or so back in the direction of the train station and the Internet café. We felt our way up the narrow staircase, pupils wide open to gather any shreds of light. Opening the glass door that was opaque with condensation, we stepped into a dimly lit, smoke-filled room lined with a couple of dozen computers in an almost night club atmosphere, a full bar, espresso and snack offering.

The room was in high gear and filled almost exclusively with young men in their twenties, their anxious faces illuminated by the diffuse light of computer screens. Hunched over their key boards they banged away, completely absorbed in video games — cigarettes dangling from their lips. We had long since ceased to find it unmanageable to work in surroundings where oxygen and nitrogen molecules were secondary components of the atmosphere. European young people seemed to feel smoking was not just a pleasure to be enjoyed but an obligation. I don't think many people came there to check e-mail or to do much surfing of the web. It was more of an arcade or Internet video game bar.

By this time, we had learned to bring small flashlights with us to Internet cafés; often these places had very dim lights, and it was impossible to read a travel book or locate towns on a map without some additional source of light. We attracted a few looks of passing curiosity between the rounds of video action when one of the participants pushed back from the screen long enough to take a deep drag on his cigarette or order another beer. After an hour or so of checking e-mails and searching for future accommodations, our eyes burning from the smoke, we stumbled back into the fastidiously clean and abandoned streets of Gunzenhausen. I imagine a faintly glowing cloud of electronically charged cigarette smoke trailed behind us in the cool evening air. The girls didn't hesitate to comment on the scent of our clothes when we returned to the hostel room. They had been dutifully reading.

After getting our bearings in Gunzenhausen for a couple of days, we boarded a train for Frankfurt where Carla had arranged for a car through a Peugeot leasing program. The plan was to travel by car through Germany, France and Italy, and drop it in Rome at the end of November, for a total of eighty days. That decision was based on the comparative cost of Eurail Passes. For two people it might have been a break-even proposition, but the car was much more economical for the four of us. The car also gave us freedom to stay in places that were removed from the center of cities we visited where lodgings were always more costly than in the outskirts or in the smaller towns. However, we would all admit that traveling by car made us feel more isolated. Train travel had a certain communal quality, and the personal interaction was something we enjoyed and missed when it was absent.

The giant sycamore trees along the River Main were beginning to change when we arrived in Frankfurt, and the sky was heavy with the grayish cast of autumn. Typical of hostels in larger European cities, the one in Frankfurt was a massive old hotel. It was crowded, and we were lucky enough to secure a room for a single night, but that was it. We would have to find other accommodations for anything beyond that. After Stockholm, Tallinn, St. Petersburg, Moscow and Prague, we had all had our fill, at least for a while, of big cities. We decided to head out into the countryside.

The arrival of September also meant the start of home schooling. Before leaving the U.S. we had purchased two complete mathematics curricula and an English grammar program. Our plan was for Carla to teach English grammar and manage the reading assignments. I would be in charge of teaching pre-algebra to Andrea and working on geometry with Lesley.

We had been trying to get the first package, the infamous Box 1, sent to us in Germany and had asked that it be sent to the American Express office in Frankfurt. However, American Express offices, we learned, did not accept packages, only letter mail. After a bit of anxiety and a couple of calls, we determined that the box had not been sent and was still safely in the hands of our business manager back home. With that under control, we got ourselves ready to embark on the next phase of our trip.

Picking up the car at the Peugeot dealer in Frankfurt, we fulfilled the last of the arrangements Carla had made before leaving Houston, except for our stay in China some seven months hence. Planning from that point on would need to be done more or less continuously or on the fly. Sometimes we planned a couple of weeks out. Other times, like in Frankfurt, accommodations for the next day were the main focus. In conjunction with guidebooks, Internet cafés became our link to the world and our main planning tool.

Around the block from the hostel in Frankfurt, we found a narrow shop lined inside with glass and aluminum enclosures. These were rather large phone booths, capable of holding two or three people, where international travelers and families of immigrants could make calls home. They also had a few Internet terminals. Going back and forth between the guidebook and computer terminal, Carla located a couple of villages and jotted down the phone numbers. While she was doing that, I worked up a short script in German that I could use to communicate our needs when someone on the other end answered the phone. The good thing about writing out a script is that it prompted me on the vocabulary that tended to slip away in the course of a conversation. I found it was also prudent to try to map out some of the variations that might occur when the party on the other end didn't know his part of the script. If I couldn't understand the person on the other end, I would just go back and try to pick up at the point where I had become derailed. It was comical, but we were eventually successful at arranging an evening at a hostel in the town of Melsungen and then a week in a historic small town an hour or so southwest of Berlin.

The day's weather had begun to take shape — chilly with intermittent rain showers; it had us dodging in and out of doorways as we made our way along the sidewalk. Dashing into the bakery a few doors down from the Internet shop, we picked up some traveling fare and jogged to the edge of the river where the car was parked under the arching branches of the sycamore trees that almost completely blocked out the light of day. Threading our way through Frankfurt's morning traffic and arriving at the outskirts, we set our little Peugeot 302 on a north by northeasterly heading. Some optimizing had to be done to get all of our stuff into the hatchback trunk; but we finally figured it out.

Driving through the Harz Mountains from the south, we passed several small towns with bright little shops and busloads of Berliners out for weekend excursions. Carla stared dreamily out at them, but we had already made a reservation at Quedlinburg a small town a few kilometers north of the mountains; we kept on going. Finally, late in the afternoon we rolled into the town of Thale, (pronounced Tal'-eh). It didn't seem to have any of the gingerbread that was so prevalent earlier in the day; in fact, in some parts old, abandoned buildings and a sprawling industrial complex looked a bit under-utilized. Shortly we would be heading out onto the plains away from the mountains.

Carla and I exchanged glances, thought longingly about being in the mountains and decided to check with the little tourist information center in the city park to see if there were any cottages or flats to rent in the area. The charming young lady spoke perfect English. She checked her computer and quickly located a flat for us. She called the owner, checked the rate and availability, and gave us directions to a jewelry shop on Karl Marx Strasse.

In a matter of minutes we were introducing ourselves to Frau Witchen who was waiting for us in front of her carefully appointed jewelry store. Our accommodations for the next week would be a flat over the jewelry store that looked out onto the tidy hauptstrasse (main street). The view from our rear window was of an ivy covered courtyard, pots of geraniums, brilliant splashes of red and salmon surrounding a little, well-manicured summer garden, not a weed to be found. After weeks of traveling, we were ready to settle in and try to recapture some semblance of order and routine. The luxury of having a kitchen again was something we had all been longing for. At Frau Witchen's urging we made it off to the grocery store before closing, since she indicated they would be closed on Sunday. We stocked up on a few German essentials and got ourselves back to our flat by dark.

In spite of the fact that the main street was Karl Marx Strasse, and we were around the corner from the Sputnik Youth Club, it did not occur to me, at least for the first few days, that Thale was in what was formerly the German Democratic Republic.

A couple of days went by. We located a pair of coin operated Internet terminals at the nearby hostel. It was a beautiful old lodge at the end of the road, situated in a fairly steep canyon along a tumbling mountain stream. We felt a slight tinge of disappointment, as we had not been able to get into this grand old inn. Since there was no one at the desk to make change, we pooled the few coins we had among us and went through the slow process of logging on. About the time we got things going, a torrent of junior high students spilled down the stairs and engulfed us. Amused and in need of something to do, youngsters looked over Lesley's shoulders, reading out loud the English as she typed in a message to a friend back home. Our decision to stay at Frau Witchen's did seem to have its advantages. Comfortably ensconced in our flat at Number 22 Karl Marx Strasse, we were in the process of preparing a dinner of bratwurst and sauerkraut with a batch of kartofel puffers. The puffers were dumplings made of potato flour. Lesley and Andrea were enjoying the process of rolling the sticky dough into little spheres and alternately complaining about getting their hands covered with dough. The kitchen was warmed up and filled with the aromas of sauerkraut and sausage cooking. Tired but satisfied after a full day hiking in the mountains, idle chatter surrounded the process of food preparation.

Paging through a travel worn edition of an English news magazine, things seemed to be rocking along as usual. It didn't look like tempers were settling down anywhere in the world. Lesley and Andrea, by then starved for news, conceded to reading anything in English, even if the magazine carried the title of *The Economist.*

Lesley let out a sigh, "I don't get it. What can they possibly be fighting about? They're all the same people. They just go to a different church." She was speaking in reference to the story about Northern Ireland. "Everybody in our neighborhood goes to a different church, and we're not fighting," she stated matter of factly.

"Old ideas die hard," I offered "That's the advantage America had when it was formed. Everyone was an immigrant, and they had to worry about eating or making it through the next winter. So they had to depend on each other and put cultural differences aside, just in order to survive."

"It's not like the Muslims and the Jews," she persisted. "They at least have different religions. Those people are all Christians!"

Dinner conversations had taken on a much more global scope. Over the months we watched our plans to visit some friends in Jakarta slip off the schedule, prompted by ethnic and religious unrest. Politics at home were still within the limits of predictability.

The following evening a knock came at the apartment door. I went around to the darkened entrance to our flat and switched on the hallway light at the head of the stairs. Herr Witchen was standing there, his athletic six foot six frame filling the doorway; he looked a bit anxious. I invited him in. He and I both realized that communications between the two of us were never going get beyond the short list of cordial greetings I had memorized, and even they were failing me at the moment.

"Do you have news of New York?" he asked.

"No, I'm sorry, what is it about New York?" I looked at him puzzled, not understanding what he was trying to say.

Frustrated by his inability to put his thoughts into English, he simply said. "Trade Center all gone! Terrorists! All gone! Pentagon all gone!" Herr Witchen was a tall handsome man in his early sixties with a full head of perfectly white hair and the air of an athlete. His degree of agitation didn't seem to fit his normally polite and reserved demeanor.

He walked past me into the living room. The foldout sleeper sofa, covered with maps and books, had not been made up. I winced when he stepped around the bed and witnessed the full scale and scope of Andrea's spontaneously exploding suitcase. We had scarcely noticed the small black-and-white television on the table. Herr Witchen fumbled around to find a socket, then a small extension cord and finally the remote. He seemed in a hurry. We stood there nodding and smiling like the bunch of linguistically challenged refugees that we were. At last he got the little television set going, and we stood there speechless at the continuous stream of reruns, watching over and over the impact of the two airliners on the World Trade Center in New York. Herr Witchen, now relieved at getting the message delivered, made a disturbed comment about having visited there only last year, offered a few gestures and words in condolence, then departed for his flat across the landing.

We watched for a while and then, as all the news was in German, turned off the television to eat dinner. It was almost as though we had been seeing clips from the latest Hollywood disaster movie. The enormity of the catastrophe was literally too much to take in. Sitting around the tiny dinner table, conversation was sparse, each of us turning over in our minds what we had seen and what it all might mean.

Finally Lesley broke the silence, "Well, what are we going to do now?

Carla and I looked at each other and had to admit there was much we didn't know. But what we did know was that we were going keep our eyes and ears open, and our wits about us.

The girls each asked a few questions. Carla and I tried to answer them as well as we could. Anything we said at that moment would just be pointless speculation.

"We have no idea who these people are," I said, "but if we pack our bags and run home, I think we will be giving them just what they want. We have only this one year together, and we are not going to let anyone take it from us."

On a shaky book shelf near where we were sitting was a large, old multiband Grundig radio with a piece of wire coat hanger attached to the jagged little stub where the antenna had once been. The strings and pulleys that controlled the dial indicator reacted in sporadic, jerky movements as I adjusted the tuning knob. The sounds, the entire scene, were those of an old World War II movie, except it was real.

Squealing and buzzing, snow and chatter, fading in and fading out, radio stations from all across Europe were alive with the news. The only parts we could understand were the words "World Trade Center," "Pentagon" and "terrorists." These phrases were being repeated in every conceivable language and accent, all the way across the radio dial. After some time, moving the knob with utmost precision, I was able to find some English. It was the Voice of America. It came and went, and every time we wanted to catch some salient detail, it would begin to squeal and fade between a Russian and a French station. Soon it vanished, and we finished the evening listening to the English broadcast from the Voice of Russia. It was a surprisingly level and sedate account of the disaster. We probably learned more from that broadcast than anywhere else.

We listened as long as possible, until the news became repetitive and the reception receded into the ether. There was nothing more to do except sleep and see what news tomorrow would bring. As we pulled back the covers, I said to Carla, "You know, next to being home, I can't think of a place on this planet I'd feel safer and more welcome than here in this little town in East Germany. These people are so solid, so German."

Over the next couple of days we began to put together some of the details and accept the facts of what happened on September 11. The first night it was the Voice of Russia, the next night an American Radio Free Europe broadcast, and the third night it was the good old BBC. It all depended on the weather conditions and the careful positioning of the homemade antenna. We spent most of the time twisting the knobs on the old radio, scanning to find a station, then holding onto it once we did.

Carla and I never really considered turning around and going home. The question was: What would we do differently, if anything, than we had planned? The goal we had all agreed upon was to travel completely around the world. We would persist in the pursuit of our goal.

On September 12, 2001, we received Box 1; it contained about three months of instructional material. Home schooling began in earnest. We would see to it that our daughters were educated and prepared to assume active and intelligent roles in the dangerous and violent world they would inherit all too soon. In the mail, along with the package, was a letter we would treasure for a long time; it was from the Bergermeister (mayor) and town council of Thale. In not quite perfect English it expressed their deepest sympathies and support for the people of the United States. They offered any assistance that we might need in arranging our return trip to the U.S. We were very proud to be Americans and very to happy to be in Germany; we felt a kinship with this community that had endured so much in their own past.

We spent the next few mornings delving into our workbooks and establishing the operating parameters of home schooling away from home. The return to discipline was a bit of a shock to us all, especially Lesley and Andrea. It meant that we had to get up, do whatever jogging we might have decided on, finish breakfast and open up our math books by 8:00 a.m. The daily routine was math for ninety minutes, a thirty-minute break, then English grammar for another ninety minutes. It also meant that Carla and I had to get up at 5:30 to allow time for us to prepare — checking assignments from the previous day and working some problems in the upcoming sections. Routines like jogging, journal writing, reading, preparing for school and other recurring events created our sense of home. We no longer relied on physical props around us. Home was us, and we were always at home.

Schooling was also a great thing to keep us focused and avoid dwelling on international turmoil over which we had no control or influence. The girls' education was paramount. It was, after all, the reason we had taken the trip in the first place.

Current events flooded their young minds at every juncture. They anxiously exchanged e-mails with their friends back home. We were still piecing together what was happening there.

Though the magazine was almost in shreds, it brought home the bad news one more time. The headline on the September 15–21, 2001, issue of *The Economist* read:

The Day the World Changed

America suffered the worst terrorist attack ever. Suicide hijackers crashed two fuel-laden passenger jets into the towers of the World Trade Centre in New York, both of which caught fire and collapsed, killing office workers and rescue workers alike.

Next to school, hiking in the hills was the best therapy. During our time in Thale and the Harz Mountains, our most memorable excursion was hiking up Mt. Brocken (1152 m / 3379 ft.) to an old Soviet broadcast and listening station left over from the Cold War. It had been converted into a museum. The trail to the station wound its way through the lichen covered pine trees and crossed into an upland peat bog environment. Narrow ditches conducted a clear brown tea as it drained from the soft peat soil that seemed to spring back after each step.

The day we made the hike, the sky remained gray and rain fell almost continuously. As the trail steepened, we stepped onto an old road composed of complicated concrete blocks embedded in the soil. It was something Carla and I both wanted to connect with — to press against it with the soles of our shoes. This was the road that had marked the line between East and West — the Iron Curtain. We were humbled, almost reverent as we walked along that infamous trace — a tangible piece of modern history. It looked so benign with little tufts of grass sprouting up between the blocks. Yet, it had held such deep meaning for the entire world for almost fifty years. Many had died trying to make it from one side to the other.

The day was short and rain steadily intensified. With the deepening color of the sky, we decided to turn back and find the trail and our car before dark. Retracing our steps along the road, it seemed as if one ominous page of history was melting into the landscape as another page had opened in New York.

From Thale, we went straight south to the tourist town of Garmish on the border with Austria. The girls waited in a laundry, working on some math assignments while Carla and I went to find lodging. With the

Mountain meadows and stock shelters near Garmish, Germany. It felt
like we were in postcard pictures. (Russ)

help of the tourist information center in the town center we located a flat
for a week's stay. We needed a little more time hiking in the hills to
settle us back into our traveling routine.

Those hills, in a fairly short distance, turn into the German Alps of
which Zugspitz, Germany's tallest mountain at 9,721 feet above sea
level, is a local attraction. The beauty of the mountain meadows is the
stuff of wall calendars. I expected Julie Andrews to come swirling out
from behind one of the little mountain shacks, belting out "The hills are
alive . . ." at any moment. This was truly breathtaking countryside.

Always planning, we found a fledgling Internet café in Garmish a
short walk from our apartment. We spent quite a few hours trying to
make some forward reservations on a course through the Black Forest
region of Germany, then over into France. Though its sign claimed it
was an Internet café, inside it was plainly a bar that had an espresso
machine and two stand up Internet terminals better suited for video
gaming.

A person was required to keep a stack of deutsch marks handy to
pump into the machine while trying to work. The spill-proof keyboards
wore a vinyl sheet with letters printed on them; a very deliberate effort

had to be made to make sure each key pressed was actually registered on the screen.

To add to the general challenge of the situation, the German keyboard is just slightly different from the one we were accustomed to using. Some of the letters were in different places. Typing speed, drastically reduced by the not-so-sensitive touch pad and having to concentrate on the locations of certain letters, made communicating a real effort. If by chance the timer on the screen ran down, the terminal would unceremoniously shut down. Then it was necessary to start all over.

We had no arrangements for the foreseeable future and were under the gun to get something worked out. Making our way down to the Internet bar in the evening was quite different from the daytime experience. Lights dimmed, the atmosphere was composed primarily of smoke produced by crowd of twenty- and thirty-somethings. Carla and I earned a few looks as we moved cautiously over to the Internet consoles with maps and books in hand, appropriated a couple of bar stools and made ourselves comfortable. We hadn't really paid much attention during our daytime visits, but the two Internet consoles were situated immediately behind what turned out to be the karaoke equipment.

With the greatest effort, we composed inquiries for potential lodgings. Fumbling with ponderous Michelin road maps and miniature flashlights, we tried to decipher our travel options. It was amazing we got anything done at all. I eventually broke down and ordered a couple of beers for Carla and me.

The karaoke tunes being played were mostly U.S. and English language rock and roll hits from the '70s and '80s. One young lady had apparently been given, as a penance, the mastery of the 1970s hit "Dancing Queen" by Abba. Trying repeatedly to reach a couple of the more elevated measures, she was determined to work it out that very night. We heard that particular number at least three times. I'm not sure if she actually got any better or the beer just took the edge off. It was comical — Carla and I with our maps, books and flashlights, providing the backdrop for the aspiring, young and not-so-young rock stars whose inhibitions had been checked at the door or dissolved by a good dose of ethanol.

Upon returning to our apartment, humming to myself the tune, "The Dancing Queen," we were soundly called to task by Andrea and Lesley for coming home smelling like smoke, while they had been suffering through their reading assignments.

The next morning we finished sweeping up, carefully segregated our trash into the appropriate receptacles, and collected our things. We headed out to the car with our gear. Our landlady, Frau Hut, was a proper German lady with efficiently cropped silver hair, in her early sixties, I figured. She had been polite but not inclined to idle conversation. She nodded, as I handed the keys of the apartment to her, and said, "You are going a long way, aren't you?"

"Yes, we are," I replied.

"God bless you all," she said and smiled.

"Thank you."

We finished packing our gear into the car trunk. I held my breath, slammed the hatch and climbed in behind the wheel. "Well, girls, in the immortal words of Ray Charles, 'Here we go again!'"

We were headed on a northwesterly course into the upper reaches of the Black Forest, the delightful land of cuckoo clocks and the incomparable Black Forest Tort. In the town of Gengenbach, we stayed with a charming family who also had a daughter about the same age as Lesley.

Our first major challenge involved a face-to-face encounter with the blue laws of Germany, the most severe of any we found in Europe. Usually we were able to get to a grocery store on Saturday evening, shortly after arriving in a new town, but for some reason this pattern broke down in Gengenbach. Here was an important lesson. The next day, Sunday, we found ourselves in this small German town with not a single business enterprise open except for a solitary gas station out on the main highway. We had not much in the way of reserve groceries in the car. Carla and I literally spent three hours driving around looking for an open establishment. We ranged out about 20 miles to Offenberg, just short of the French border, and still found nothing.

Second only to her legendary skill as a navigator, Carla has the ability to conceive of meals made of next to nothing. In desperation, we finally pulled into the only open business in Gengenbach, the gas station. There was no shortage of beer. After all, we were in Germany. The rest of the shelves were almost barren except for a few bags of chips and candy bars. Carla found a couple small packages of pasta and some other items she whipped into a sauce that turned into a meal of surprising satisfaction. The PayDay candy bar dodged the bullet one more time and remained safely tucked away in my daypack. It is worth knowing that in many smaller towns all commerce and activities outside the home literally close down on Sunday. That experience provided a guiding principle for our travels in Europe.

The week passed with excursions to a thoroughly fascinating Black Forest folk museum and, of course, the quest for a cuckoo clock to be shipped back to Houston. Our landlady Frau Otter and her husband led us one evening on a short hike up to a tiny beer garden tucked away in the hills overlooking Gengenbach. Opportunities to truly connect like that were treasured. Struggle as we all did with language, a flagon of Most, an apple wine of some sort with a sampling of German fare and the cool September breeze, went a long way to smooth the slightly strained dialog into a memorable time.

After several visits to the one and only public Internet connection in the area, Carla was able to get a tentative fix on a flat in Paris. The Internet connection was located about ten miles away in a youth hostel. This particular hostel was a converted castle up on a ridge overlooking the Kinzig River Valley and surrounded by vineyards.

With a Paris destination, we headed off across the broad flood plane of the Rhine River to the French border. Carla worked the maps while I negotiated our way through Strausbourg traffic with an off-key rendition of "Dancing Queen" playing over and over in my head. Germany had been fun. The opportunity to slow down and get the feel of a few small towns put us all on an even keel. We looked forward to a similar experience in France.

France

The need to stretch a couple of pairs of youthful legs had us pulling over for a snack at a service plaza. No question about it, we were in France. Positioned directly in the path of the entry to what might otherwise be a convenience store was a large stand-up espresso bar.

I thought to myself: I think I'm going to enjoy our time in France!

Without hesitation, Carla and I found our positions, put an elbow on the bar, a foot on the rail and called for a couple of coffees. I was almost tempted to run my hand backward through my hair, tie my sweater around my neck and dangle my sunglasses from my ear. Fortified with a round of double espressos, we drove off into the Alsatian countryside and made excellent time for the duration of our drive to Paris.

Showing up at our destination on Saturday around dusk and in the rain was a recurring event; this time an initiation into Paris traffic.

Driving in Paris is a sport — but a civilized one. I don't think road rage is common in Europe. Europeans just don't expect to get places without some negotiation for the right to occupy space on the road. The Vespa and Piaggio scooters were like swarms of gnats, and they drove with all the abandonment of 18-year-olds.

It turned out that the apartment we thought was secured had been rented to another party. We pulled up along side a phone booth as the gentle evening drizzle began. I was just happy to sit by the curb and not drive for a while. Upon crossing the Rhine, Carla had been put in charge of language and communications. She got out and purchased a phone card at a local tobacco shop. Armed with our guide to France, the two of us crammed into a phone booth and located a hostel on the outskirts of Paris for the evening.

The youth hostel in Paris was a towering old building along a nondescript avenue. It was suffering the strains of intense usage; while clean enough, it was in a category with some of the less maintained college dormitories I've seen. I noticed a few door frames had been recently repaired. Security, we surmised, might have been more of a concern than in some of the places we had stayed. Nonetheless, it was a friendly and highly energized atmosphere as young travelers came and went, filled with the euphoria of being in Paris. The lobby was a cross between a train station and an insane asylum

After an evening at the hostel, we secured a room at the Hotel Ibis out on the northeast end of the underground system. It was on the upper end of our budget, but we felt fortunate to get anything at all reasonably priced in Paris. A week seemed like an appropriate commitment of time for a first visit to the City of Light. It is just so packed with things to see and do. The nice part about the Hotel Ibis — it was located in a residential part of Paris where people went about their daily lives. It was always relaxing after spending the day in the city jostling with other tourists to come up from the underground and stroll along familiar streets, looking in shop windows, stopping to pick up snacks to eat later during homework time in the room.

Paris is filled with famous sights: Notre Dame Cathedral, Eiffel Tower, Champs Elysees, Arch de Triomphe, and the list goes on. It requires no less than a week to see the most prominent sights. There are the two big ones, Versailles and the Louvre. Each is easily a full day's commitment. Any longings for the pastoral bliss of the countryside were put on the shelf for the week.

The stay in Paris was an urban cultural overload, and we all loved it. Proficiency with the underground system was quickly gained, and we found our way to all corners of the city. As was typical for us, we walked miles every day. Carla and I decided that despite the fact that we were paying for the car and despite the fact that we were paying a fee of ten dollars a day to park it back at the hotel, it made absolutely no sense to try to negotiate Parisian traffic, then spend half a day looking for an even more expensive place to park it. We just locked it up, let it sit and took the subway

While there are elevators, the only way to really appreciate the Eiffel Tower is to climb the stairs. When they arrived at the top Lesley and Andrea were at odds over the number of steps. While the girls went bounding back down to the lower landing to do a recount, Carla and I caught our breaths and looked out over the sprawling city of palaces and parks. No garish high-rise towers of glass and steel but blocks of buff colored apartments, all with uniformly gray zinc clad roofs neatly sectioned by tree-lined avenues. It would be easy to fall in love with Paris and never leave.

Of all the Parisian landmarks, Notre Dame Cathedral was truly a highlight. Located on a small island in the River Seine, it was one of the ultimate pilgrimage sites. I had to remind myself of the fact that construction of this medieval masterpiece began in the year 1163, and it is still used today on a regular basis. Construction continued more or less unabated for 180 years; this technological and engineering feat was unequaled.

That period of history also saw the rise of Venice, the second and subsequent Crusades, arrival of the Turks and the Mongols of the Golden Horde from the Asian Steppe, the sacking of Constantinople by the misguided participants of the Fourth Crusade, the life of Marco Polo and far to the east the beginning of the construction of the Forbidden City by Genghis Kahn's grandson Khubilai. The world, at that point, came alive, and the seeds of globalization germinated and brought together the cultures of Europe and Asia. Then, spreading more rapidly and indiscriminately than any of the eastern nomads, the Black Death arrived in 1346, bringing an end, at least temporarily, to time of unprecedented global change.

Unmoved by all this, Andrea and Lesley were beginning to reach museum saturation. They had been through the British Museum, Munch

Museum, The Viking Ships and Wasa Museum, The Hermitage Museum, Museum of the Peoples Revolution, Museum of Musical Instruments, and countless other small roadside attractions and open air museums. Detecting signs of indifference, we had a motivational talk about the significance of the Musée du Louvre and all agreed, notwithstanding what we may have seen, this was the big one. We skipped school on the day of our Louvre outing and planned it out carefully, standing in line for tickets by 10:30. Our start was a little slower than we hoped for.

A cup of strong coffee for Carla and me, and a snack for the girls were in order before our first sally into the cavernous halls. Never one to hide her feelings, it was clear our previous day's motivational talk was lost on Andrea. So, as a refresher, I recalled that we had all agreed that we would maintain an upbeat disposition.

Our first objective was to see the Mona Lisa. After a glimpse of Leonardo's masterpiece, we meandered through the large format French paintings, then the German, Flemish and Dutch paintings and finally down through the sculpture. If there were any unanswered questions in the girls' minds about the details of anatomy, prior to the sculpture

The Musée du Louvre, Paris, France. Carla, Lesley and Andrea recover from museum saturation in front of the Louvre. (Russ)

exhibits, they had been summarily laid to rest upon our final exit into the warm evening air of the great courtyard with its glass pyramid. It had taken commitment and endurance. The entire Musée du Louvre cannot be seen in one day unless a person ran through the halls and didn't look at anything. A second day — I am not a student of fine art — would have been well beyond my capacity for squinting at captions. In the end we all agreed it was a day well spent and worth every bit of the effort.

10/03/01 — Andrea

Today we had no school and went straight to the Louvre Museum, the biggest art museum in the world. And luckily it wasn't half as boring as I thought it would be. I actually really liked the sculptures.

At the conclusion of the long and enlightening day, we found ourselves once again strolling the Rue Di Rivoli that runs along the north side of the Louvre Palace. Two out of three English bookstores are located in the area, and we were in need of maps and tour books of Italy and Greece. We emerged back onto the street an hour later and 15 pounds heavier. Buying books is great fun, carrying them is not so great.

Along the Rue Di Rivoli and across from the Louvre is a small plaza where a group of in-line skaters congregated each day to socialize and polish their techniques. The challenge at that particular time was to perfect a miniature slalom course consisting of plastic drink cups set about three feet apart by weaving feet in and out in an alternating pattern. It was an entertaining sight, and each time we were in the neighborhood we stopped for half an hour or so to watch. Andrea, an avid roller-blader, was hard pressed to contain herself. If not for the lack of skates, she would have been lining up to have a go at it. Some accomplished amateur skaters were participating with a few dramatic wipeouts from other skaters. The skaters did their best to keep the pain from showing in their faces, but the pavement in Paris is just as unyielding as anywhere else.

The sidewalk café culture reaches its zenith in Paris. Leaving the skaters to further refinements, we headed in the direction of the Madeline Cathedral. Overcome by the odor of food, we pulled up to a precisely arranged row of tiny tables, each with four straight back chairs and a few centimeters of space. This activity is a must for a complete and unabridged visit to Paris. It was, for us, the first time we had sat down to relax since our morning snack in the Louvre. And sidewalk cafés are not to be missed.

We had all come to know a bit of Paris, and getting around on the underground system was easy. After a week our time was up and our budget could only handle so much urban drain. I paid our parking bill, got the car packed and off we went into the French countryside. The direction was southwest to the Loire Valley and the small town of Gennes, about 160 miles from Paris between Tours and Angers.

The French have organized a truly unique program for accommodations called Gîtes de France (pronounced zheets). We highly recommend this option as the way to see France. Each one of the gîtes is a small rural cottage or house. They are located in many of the smaller towns and are always fastidiously kept and fully equipped. Bring your own groceries, and you are ready to enjoy a week of relaxed sightseeing in the surrounding areas. After a hard day of touring castles, shopping for groceries in the market place or hiking in the countryside, it is nice to have the space to take off your shoes and relax. Preparing meals also meant we could draw the cork from a bottle of local vintage, make ourselves a snack of escargot with a baguette and not have to put up with all the hassle of going to a restaurant.

One problem we ran into in small towns was the conflict between our school schedule and the early afternoon siesta; the siesta is not confined to Spain. The girls were freshest and most compliant in the morning, so we conducted school from 8:00 A.M. until noon or one o'clock, depending on how things were going. By the time lessons and lunch were finished, we would venture out into the village only to find shops and businesses shuttered until three or so when they would re-open for a few hours in the afternoon and early evening. Experimentation with a couple of different scheduling options brought us back to the original plan. If we were to get any schooling accomplished, it had to be first thing in the morning. The disadvantage was this schedule kept us from traveling too far from our lodging as winter approached and days became shorter.

The Loire Valley and the surrounding countryside seemed unremarkable at first. Everything has a soft, slightly golden hue. Low cliffs of buff colored stone set back from the river are rounded by centuries of mild erosion as the Loire River meanders its way to the Bay of Biscay. Houses and villages all seemed to have the same uniform soft butterscotch hue that blended into the surroundings. Amber fields of stubble and early autumn colors added to the sameness of the broad open country. It reminded me of eastern Nebraska.

As we wound our way along the Loire River toward our destination, it appeared the cliffs were pockmarked with depressions and other more regular shapes like windows and doors. Soon we noticed that many of the houses were built very close to the cliffs. They were not much more than a shallow façade extending from the face of the natural slope. Many of the older homes had actually been carved into the banks of the river. After digging into the tour book, we discovered that for several hundred years this entire region existed largely underground. Carla had some knowledge of these troglodyte communities, but none of us really grasped how wide spread this form of living was.

Given the name troglodytes by surface dwellers, fully half of the population along the stream from Saumur to Angers lived underground in the twelfth century. Away from the river, entire villages had been excavated from the small depressions in the local topography. The troglodyte community of Rochemenier was only abandoned in the 1930s. However, an old hippie, of the French variety had steadfastly hung on to his way of life. For a few francs, he provided bent, spindled, mutilated and folded copies of a brief tour itinerary for his portion of the underground community. It was well worth the cost.

Pulling into Gennes in the late afternoon, Carla recounted the directions she had been given; we must be somewhere in the vicinity of our cottage. Finally we parked the car and got out to look around. Since Carla was our French speaker, it was now her job to knock on the door of the tidy stone house to ask for help in locating our accommodations for the week. Answering the door was our soon-to-be landlady. She spoke only French. Within minutes Carla was nodding, smiling and doing her best to sort out the details in French. Those years of high school French had not been buried too deeply and finally paid off.

As we unloaded our possessions from the car and were settling groceries into the refrigerator, a knock came at a rear kitchen door. It didn't look as though the owners were promoting the door's use, but we moved a stool and a few other items aside to get it open. Andrea entered in a fever of excitement. It seemed this door led to what remained of an ancient residence that had been carved into the hill immediately behind the cottage.

An archway opened up to what was once a kitchen. In a smoke blackened recess were remains of a cooking hearth, shelves and an entry from the outside, apparently the route Andrea and Lesley had discovered. Barely containing an overwhelming sense of adventure, we dug flashlights from our packs and started down a narrow passage. Choosing steps carefully, we crossed over a pile of rubble and entered into a vast network of caverns with straight walls, flat floors and ceilings. Literally acres of land had been turned into man-made caverns; at first, we could not conceive of a reason for this enormous effort.

Native building stone, despite its seemingly soft consistency, hardened when exposed to the air and was the material of choice for the nearby castles, chateaus, fortifications, homes and businesses that we passed as we followed the meandering highway through the villages of the Loire. Hands-down, this location moved to the top of the list for being the most awesome up to that point. The girls couldn't get enough time to spend poking around the adjacent ruins and abandoned caverns.

Many of these cool caverns that were in over supply had been pressed into service as wine cellars. A particular carbonated wine, Saumur Brut, was the regional specialty. Naturally, after a tour of the winery and storage caverns, we succumbed and ended up with a few heavy bottles to carry along, presumably for some special occasion. The problem was that we had little space in which to accumulate anything. We would just have to consume them to enhance our French experience. The vast underground spaces had also given rise to commercial-scale mushroom production that yielded 100,000 tons per year of edible fungi.

Gennes retained a slowly paced village way of life. The tiny corner store had the essentials. Each morning delicious pies, made with local specialties like blackberries and peaches, were carefully arranged in the window of the patisserie next door. The warm compelling aroma of freshly baked baguettes was carried along by the soft October breeze.

Though Gennes is not a major tourist town, pre-Roman stone structures stood silently in an otherwise featureless farmer's fields. Gennes, it seems, had been a Gaulic stronghold prior to Julius Caesar's push to extend his empire in 56 B.C. A Roman amphitheater, from the time of Emperor Claudius in the first century A.D., captured an afternoon of our time, but nothing there brought buses of other tourists to trample the paths. We felt very fortunate to have discovered this little town on our own.

One slightly gray autumn afternoon we were lucky enough to happen upon a village wine festival with lively grape stomping in the town of Martigne-Briand, a few miles from Gennes. But the highlight was an evening meal in Le Caveau, a restaurant situated in a twelfth century troglodyte dwelling. Fully underground, the only surface expression was a small wrought iron gate and sign nestled among an otherwise nondescript block of shops and businesses. Descending below the shops, we dined on Fouaces, small circles of perfectly elastic bread like mini-pitas, baked in the excavated stone, underground ovens and served hot with local troglodyte specialties: potted meat, white beans and pork, mushrooms and some pretty strong goat cheese.

Lifting a glass of local red, Carla and I paused briefly to acknowledge the end of our fourth month on the road. We reflected on the past month and asked ourselves if we had genuinely paid attention to what we were experiencing. Had each of us done his or her best to ensure the experience was positive? Within the limits of human endurance, I think the answers were "yes." With the passing of each month, Carla and I were both aware of the finite nature of this experience and attempted to suppress the twinges of sadness as we watched this magical time pass before our eyes. My mantra became: "Pay attention!"

As autumn temperatures set in, our migration continued in a southerly direction. Trees had begun to lose their leaves as we packed our belongings again into the tiny hatchback trunk of our Peugeot. Next destination was Cadouin, a tiny village with an eighth century monastery (a youth hostel). It is situated about eighty miles east of Bordeaux near the Dordogne River. Finding our modern but quite remote cottage involved no small amount of dumb luck.

We spent two or three hours driving around the countryside asking directions and making phone calls to no avail. It was dark, raining, and the wind was up. This was typical Saturday evening fare. Heading down a single-track, one-way lane in the wrong direction, we were forced to reverse our way out to permit an oncoming car to pass. Not disheartened but still disappointed, I backed into the driveway of a small house in the dark. Our backup lights illuminated a sign on the cottage, not really visible from the road. Of course, that was it. Checking the instructions Carla had managed to get in French, the key was just where it was supposed to be. On the kitchen table, the owner had left us a large bag of fresh walnuts that grow wild in the area and a bottle of red wine. With a sigh of relief and an eye on the bottle of wine, we settled in.

The Dordogne region is more rugged and forested than northwestern France. Rivers and streams have cut their way through the soft yellow sandstone, creating verdant flat-bottomed valleys and pasturelands bounded by vertical cliffs. For the last 20,000 years, the water-cut shelves and overhanging cliffs have provided shelter for countless tribes and human societies.

The Lascaux Caves, site of some of the oldest Western cave art of the late Ice Age Cro-Magnon era, are in the Dordogne Valley. The original cave paintings are protected and not accessible to the general public.

However, modern computer-aided sensing and design techniques have enabled French archeologists to completely and, I might add, convincingly reproduce in its entirety the original Lascaux cavern. The display is named Lascaux II and is located near the town of Montignac. It may seem like a bit of a Disneyland-type trick, but I left the man-made cave feeling as if I had been to the original cave and seen the actual renderings of the Paleolithic artists. Truly remarkable are the artist's use of shading combined with the contours of the natural rock surfaces to give the creatures a three dimensional quality.

Returning from our daily excursions and stopping in villages and towns for groceries or sundries, we took full advantage of the opportunity to sample the local wines. After all, we were in France, and we were on the edge of the Bordeaux region. Everyone has heard that in France a person can find truly excellent wines for a song. Well, from our experience, any stories you may hear about remarkable wines for as little as $1.50 a bottle are entirely true. We paid ridiculously low prices for what we considered first class offerings. *Carpe diem*, and that we did!

Our tour of France continued in a grand arc that bent to the east from Cadouin to another small town, Chenac, about 65 miles northwest of Nimes. Located on the flanks of the Massif Central or central highlands, the area is renowned for spectacular hiking along deep limestone canyons that are replete with cave dwellings and abandoned villages sprinkled among the pines trees, brush and exotic erosional landforms. The country reminded us more of the Texas Hill Country than anything we had expected to see in France.

We prepared many of our own meals as long as we had access to some form of kitchen. At least once during each stay we also tried to get out and sample the regional specialties. After a hard day of hiking in the striking Gorges du Tarn area, we decided to see what southern France had to offer in the way of unique foods. Andrea claimed to be starving. She craved a good helping of red meat or sausage of some sort.

The menu in a small hotel restaurant listed andouille with a side order of vegetables. We have a respectable Cajun population in East Texas and andouille is typically a coarsely ground smoked sausage with some pretty reasonable spicing. However, Andrea's andouille arrived looking a little gray. Undaunted by appearance, she laid into it with knife and fork. I watched her eyes widened as the first breaking of the sausage skin revealed some rather springy components that started to extend and unfold themselves after being cooped up in its sausage casing. The more she cut, the more its filling began to spring forth to reassume its original shape. It became increasingly obvious that this wasn't the andouille from back home. The majority of it did not fall into the category of meat as we know it — mostly, internals. To Andrea's credit she made an admirable showing, but even I had to admit it was chewy and only faintly resembled meat. Lesley and Andrea were determined not to be viewed as picky American kids; and so, Andrea felt obligated to press on and even considered putting it in her pocket.

From our position in southern France, the influence of ancient Rome was becoming more apparent. Remnants of the Via Domitia, the Roman road that stretched along the Mediterranean coast from northwestern Italy near Turin to the border of Spain can still be seen. This extraordinary Roman highway then continues through Spain all the way to Cadiz, which is on the Atlantic side of the Straits of Gibraltar. The distance from its start in Turin to Cadiz is more than a thousand miles.

The city of Nimes in southern France has a couple of very well preserved Roman structures. But we found the most impressive was the Pont du Gard or the bridge over the River Gardon. It is actually an aqueduct that was part of a system of canals that brought water to the city of Nimes, then called Nemausus. This 900-foot long structure connected the water supply channels that were dug into the adjacent hills and comprised three elegant courses of classical Roman arches sculpted in golden sandstone. Standing 157 feet above the river, this symbol of the engineering skill and craftsmanship of Rome in the first century A.D. is hard to describe; this near perfectly executed structure is a marvel. Pedestrian traffic is still permitted, and hundreds of tourists make the crossing every day as they have for almost 2,000 years.

I often tried to make the point to Lesley and Andrea that people didn't sit around cooking up all the mathematical contrivances we had been studying just to annoy their kids. Pont du Gard offered some excellent opportunities to bring the seemingly esoteric studies of algebra and geometry back into focus. We spent a couple of morning math sessions trying to understand some of the problems the engineers had to solve.

The canal system, of which Pont du Gard was a part, followed the contours of the rugged hill country for some fifty kilometers (thirty-one miles). Along that course it drops in elevation a mere 12 meters (39 feet). The slope is an almost insignificant 15 inches per mile. It was difficult to imagine what tools and measuring devices the Roman engineers had at their disposal to ensure that the water actually flowed in the right direction.

Heading off for the Mediterranean and the Italian border, we looked back at all we had experienced in France — the diverse culture, geography and history. From the broad open prairies of the northwest and the sandy cliffs of the Dordogne, to the limestone gorges and brush-covered highlands of the Massif Central, the French countryside constantly changes. It is hard to equal France's natural beauty and its historical resources when one considers the evidence of early man, the Roman occupation, troglodyte communities and on to the Renaissance and Baroque architecture of Paris. The characteristic national pride and infatuation the French people have with their own countryside seemed to us well deserved.

Italy

We arrived in the town of Albenga, about an hour up the coast from the famous 370-acre principality of Monaco. It was dark, and we had nothing more than an address and a general idea that the vacation apartment we had reserved was somewhere close to the beach.

When making a reservation for a cottage we always tried to make it clear that we were traveling and would not be at our mailing address back in the U.S. to receive the confirming voucher and directions. But often the idea that we needed an e-mail voucher or a FAX to the destination, referencing a passport number or something like it, just didn't get through. The helpful and polite young customer service representative would dutifully send all of our documentation back to our mail box in Houston. As a result, we now groped around Albenga in the dark. With a map purchased in a local bookstore, we drove along the coast to the south looking for something with the name of the lodge. I have only so much patience for driving around in the dark. Before long, I pulled over to a little seaside restaurant; map in hand, hat in hand, I went in to ask for directions. Fortunately the dinner rush hadn't hit yet.

Very few words of English in this establishment, I thought to myself, stepping into the softly lit trattoria with slender candles and white tablecloths. And even fewer words of Italian on my part, I concluded; and I was right.

Persistence is a prerequisite for this kind of travel. Between the bartender, the assistant cook, the bus boy and two waiters, accompanied by much waving of hands, we got pointed in the right direction, the opposite direction. I *ciao*'ed, and *arrivederci*'ed my way out into the street and back to the car where Carla was waiting with two travel weary girls.

The apartment had everything we needed, a pull out couch for Lesley and Andrea, a bedroom, kitchen and shower. It also featured one of those little hexagonal espresso pots, the sort I had seen the Italian couple guarding carefully back in the hostel in Bergen. After four months of sleeping in strange places, the occasional passing train had absolutely no effect. A little walkway ran beneath the tracks to the rocky shore of the Mediterranean. Not a seaside villa exactly, but who was going to spend much time in the room?

Morning math class was a time for the girls to study quietly, and a time for Carla and me to enjoy a cup of strong Italian coffee while doing some planning. Internet services were nowhere to be found in that part of Italy. Communications relied mostly on the use of FAX.

Meanwhile, the warm rays of early November sun bounced off the white plastic table making it glow. Math papers scattered by a delinquent gust of sea air gave the girls a short reprieve from the repetitive monotony of geometrical proofs; side angle side, internal angles theorems and the laws of powers and roots. When the sun crossed the meridian we were off to explore the surrounding hills.

Albenga is a sleepy little resort community with an attractive old-town area. It is complete with medieval chapel and aristocratic family residences nestled among shops, restaurants and whatever else a person might need.

From our experiences in France, we could sniff out the InterMarche and Carrefour supermarkets in most towns. We had learned from our time in Germany not to run out of food. When all else failed, there were always salami and maybe some olives in my backpack. Fortunately, Italy had plenty of opportunities for grocery shopping. The old fashioned market place is always entertaining, but an Italian supermarket is just about as much fun — local cheeses, fresh breads, olives and wines.

Hiking in the hills along the coast was not a highly publicized activity. The trails running through the hills strike out from any of several small towns between Albenga and Imperia. Mostly they are marked and head to the west, in some cases following a narrow Roman foot path through villages and olive groves. Life in those hills continues as it has for centuries. Middle-aged women in skirts and babushkas beat olive trees with cane poles, harvesting the bitter fruit in nets spread on the ground. Their husbands, in worn woolen sweaters with wind burnt faces

and tussled hair, gathered the fresh olives and sacked them for processing. Olive oil is such a defining part of Mediterranean life that some
Italian families have their own small groves of trees. After harvesting, they
take their olives to a local press to insure a supply of the most virgin olive oil
of their own. There is a small custom olive press and museum in Albenga.

Dogs barked and donkeys brayed as we picked our way along the
steep, shaded trails. Small stone villages dotted the hills. Rocky spires
on crumbling walls, ruined castles, churches and long abandoned fortifications reminded us how important defense was as generations of families struggled for dominance over a rugged land that yielded little more
than olives and goat cheese.

Lesley, the master of rhetorical questions, observed, "Is everything
in Italy built on a hill? It looks like everything has some kind of a wall
around it too. Why is that?"

"What do you think they were trying to accomplish by building that
way?" I prompted. "You don't suppose they were trying to keep people
in, do you?"

"But all the old buildings are like fortresses," she persisted.

"Well, in medieval times, much of Europe was broken up into little
principalities, duchies and various political units. They were all basically
tribes. We might call them clans and their leaders warlords today. It is
going on in Afghanistan right now. Left to their own devices, people
will always come up with some reason to pick a fight with their neighbor, even if it is just for a better goat pasture. For thousands of years
people in Europe were constantly bashing each other for one reason or
another. So defense was always foremost on their minds, no matter
what they did. We live in such a secure environment it is hard for us to
imagine being carried off by a competing clan."

"So what would happen if you were captured?"

"You might end up as a slave for a prominent family, helping in the
kitchen or cleaning the castle. Or you could end up being sold on the
slave market or traded for a donkey or something."

This gave her plenty to think about as we followed the Roman foot
path through the narrow archways of a tiny village and back over the
ridge. The sun had set the clouds on fire. The pink and orange streaks
reflected in the glassy surface of the Mediterranean created an impres-
sionistic haze.

I think we could adapt to living in Italy. It has a very steady and
reasonably paced way of life. Who needs all the administrative hassle of

trying to run an empire consisting of the known world? The Romans took their turn at it a couple thousand years ago.

A driving excursion to Genoa one afternoon reminded me of the Caribbean — snorkeling in a school of ten thousand tiny fish. Approaching the city, the Vespa two-wheeled suicide squads surrounded us as four-wheel traffic ground to a halt. They moved like a wildly colored fluid seeking out the path of least resistance and rushing to fill any opening

The market in Genoa, a block off the waterfront, is an experience that, were it not for a couple of ratty looking strings of electric lights, transported us back to the thirteenth century. It was a time when Genoa, one of the world's most powerful city-states, was in heated competition with Venice. In unprecedented demand were Oriental silks from Antioch, fine cotton from Alexandria and Indian black pepper coming through the Red Sea to Cairo. It took almost no imagination to conjure an image of tiny shops clustered along that sunless winding passageway. It was plainly obvious why, in those days, an ordinary citizen kept a dagger tucked in his belt.

With only slightly more directions than we had for our arrival in Albenga, we set off down the length of the broad agricultural Po River Valley to the romantic floating City of Venice. Engineers tell us Venice is probably sinking. But never mind. Off we went.

We had read all sorts of horror stories about tourists having their cars broken into and everything removed in Italy. When we pulled into the filled-to-capacity, six level parking garage at the Piazzale Roma in Venice, the sign said, "Leave your keys in the car and the doors unlocked." Our instincts just couldn't support that, so I discretely looked around at some of the other cars and noted that no one had left his keys in the car and the doors unlocked. I expect that the sign was a means of absolving the lot owners of any responsibility for break-ins.

The directions I had received over the phone from our English speaking contact were precise. We were very shortly hauling our packs up the narrow flight of stairs to a flat at #4 Tobacci, overlooking the tiny plaza of Campo San Stin. It was about a block, if that really means anything, in Venice, north of the Frari Cathedral.

The week we spent in Venice was almost an illusion. We were far enough away from the Piazza San Marco that it was a comfortable jog in the mornings but not isolated from the festive atmosphere that permeates the city. All of Venice is a veritable museum. It reminds me of a tropical island, full of tourists and people whose sole purpose is serving the tourist industry. But it is a very comfortable and easygoing brand of tourism.

It took only a single evening for the girls to work out the route to a neighborhood Venetian bakery, then the next night a carry-out pizza place. Small grocery stores and shops were hidden here and there. We had stopped at a supermarket on the mainland before putting the car away for the week, so we were pretty well stocked upon moving in.

Starting the day before sunrise, our jogging route took us along passageways that were scarcely wide enough for a second person to pass. We jogged along in front of the darkened shops, across the Rialto Bridge, on to Piazza San Marco, then back. The sun's rays inched their way down into the plaza as we returned from our morning run. Young boys kicked their soccer balls against the wall for a few minutes before school. A small stone fountain off to one side flowed intermittently. Except for window pots, not a blade of grass could find a protected corner to gain hold and prosper.

Cooling down from our run, the girls had some breakfast. I stood at the window with its tiny balcony looking out onto the Campo San Stin, sipping a cup of strong black coffee, while watching a drama unfolded just across the way. A neatly dressed, middle-aged man arrived at his shop door. It was a closet-sized shop of cleaning supplies and household items. He unlocked the door, then removed the security panels and carried them to their usual resting place in the rear of the shop. A few swipes of his worn broom prepared the polished paving stones for the rectangular doormat. Then he took off his jacket, changed into a gray cardigan sweater and began the methodical organization of wire racks that displayed an assortment of brightly colored brooms and dusters. A selection of shopping bags, suspended in galvanized wire frames with wheels were allocated space under the front window. Since no motorized vehicles are allowed in Venice, anything with wheels is very popular. Then he set out a shelf of soaps and cleaning aids along with several other convenient displays of scrub brushes and polishes. When everything was in its prescribed location, he went back into the shop and did not reemerge until around one o'clock in the afternoon; then the process was reversed in the precise order it had occurred, until evening business hours, only to be repeated again.

Each morning the warm sun streamed through the tall rain-spotted windows of our apartment. The man in the cardigan began his routine while the girls sat at the kitchen table, heads bent over their math workbooks. Andrea's bare feet restlessly squirmed beneath her chair, and Lesley idly twisted a lock of her chestnut hair around the end of her finger. Carla thoughtfully prepared for a session of English grammar. All was silent except for the scratch of pencils on paper and the sputtering of the recently acquired espresso maker on the small burner of the kitchen stove.

For the first half of November the weather was mild. A light jacket was all that was required. In the U.S. we think of Italy as being southern, balmy, and very Mediterranean. It may be Mediterranean, but it is interesting to note that Venice (Latitude 45.4N) is about sixty miles farther north than Green Bay, Wisconsin (Latitude 44.5N). Geography always has its surprises.

I could think of no better place to spend a week or maybe a lifetime than exploring the narrow passageways, footbridges and canals of Venice. Our week allowed us to get to know the place. From our first floor apartment we were afforded a glimpse of the lives of the locals. We had earned the right to look on with amusement at the clusters of visitors, just like us, trying to read the tiny print on the tourist maps to learn where they were. Finding your way around Venice isn't all that hard, but you do gain a certain sense of accomplishment just getting to your chosen destination. Yes, we took our compulsory gondola cruise through the back canals, and it was worth it!

It is difficult not to go on and on about Italy. It has no end of diverse and utterly engaging mountain villages and historic cities such as Assisi, Gubio or Perugina.

Andrea celebrated her thirteenth birthday in Citta di Castello, which translates into "city of the castle," a fortified medieval city in central Italy. We found a gourmet restaurant tucked away in the wine cellar beneath the cobblestone streets. The collection of insignificant little birthday gifts bought in the marketplace were lovingly wrapped by Lesley and Carla as before in well-used travel maps that had become obsolete.

We worked our way south through central Italy to Naples with the goal of satisfying my childhood fantasy of walking the streets of Pompeii. Finally, there was Mt. Vesuvius like an old man reclining in a soft upholstered chair blanketed in a deep green mantle of pines, dozing and occasionally opening an eye to gaze out over the sparkling blue waters of the Mediterranean. Vesuvius had last been called out of provisional retirement in 1944 to ease the build up of pressure where two massive tectonic plates rub up against each other. Like residents of San

The Roman amphitheater at Pompeii, near Naples, Italy. Russ contemplates life in Pompeii, and his lifelong dream to visit Mt. Vesuvius finally realized. (Carla)

Francisco, Napolitanos go about their daily lives under the constant threat of disaster. Aided by modern scientific data, the quickening of its pulse and respiration are not likely to go undetected. Meanwhile, old man Vesuvius stands in the background — quiet, vigilant and still smoldering.

Our objective for dropping south to Naples related to my recollections of *National Geographic* articles that chronicled the gradual rediscovery of Herculaneum and Pompeii. These cities were not primitive cave dwellings or hastily constructed lean-tos. The paintings, sculptures and mosaics that still remain stir any mind to wonder how much more advanced we would be if the empire had not disintegrated.

It is difficult to imagine the choking gloom and utter blackness that prevailed on the twenty-fourth day of August in A.D. 79 as the towns of Pompeii and Herculaneum were gradually buried by six to eight inches per hour of hot volcanic ash. A brief pause, and the ash fall was brought to an abrupt climax as incandescent cloud of hot gas and lava, traveling between sixty and one hundred miles per hour, seared the land surface, sparing nothing in its path.

With today's population of well over a million people, Naples would undoubtedly be frozen in its tracks should Vesuvius act again. The scale of the evacuation makes one wonder if the residents of Pompeii might not have had a better chance.

Rome was the dropping off point for our car. It all went very smoothly and without any hidden surcharges, usage fees or collision damage waivers. We just drove up to the airport departure terminal, handed over the keys and that was it, eighty days and 9,536 km (5,925 mi.) later. Having a car is a convenience, but I'm always relieved to be able to give it back to its rightful owner in one piece. We had absolutely no problems with it, and it would have been impossible for us to have seen as much and done as much on public transportation at anywhere near comparable cost. Catching the train back to our apartment in downtown Rome, I felt a sense of sadness at so unceremoniously breaking off the relationship with our little Peugeot.

Rome was an experience all to itself. We had been fortunate enough to secure a week's stay on the Viminale Hill district, about two blocks from Stazione Termini, Rome's main train and transportation hub. Finishing each day outside the terminal with a small brown paper bag of hot, freshly roasted chestnuts became our ritual. Lesley and Andrea absolutely fell in love with those starchy, slightly sweet nuggets in France and Italy.

Many people may have a different recollection of Rome than we do, but Termini Station figures prominently in our minds. Before our departure, we had explored all the environs of Termini, and I must admit in all honesty and with some reluctance that on at least one occasion we caved in, indulged our more corporal cravings and visited one of the three Dunkin Donuts shops. They are strategically positioned to snare the passing U.S. tourists and ex-pats. I discretely slipped the familiar bright pink-and-purple box into my plain daypack and with renewed spring in my step stole back along the narrow streets and back alleys to our flat.

On a couple of mornings, we started with a two or three mile run through the city as Romans quietly renewed their commitment to another day and prepared themselves for the upcoming holiday season. One morning we ran down and made a loop around the Coliseum and back around the third century Aurelian Wall, on another morning we ran over the Spanish Steps and back up and by the Quattro Fontane, a real hill climb. Running through a city early in the morning always gives one an entirely different perspective. It is rather like seeing it get out of bed with worn slippers and tattered bathrobe as it finds the paper and first cup of coffee. It is a personal side that is inaccessible through organized tours or travel books.

The most characteristic landmark of Rome is the Coliseum. It is the epitome of a pilgrimage site. I had to tag base every time we went by it. Why, I had always asked myself, does it look like it is still under construction? As it turns out, most of the decorative marble that was carefully placed on the visible surfaces had been just as carefully removed by pilfering stone masons who were engaged in various projects, not the least of which was St. Peter's Basilica. It is easy to be critical of a culture that would treat this monument to civilization with such disregard. Then I tried to imagine what the Astro Dome in Houston, now replaced by a more modern sports arena, might look like 2,000 years from now.

The more mundane activities, laundry and grocery shopping were part of our daily existence. The nearest grocery store was down on a lower level and around the other side of Termini Station from our apartment. It was probably a kilometer in distance and not the best part of town to frequent at night. The easiest way to get there was to go through the station, along the platform to the end and down a couple flights of stairs to Via Giovanni, the street on the other side, which is what we normally did.

It is customary in many European countries to bag your own groceries as the checker enters them into the cash register. With glazed expressions on their faces, Lesley and Andrea squeezed past and started loading things into the plastic bags. They were both hungry and tired after a day's hiking around Rome.

Stepping out from the grocery store with several heavy bags, we began walking back toward the apartment. With the solstice only about three weeks away, the sun had gone down early, and a cold wind was blowing. An alternative route back to the apartment was along Via Tiburtina, a road dating back to the fifth century B.C., that ran through an exhaust-choked tunnel that ran under Termini. It was arguably shorter to go that way.

Andrea chose the heaviest of the bags, the ones with the milk, and set off through the tunnel. Lesley with her load followed close behind.

With six lanes of city traffic, the noise was deafening and the exhaust fumes almost overwhelming. It was cold and dark. Andrea's bright white socks were visible below her ankle length pants. She had grown at least three inches since we left home. Lesley in her well-used fleece vest had the collar up around her neck and ears. We walked in silence through the noisy tunnel. The fumes made my eyes water. I looked at the girls, fifty yards out ahead of us, soldiering along in the gloom. I wondered to myself: When we return home and someone asks them what is it like to go around the world, what will their answers be?

Overwhelmed by the scale and profound history of Rome but left with fond memories, we cleaned the kitchen, swept the floor and stripped the beds as is customary in hostels. Andrea and Lesley were by this time good at getting their things recaptured after a week, being sure to check under the couch and beds for errant socks or books. I packaged up the four-inch stack of schoolbooks and papers, the last items to go into my pack. One of the more characteristic sounds of the trip was the zipping sound as closure was achieved and packs lined near the door for final accounting. It was just a short pull over to Termini for our final engagement. This time we would be joining the crowds of arrivers and departers, not just strolling through as we had for a week. We boarded a morning train to the ancient east coast town of Bari about 250 miles from Rome, where we connected with a ferry to Greece. Afternoon found us on the downhill, eastern slope of the rocky backbone of the Italian peninsula, an open expanse of grayish tan fields ploughed and ready for spring planting. It could have been West Texas.

We relaxed and looked out the window of the train, passing around chunks of salami and smelly cheese. For desert we savored delicious Perugina chocolates. Life was good. Our only concern was that we had not been able to find Greek language books written in English, just a couple of used phrase books. In the past, we had been better prepared to enter a new country.

Chapter 5

The Mediterranean – Greece, Turkey and Egypt

THE FERRY TRIP FROM BARI ON THE EAST coast of Italy across the Adriatic Sea to Igoumenitza on the west coast of Greece is about 220 miles as the crow flies. Favored by good weather, the ship executed a smooth crossing through the Strait of Otranto, a stretch of water between the boot heel of Italy and the country of Albania, then around the island of Corfu.

The heavy cabin door rebounded on its hinges as the steward hurriedly pounded out a wake up call, delivering his announcement along the ferry's passageway — perhaps in Italian, maybe in Greek, even in English, it didn't make any difference; it was time to get up.

I fumbled for the switch over my narrow bunk, flicked on the little reading light, pushed back a coarse woolen blanket and checked my watch — 4:30 A.M., only five and a half hours sleep. We dressed in silence, putting on clothes we had been wearing since leaving Rome almost twenty-four hours earlier. The cabin was too small to accommodate more than the four of us. Our packs had been stored on the lower deck. All we had kept out were toothbrushes and hand towels.

The ship shuddered as props changed direction in preparation for landing. We stumbled down to the main vehicle deck; diesel fuel and exhaust fumes filled the cold, damp air. The giant ferry was less than half full — no more than a dozen semi-rigs in orderly rows.

We stepped out onto the deck to free our things from beneath a net that had been thrown over the top of them. Andrea, still expressionless, flung on her ponderous daypack, then she and Lesley sleepily worked their way toward the gangway. We smiled and waved goodbye to the deck hand.

Greece

By the time we had our daypacks on and took account of our possessions, the crew of the enormous ship had skillfully backed the ferry up to the landing and let down the main vehicle ramp. Two semi-rigs moved out. No time was being wasted here at Iguomenitza.

The plastic wheels of our roll-on packs were cold. They clattered over the rough diamond plate ramp, the vibrations rattling our shoulder joints until we reached the smoother blacktop surface of the dock. It seemed only a matter of minutes before the ferry was pulling away, upper deck lights blending into the darkness of the sea and sky. I had a momentary flash of us all dressed in heavy woolen clothing with our belongings on a large wooden-wheeled handcart, refugees in a foreign land. It was then that we began to assess our situation.

A couple of semi-tractor trailer rigs were parked and waiting for another ferry boat; half a dozen darkened taxis were parked out on the road. In the opposite direction of what appeared to be the center of town was a small brightly lit café.

The air was still, the temperature cool, maybe forty-five degrees Fahrenheit. Lesley and Andrea were wearing their blue rain jackets with the stripe of reflective tape across the back. The girls disliked those jackets, but they made good windbreakers when conditions warranted.

Since no agents were at the Passport Control office, we rolled our bags through the barricades toward town. Pausing to get some local currency at an ATM, we walked on. A fellow sleepwalker behind the wheel of a cab rolled up alongside. With half-opened eyes and hair in all directions, he asked, "Where are you going?"

"The bus station," I answered. English, what a relief, I thought.

After an exchange involving direction and distance, we loaded our bags into his trunk, tied the lid with a ratty piece of rope and bounced along the winding main street into town. It was probably no more than a mile, but on empty stomachs at 5:00 A.M. it was well worth the price.

The only other occupants of the chilly bus station were a couple of old ladies cut from the pages of a *National Geographic* with the black skirts, black sweaters, rolled down stockings and black babushkas. They sat on a hard wooden bench and only faintly acknowledged us when we came through the door.

As we entered, the ticket agent glanced up. Immediately her face took on a questioning look that we'd grown accustomed to seeing. It was a mixture of surprise, confusion and pity, clearly wondering what set of challenges we might present. Fortunately for us, she also spoke English.

"Four tickets to Ioannina." I took a chance and followed this with, "Is there a place to leave our bags while we look for something to eat?"

"Over there." She pointed to the adjacent office. "He will be glad to help."

Well, maybe not glad, but he was accommodating. Our four large packs and three daypacks just about finished off any unused floor space in his cluttered little cubicle. We smiled and made a hasty retreat into the street before he changed his mind. It was warmer outside than in the unheated station.

Soon we would learn that in Greece, the distance to a warm, often-extravagant bakery or patisserie is never more than about 100 feet, no matter what town you're in. Some pastries and milk for the girls, Greek coffee for Carla and me, and all was well. We had made a successful landing in Greece. Relishing the grainy Greek coffee, I reminded myself of the simple formula for happiness I had developed over the past six months of travel.

A full stomach, a ticket forward and clean socks.

Two out of three wasn't bad.

The brewing process for Greek coffee is slightly more complicated than your basic American style drip. It is concocted in a narrow, open-top pot with a single handle called a *briki*. The coffee and roughly an equal part of sugar are added to the water. Heat is applied until the foam, created by the volatile oils of the coffee, rises. Depending on the school of thought, there is the two step process; the foam should rise twice, once for the coffee and once after the addition of the sugar. The coffee solids, pulverized to the consistency of talcum, are allowed to settle to the bottom of the cup. While there is always the temptation to get that last little taste, bottoms-up is not recommended.

Presently we were comfortably snoozing our way into the rugged limestone mountains en route to Ioannina (pronounced yo-AH-nina), a medium-sized city on the west side of the Pindos Mountains; this was the destination for our first day in Greece.

It seemed the decision to leave Italy on Sunday, so that we arrived in Greece on Monday, had some merit. Sunday was quiet in many parts of the Christian world. But remembering the quest to find food in Germany on the Sabbath, we didn't want to risk spending a day groping about for necessities.

By Monday afternoon we found ourselves in familiar circumstances on an unfamiliar sidewalk, standing outside the bus station, paging through our travel book, trying to orient ourselves on the four-by-six inch map of the city. The tourist information office had been relocated, maybe a couple of times, and so we pulled our bags here, and we pulled our bags there. Eventually we found a spot in the sun and let the girls look after our bags while Carla and I did the reconnaissance work. It was a bright sunny December day, the sun felt good and luck was with us. It didn't take long to secure a room for a couple of nights at the Hotel Bretania. The hotel owner was anxious to point out that they also prepared breakfast. The room was maybe a bit on the plain side, but the patisserie downstairs on the street level, at least in our limited experience, was beyond extravagant.

The sidewalk café culture in Greece during the winter months was more of a coffee shop culture. At around 11:00 A.M. and again at 7:00 P.M. the shops are full to capacity, mostly coffee drinkers. No one appeared to be indulging in all the sweets arranged into great pyramids and arrayed in rows on long tables; however, it seems it was customary to bring a few pastries home each evening. Any social visit is always accompanied by an offering of pastries in a small white box with corn syrup soaking through at the corners, tied by means of a narrow red ribbon. The amazing part — we saw very few overweight people in Greece.

This unpretentious city yielded a low key introduction to Greek life as we explored the streets and alleys and peered into shops. Lesley and Andrea probed every inch of the ruins of an old Ottoman fortress built by the local pasha who went by the name of Ali. It seems he was able to manage the rugged northwestern region, known as Epirus, as his own personal realm until 1822 when he was shot. After catching our breath in Ioannina for a couple of nights, we boarded an early morning bus headed across Katara Pass for Kalambaka and the medieval monasteries, known as Meteora.

Our transport looked like a 1960s vintage bus, very clean and well maintained despite its age. The cold vinyl seats confirmed that the temperature was well below freezing. Our breath condensed and formed vaporous clouds that remained suspended above our heads in the still, frigid air. Andrea and Lesley wondered out loud when the driver would arrive to start the engine and hopefully the heater. A few other tentatively committed early morning travelers climbed aboard. Quiet conversations began to penetrate the silence. Eventually the driver arrived and brought the clattery diesel to life. I don't know if he ever turned on the heat or if the bus just warmed up from the body heat of the passengers.

We had read that Katara Pass could be treacherous in winter months, and so we opted to delay renting a car until we were on the eastern side of the mountains. As it was, the roads were clear, but the snow was already accumulating on the upper reaches of the pass and farther down on the eastern side.

The significance of the town of Kalambaka is its proximity to the medieval monasteries known collectively as Meteora. Construction of the precariously balanced structures on slender pinnacles of rock began as early as the ninth century but flourished in the thirteenth century as Christian sects sought refuge from the ebbs and flows of human migrations and invading hordes. As many as twenty-four monastic communities existed at the peak of the Ottoman Empire in the fifteenth and sixteenth centuries.

This apparent obsession with isolation makes more sense when one realizes that starting about the fifth century, the northern Balkan peninsula was trampled by the likes of Attila known locally as "the scourge of God" and his band of Huns, only to be followed by the Ostrogoths and Gepids, the Kurtigur Huns, the White Huns and the Avars, until they were edged over by the Patzinak Turks from the Asian Steppe and subsequently the Cuman Turks. The Serbs carved out their homeland around 1025. Finally came the passing hordes of French and German religious fanatics on their way to retake the Holy Land in 1095. This was not an easy place to live. Each arriving horde ravaged the land and plundered the villages and monasteries. With all this coming and going, it is easy to see why the monks placed such emphasis on defense through isolation.

We spent a few days hiking the trails under azure skies and the occasional dusting of snow. The five remaining active monasteries are at least in part, museums. Welcomed by white bearded monks in long black robes we were some of the few tourists in early December. Exploring every nook and cranny, Lesley and Andrea got a chilling surprise peering through a crack into a darkened recess. Staring back at them was a stack of human skulls and femurs belonging to some of the previous residents.

On our first chilly night in Kalambaka, we set out in search of some dinner, envisioning a truly Greek experience. While breakfast was included in the price of the room, the little Hotel Meteora was not equipped to prepare dinner during the off-season. Walking down toward the plaza in the night air, a few degrees below freezing, we were each wearing practically every article of clothing we had brought. The wind was up, and we moved along at a good pace to stay warm, straining our ears as we went to make out what seemed to be a familiar melody off in the distance. As we approached the brightly lit fountain, fully decked out in Christmas regalia, a hastily arranged PA system rocked and gyrated in the cold wind. With slightly more clarity now, yes, it really was *White Christmas* and as incongruous as it seemed, it really was none other than Bing Crosby doing the crooning. It just seemed so absurd to be walking down the main street in a small town in Greece listening to Bing recount the virtues of chestnuts, open fires, Jack Frost and all that!

We ducked into a busy little gyro shop and ordered a round of pitas. With tsatziki sauce running along the backs of our hands down to our elbows, we warmed ourselves and listened to the ominous refrain of *Let It Snow*. Old Bing sure got around. A truly Greek experience all the same. There didn't seem to be any reluctance to incorporate bits and pieces from other cultures to which the Greeks had also contributed over the millennia. It is easy to understand their willing assimilation and adaptability in light of a history of occupation and the waves of culture that washed across the Balkan Peninsula for nearly 4,000 years. The Greeks don't have any questions about identity.

The small family-run Hotel Meteora, up on the end of a near vertical street that abruptly terminated in a sheer cliff, had been a lucky choice. The tidy little lodge looked out onto the rugged snow capped peaks of the Pindos Mountains. In the valley below the Pineios River rushed down from the steep mountain gorges and out onto the vast plains of Thessaly where archeologists have uncovered some of the earliest known sites showing evidence of cereal grain cultivation.

The hotel lobby and restaurant on the ground floor also served as a family living room and was the center of a continuous flow of family members and friends. Always a fire going in the hearth, Grandma sitting at a table doing her needlework, Grandpa coming in from his chores to warm his hands, while the sons Dimetrius and Nikolas kept the business running and looked after guests.

Lesley and Andrea spread out on one of the tables close to the fire and ground away on their home schooling assignments. Carla continued planning for Egypt and India, while I found a place for my espresso pot among the embers and worked up the monthly budget summary. It seems we had earned considerable surplus in the food category while traveling in Europe. That surplus would offset the costs of arranged travel in Egypt and China.

The forecast for the Balkans and the northwestern mountains was for heavy snow. We decided to head east to lower elevations on the eastern side of the peninsula to catch a glimpse of the Aegean Sea.

The land east of Kalambaka was flat and open. It fell away quickly from the rugged peaks of the Pindus Mountains that rise to over 7,200 feet down to the coastal plain of the Aegean. It was a chilly bus ride out across a desolate gray agricultural area. Farming co-ops and ag-chemical dealers had stacked their equipment alongside storage bins. Our bus rumbled in high gear through small farming communities whose residents, waiting out the cold dry winter months, had turned their attention to the holiday season. Hints of Christmas regalia began to appear in shop windows. A couple of stops along the way and the bus gradually filled with day-trippers headed to the cities of Larrisa and Volos for holiday shopping. There was a palpable sense of anticipation as the Christmas holidays approached.

Clear blue skies and the friendly crowd soon had the old bus warmed up to where we could take off our hats and gloves. Heads began to slump forward, swaying from side to side as the warm sunlight streamed in through the windows. An occasional cry from a baby goat, whose fuzzy white head protruded from a plastic grocery bag, brought us all back to consciousness from time to time. A bewhiskered old gentleman, wearing a tattered sports coat and tweed hat, sat in the back keeping a warm hand on his wooly young traveling companion and smiled amicably.

The temperature outside was a few degrees above freezing, and the warm sun of the bus ride began to lose some of its intensity as a few billowing gray clouds gathered over the mountains where we had started earlier in the day. Arriving in Larrisa, we pulled our collars up, dug out our rain gear to break the wind and pulled our bags about a mile from the bus station into the center of town. Lesley and Andrea stood by the bags while Carla and I searched for the rental car office as the first flakes of wet snow drifted to the ground. It was a role the girls had grown accustomed to, but it was cold, and I felt badly abandoning them on the street corner in a strange country to fend for themselves. Parental instincts had to be put aside in the name of expediency. At the rental car agency a friendly round-faced agent welcomed us into the warm office. While I filled out the paper work, Carla went back to find the girls.

In a matter of minutes we were together again, and I was muttering half audible threats and epithets as I wrestled our things into yet another scarcely large enough trunk (boot in the Eastern dialect). Just about the time I had everything fitted in and as an apparent afterthought, the rental agent brought out a set of cable chains for our tires, just in case. Filled with self-satisfaction at the fine packing job I had just completed, I looked at the tire chains with reservation. Out of politeness I thanked the agent, pulled out a daypack that would now have to go in the back seat with the girls and slammed the trunk lid closed.

With the heater blasting, Carla navigated us through town, and we set out driving around to the other side of Mt. Pelion, which looked out onto the Aegean Sea. Pelion was the fabled domain of the Centaurs. In those dense green forests Chiron, king of the race of half man and half horse, reared and fostered the demi-god Heracles, Jason, son of Aeson, and, of course, Achilles, hero of Troy.

We continued on through the port city of Volos, also known historically as Iolcos, the point from which Jason launched his ship The Argo in search of the Golden Fleece. Climbing through mountain villages, the roads became ever more narrow and steep.

About half way up the west side of the mountain, the snow was getting to be a challenge to drive through as it accumulated on the road surface. We decided to go on, but the grade was steep. By the time I finally resolved to try the tire chains, the snow depth on the west side of the mountain was approaching four inches.

The tire chains were tricky, but after a couple of attempts, Carla and I figured out how to get the cables around the tires and fastened. We continued on and so did the snow with no signs of letting up. At the pass the wind was creating small drifts over the two-lane highway. On the Aegean side of the mountain, progress was slow. Very little cut and fill had been involved in making the road, so we worked our way in and out of every canyon as we followed a contour about 500 feet above the sea.

Daylight was in short supply. The sun was fighting a losing battle against a thickening blanket of clouds and the snow was falling harder still. Carla checked the map and found what looked like a coastal road. We dropped down a couple hundred feet to see if we could find it and get out of the snow. There was no snow, which was some relief. The tire chains were noisy on the wet pavement and kept us from going much over about 25 miles per hour. I was reluctant to take them off.

After groping around for half an hour, we came to a place where the two dirt tire tracks we were following disappeared into a small, presumably shallow, inlet. The sea was to our right, the beach and the mountain to our left, and we were in total darkness. No clear evidence of a road revealed itself on the other side, and we had no idea how deep the water was. Surrounded by darkness and in an unfamiliar car, we decided to head back up to the two-lane highway where the snow accumulation had reached about eight inches.

The directions we had gotten on the internet were perfectly accurate, but identifying landmarks was becoming more difficult in near whiteout conditions. We felt a wave of relief as we passed the sign for Zagora, accent on the last syllable. Stopping to ask directions at a nearby house, we continued down a road that was visible only as a vague impression in the otherwise smooth white surface. Cautiously feeling our way down the steep hill along the narrow tree-lined lane, branches were beginning to bend under the weight of the fluffy white burden.

We parked the car in a wide spot at what appeared to be the end of the road. Down the slope to where I knew the Aegean Sea was supposed to be, the visibility had dropped to less than a hundred feet. The snow was now well over our ankles. It was a relief to be out from behind the wheel. We were greeted at the door of the Villa Horizonte by our host Wolf Kiel; he wore a welcoming but slightly curious smile as this bunch of wandering Americans emerged from the darkness and the blizzard.

"Not a fit night out for man nor beast," I offered and went on to introduce our group.

Wolf had a fire raging in the artfully engineered hearth at the end of the long narrow dining table. The walls of the spacious common room were pure white stucco, except for the wall facing east, which was mostly glass and looked out onto the sea. Masterfully crafted hand cut trusses supported the high ceiling. Heating such a room with conventional forced air would have been impossible, but the design included heating cables in the concrete floor. It was a pleasure to walk around in bare feet, even as the temperature outside was well below freezing.

Wolf helped bring in our things and showed us to our rooms. We spent the remainder of the evening looking out in disbelief at the deepening snow. Carla's skill as a navigator and a dose of luck had got us to our destination. We had also been fortunate to have chosen this particular place instead of an empty cottage somewhere along the beach.

Southern and eastern Europe were snowed in from Vienna to Ankara and down to Corinth, one of those climatological events that happened every twenty or thirty years. When all was said and done we received over three feet of snow. We spent probably the most memorable eleven days of our trip at the lodge with Wolf Keil and his charming wife Ingrid Brink. Wolf and Ingrid had left the countries of their birth, Germany and Sweden, sometime in the late 1970s to adapt to a culture of tradition and orthodoxy. Besides their native tongues and English, they both spoke, as far as we could tell, flawless Greek.

Catching up on home schooling was foremost on our daily agenda. It had been hit or miss since we left Rome, so the girls hit the books. Between schooling and playing in the snow, they received daily drawing lessons from Ingrid, an accomplished artist.

Under the circumstances, activities were limited. Our regular exercise consisted of hiking through waist deep snow up to the tiny grocery store, filling our daypacks with whatever we could make into a couple of meals and hiking back. I worked my way through Wolf's music collection. His tastes, like mine, were rather eclectic and ranged from European electronic pop to Mid-eastern ballads. While the girls spent hours playing in the snow, I updated our budget sheets, kept the fire going in the fireplace and mastered the art of making espresso in the pot that I had purchased in Venice. Carla continued her planning work using Ingrid's Internet connection.

The columns of the tattered edition of our English news magazine painted a mixed picture of the state of the world. Headlines proclaimed the arrival of 1,000 U.S. Marines in Afghanistan to set up a forward base in Kandahar, and a state of emergency declared by the Nepalese government as Maoists rebels attack police and army posts.

Our visit to Nepal was in serious question. I thought Mao's little red book had gone out of print a long time ago. In spite of the discovery that Egypt had been the birthplace of al Qeada, we were still planning to visit there. An e-mail from a travel agent in Rome, however, indicated some problem with the tour we had booked. Maybe we could sort it out when we got down to Athens. We could only hope that tensions would subside before we left the comfort zone of Europe.

The huge dining table in the Villa Horizonte could have seated twenty people. We had our projects spread out and still had room to eat. Dinner was when we discussed business items like planning and budget.

"I've finished totaling up our expenses through the end of November," I announced one evening.

"Are we doing all right?" asked Lesley "Or are we going to have to stop eating for a while?"

I launched into my budget review. "At the end of November we had been on the road for 172 days. We are well below budget on food. Including our stays in big cities where we ate in restaurants, we averaged $43.01 per day to feed the four of us. That's $29.00 below budget, predicated on eating out every day. We are ninety cents a day under budget on room and $5.76 cents under in transportation. In admissions and miscellaneous categories we are okay as well."

Andrea looked up from her drawing pad, "So what does that mean? Is that good?"

"What it means is that we will cover the cost of package tours that we arranged in Egypt and China," I responded.

"Why do we need to take package tours? Andrea interjected. "I like traveling like we are."

Carla, who was immersed in a travel book on India, looked up and said. "You can't just go to those countries and travel around like we have all over Europe. The tourist policies are much more strict, and you have to be under the control of an organized tour provider."

"Well, I prefer traveling alone like we are," insisted Andrea.

"We do too, but we just don't have any choice. Egypt just can't afford to lose any more tourists, so they are very careful about letting Westerners just wander from place to place."

"Why? Did they lose some tourists somewhere?" asked Lesley.

"In 1997 a busload of German tourists were gunned down near one of the temples. The terrorists were hoping to ruin the tourist industry and destabilize the government," Carla ended by way of explanation.

"The world is a turbulent place. From what I see in this article I am reading," I said, "we can pretty well put Nepal into the same category as Indonesia. If these Maoists keep up their antics and start targeting foreigners, it would be foolish for us to go there. We may have to extend our time in India by several days."

Hiking up to the village was always an adventure. After a couple of days, we had tramped a path through the snow to where it was no longer waist deep, only to be obliterated by a second wave of weather that dropped another foot and a half.

We worked our way through the aisles of the dimly lit old grocery store, trying to conceive of combinations that would constitute an acceptable meal. Then across the tiny plaza, past the Orthodox Church, we trudged onward to the meat market and finally to the bakery.

Wolf, who accompanied us on our trek up to the village, had gone about his business, and we regrouped at a coffee shop on the plaza. Greek coffee is an entirely unique experience and should be enjoyed in an appropriate café or taverna. At ten in the morning, the café was a male dominated environment. Entirely devoid of adornments, the stucco walls had acquired a yellow hue from years of tobacco smoke and recondensed coffee volatiles. The heavy wooden chairs and tables arranged in clusters revealed that this was the epicenter of local discourse and politics. Normal life that proceeded at a slower pace than in a big city had for all practical purposes come to a chilly standstill. There were animated discussions among the men of the village, as they discussed frozen water pipes and the condition of the highway back across the mountain.

The town drunk teetered through the door of the café, fell into a chair and cracked open a twist top bottle of retsina. He earned a couple of disgusted looks as he took a healthy swallow. A few drachmas fell onto the table in front of him; they were donated by a couple of passersby who considered a town drunk an essential part of any well rounded community. It's a tough job, but somebody has to do it.

No one seemed bothered by the presence of outsiders, even Americans, even women. Wolf and Ingrid, who had been in Zagora for several years and brought a fresh source of revenue into the community, would always remain outsiders. Rumor had it that they were Buddhists. As far as I could determine, Wolf was still a Lutheran. No Buddhist altars or incense burners were to be found in Villa Horizonte. Even though they spoke Greek fluently, they just didn't look Greek.

After eleven days there was a break in the weather; we headed back across the mountain and south for Athens. We inched our way over the pass along a narrow single lane bounded by ten-foot sheer walls of snow. I finally took the tire chains off when we got down to Volos. The national highway was perfectly clear. I can only imagine Wolf's sense of relief at seeing us go. We had probably burned up a whole season's worth of firewood, since we were cabin bound most of our stay. We will always have the fondest memories of our days spent in Villa Horizonte. It was a chance to relax, catch our breath and reaffirm our resolve to complete our adventure.

Athens

Rolling into Athens on the twentieth of December the sky was clear with no sign of winter. Christmas was approaching rapidly and Carla's mother Norma, her husband Max and other family members would be arriving in two days. Carla's sister Debra and her two daughters Mariko and Kiri were coming in from Albuquerque and her youngest sister Shari and husband Steve were flying in from Salt Lake City. The entourage ranged in age from eleven to seventy-seven. It promised to be great time, and we were all primed. Athens was the perfect place for our annual family reunion. And if there is one thing the Greek people know how to do, it is to celebrate Christmas. A knowledgeable travel agent in Albuquerque had found a hotel for us right in the center of Athens.

It didn't take long to scope out our surroundings: an Internet café with excellent espresso, a sandwich shop, a quick gyro shop and, of course, several pastry shops. The underground commuter railway was clean and fast, and we had no trouble making our way through the Athens system. We found the area around the central market, the real heart of the city, to be the most enjoyable part of Athens. We often ended up there surrounded by people who did not speak English as a first language. The meat market is not for the faint of heart, while the fish market is a riot of activity and good-natured buying and selling. In either case, smiling young men in stained white aprons cried out to draw attention to their offering of the day. The atmosphere was festive and the cacophony infectious. It was easy to walk out with more than you might have the capacity to cook in a hotel room. I restocked on salami. What better place?

Across the street were fruit and vegetable vendors situated in canvas and plywood stalls, purveyors of olives and mountains of nuts, seed and spices. Interspersed were everything from batteries to pipe wrenches, hairnets to socks, and various household items. It was our favorite part of Athens.

The Parliament Building in Athens, Greece. Andrea had developed a preoccupation for men in uniform and had a picture taken with them whenever possible. (Lesley)

With only a few days left before Christmas and the imminent arrival of Carla's family, we scurried around from stall to stall and shop to shop buying bits of Christmas paraphernalia to liven up our rooms. A few strings of cheap lights, some garlands, a couple of banners with little cardboard Santas, saying, "Merry Christmas," in Greek, olives, some more indigenous salami, a big bag of pistachios, a bottle of Metaxa, a few other support items, and we were ready to let the good times roll. We spent several family days, just enjoying each others company, eating, drinking and exploring the diverse environs of Athens.

Lesley and Andrea were glad to see their cousins, Mariko and Kiri, especially after spending the previous six months isolated from friends and peers. This was no small feat of patience and restraint for 13- and 14-year-old girls. They chattered on, laughed, told stories and compared detailed enumerations of the idiosyncrasies of their parents.

It was nice to let the girls make unsupervised excursions out into the chaos that was Athens at Christmas. We had no reservation giving them the freedom to do some exploring on their own. They always made it back to the meeting point at the designated time. We developed a strong feeling of trust in the girl's ability to stay together, look after each other and find their way around. In return, they had time together outside the range of critical parent oversight.

Rising a hundred feet of so above the heart of the city, the Acropolis rests on a prominent limestone platform. Among the ancient structures are temples and theaters that predate the ascendance of Rome. What is visible to the modern visitor is a complete time line of early Western history, and it is difficult for a visitor not steeped in regional history and lore to make much sense of it. Like kremlins in Russia, there is more than one acropolis in Greece; the word acropolis simply describes the central temple and fortification of an ancient Greek city.

Most evidence of Neolithic communities dating back to 2,800 years B.C. and on through the fifth century B.C. was obliterated when the rival Persian Empire sacked Athens in 479 B.C. No two stones were left standing.

Numerous structures were built in the Acropolis in classical times. The work of the general and politician Perikles is most remembered by the construction of the Parthenon, a temple to Athena and the Odion of Perikles around 450 B.C. The Parthenon served many years as a political center, then became a Christian church dedicated to St. Sophia. Minarets were added, and it was converted to a mosque during the second Turkish occupation. The Turks pulled down the adjacent temple of Nike to use its building stone to make a rampart during their war with the Venetians. The Parthenon was converted to an arsenal in the seventeenth century. Gunpowder stored inside ignited with an explosion and fire causing the roof to collapse. It is remarkable that anything is left at all.

We were spared the return of winter weather while in Athens and had a perfect family holiday. The high living of Athens was interrupted for a few days of exploring down on the northeastern corner of the Peloponnesus, the big peninsula to the south. Napflion, a small city on the eastern Pelopennesus, looks out onto the Gulf of Argolis, named after the Mycenean fortress of Argos. The palace cities of Mycenae and Tiryns, a short drive from Napflion, are considered some of the oldest organized civic centers on the Greek mainland. Mycenae reached its zenith around 1600 B.C. and was all but abandoned by 1200 B.C. as the Greek Dark Age began. The fortifications at Argos ensured the survival of that small town to the present day, making it the oldest inhabited city in Greece.

Carla's skill as a navigator was put to the extreme test as she guided our caravan through hills and down unpaved lanes that sometimes disappeared into the groves of gnarled olive trees. Having survived the previous two millennia in rugged symbiosis with the human inhabitants, I don't think there is anything that more aptly captures the essence of southern Greece than the contorted gray trunks of the olive trees. Each one is a work of art, sculpted by the careless hands of nature.

Moving On

Bidding a safe return to our loved ones, they set out for the airport well before dawn on the second of January. It was a time of private reflection after ten days of intense family revelry and six months of travel, which had brought us though much of Europe. Silently the Christmas garlands and strings of lights came down. Carefully folding them, Lesley and Andrea packed the decorations discretely into the wardrobe to be discovered by hotel employees or some unsuspecting traveler. We extracted our car from the deep recesses of the underground parking garage. Fitting each piece of our gear into its assigned location, I looked down with some reservation at the nearly worn out set of tire chains in the trunk. I had already repaired them twice. I hoped that they would remain in the trunk for the rest of our time in Greece.

Before starting our trek up to Thessaloniki we set out for a quick visit to Delphi. The moderate weather we had experienced while in Athens gave way to the second major snowstorm to hit Greece that winter. Carla and I talked over breakfast about heading due north from Delphi in the direction of the ancient city of Thermopylae, but that would take us across the top of the mountains. This was the same mountain pass where in 480 B.C. Persian forces under the leadership of Xerxes annihilated that heroic contingent of 300 Spartans who remained to defend central Greece. I wasn't feeling lucky, so we headed east toward Thebes, plowing our way through heavy snow. I was happy I hadn't thrown away the tire chains. Near Thebes a patrolman was stopping those who were not equipped with chains.

Another 20 miles down the road we neared the intersection with the national highway. We picked our way through a litter of semi-rigs and other vehicles that were beginning to accumulate and appeared as an impromptu truck stop in an otherwise monochrome wasteland. Working my way to the front, the highway patrolman asked if we were headed south to Athens; I indicated that our preferred direction was north to Thessoloniki, but we were flexible. The national highway, he informed us, was completely shut down in the southbound direction of Athens. The roughly forty mile traffic jam would have thousands of people spending the night in cars and buses as the next wave of snow descended on Athens. I told him we would be heading north and asked how conditions were up toward Volos. He just looked at me, tilted his head slightly and said, "Good Luck." Conditions steadily improved as we traveled north.

After a couple of hours we were finally able to stop and take off the chains. We made good time up to Thessaloniki and rolled in about dark.

The next morning we returned the car. Bringing it back in one piece, after all we had been through, involved no small amount of luck. But we were, once again, afoot. Weather in Thessaloniki was bitterly cold, though most of the snow had melted off or blown away. The second wave of snow, the one we had passed through in Thebes, had hit the southern part of the country harder than the north.

We gathered our wits about us in Thessaloniki, got the laundry done and spent some time at an Internet café. Ingrid, back at Villa Horizonte, had called ahead and arranged a room at a discounted rate for us. The weather was cold, but sunny afternoons made hiking around the ancient ruins and city walls an enjoyable experience. Walking the winding fortifications that fringe the hills above the city, took me back in history in a way I had not really felt in many of the other cities we visited.

It seems that by the end of the third century A.D., Rome had been all but abandoned and provincial capitals like Thessalonica had ascended to imperial prominence. Around 293 the Emperor Diocletian divided the empire for more efficient administration, and Thessalonica became one of four regional capitals. Resources flowed to the capitals where troops were garrisoned, governors saw to administration and courts convened. Nestled among the shops and apartments of central Thessaloniki are aqua ducts, theaters and residences that date back to those times.

Thessaloniki is not all that well represented in some of the tour books, but with the incorporation of many ancient structures into a modern city, a feeling of continuity is fostered, making history more tangible. It permeated the air and infected the soul with a deeper appreciation of the purpose and commitment that ran through the people of Greece and the eastern Mediterranean.

After a full day of hiking in the cold air, we returned to our hotel room. It was cluttered with clothing and artifacts of travel, and we were soon tripping over each other's luggage, looking for places to stretch out. In our normal fashion we began discussions of our options for dinner, polling each other for any preferences. Andrea sat on her bed, back turned to us, insisting she was not hungry and her stomach hurt. This refrain held very little diagnostic information. It is difficult for young girls to regulate their eating habits to conform to those of a group. "My stomach hurts" sometimes means, "I'm hungry." All of us began to talk at once, offering suggestions, asking for input, chattering and stumbling around our untidy little room of four beds draped with clothes. I happened to look over at Andrea, sitting in her puffy down vest with her head bowed, one leg propped up on the other and witnessed a large crystal-like tear fall slowly through space and splash almost audibly onto the faded blue of the ill fitting jeans she had bought way back in Tipperary. Her shoulders convulsed with a sob, and I knew this was serious. The flu finally caught up with us in Thessaloniki. Andrea got it first. She laid low and stayed in the hotel room for a couple of nights, while the rest of us went out to perform laundry, chores and make travel arrangements.

We brought things back for her to eat and let her rest. The best recipe for the flu is the pediatric BRAT diet; bananas, rice, applesauce and toast with some variation for local fare. A favorite sidewalk snack in Greece and Turkey are freshly baked bread rings with sesame seeds. They are great for an upset stomach and other lower GI problems. I began feeling symptoms and relied heavily on the sesame bread rings to bring things under control and provide readily digestible carbohydrate.

After a couple of days, Andrea began to recover. We located the main bus station and booked some seats over to Istanbul. The bus to Istanbul departed at 2:30 A.M. The evening before departure, we checked out of our room and tried to catch a couple of hours of sleep on the couches in the second floor lobby. It was below freezing when we loaded our stuff into the cab and arrived at the bus station at around 1:30. The bus depot was an adjunct to the train station, and we stood in frigid air waiting to board the bus. Andrea appeared to be in good enough shape to tolerate the trip.

Any thoughts of taking the train to Istanbul had been dismissed. We had watched the story unfold on the television; several hundred people who had become stranded for three days in a snow bound train on the line between Thessaloniki and Istanbul was a lesson in itself. Having negotiated two major blizzards, we were not inclined to rely on luck. Logic told us that the first priority would be to keep the roads clear. Therefore, the bus was our choice.

Sleep had been intermittent, and the first light of day found us somewhere along the road to the Turkish border. The broad coastal plane of Thrace was to our left, the uppermost reaches of the Aegean Sea to our right. The Rhodope Mountains that mark the border between Greece and Bulgaria rose farther to the north and were mostly lost in a shroud of cold gray clouds. An hour or so later we arrived at the border cross-ing, got out to stretch our legs and purchased tourist visas. I dug into the snack pack, as my daypack had come to be known; it was the one with the perpetual supply of candy, crackers, salami, juice packets and cof-fee. We passed around some cookies to hold us until the next stop where we could disembark for breakfast.

Turkey

It was a gray, dingy day. A mixture of snow and rain was falling when we arrived at the cavernous bus station on the outskirts of Istanbul. Nowhere else in the world can a person see as many varied and colorful buses as the Istanbul terminal. Bus is the only way to travel in that part of the world.

No one connected with the bus line told us that if we stayed on the bus, after leaving the main terminal, it would go downtown. Fortunately, for us, a few noisy American disaster relief workers, who had kept us awake all night recounting their not exactly riveting experiences, clued us in. So we stayed put and ended up saving the cab fare from the main terminal into the heart of the city. I felt a little chagrined that I had not been more cordial to them during the night.

Stepping out into the icy slush and rivulets of frigid water running along the curb, Andrea and Lesley pulled our packs from the belly of the bus. Carla and I began an assessment of our next course of action as it began to rain.

Since we were without local currency, we found an ATM and ac-quired a pocket full of Turkish lire, 1,375,000 per U.S. dollar. The 385 Greek drachmas per dollar seemed easy enough now. The 2,100 Italian lire per dollar was a little more difficult. But counting the number of zeros on the Turkish currency was the challenge.

We had called ahead from Thessaloniki to a little hotel in the old town area of Istanbul. Once again, pure blind luck and some accurate reviews by our travel books led us to an ideal location for discovering Istanbul on foot, a little family-run hotel named the Side Pension.

Over the period of a week the Side Pension really began to feel like home. Breakfast came with the price of the room and included a couple of eggs, toast and a bowl of salty black olives. It was always enough to keep us going until noon. For reasons that escape me now, I didn't press to get a bottle of gas for the stove in the room, and we ended up

Hagia Sophia in Istanbul, Turkey. The largest building in the world when it was built in A.D. 532 by the Emperor Justinian. (photographer unknown)

eating our lunches and evening meals in food shops and restaurants along the main street. The food was good and economical.

We got home schooling fired up again and spent the cold Istanbul mornings going through theorem and proofs, participles and prepositions. With some amount of interest we tried to keep ourselves advised as to political developments that might influence our path. Andrea was still suffering the effects of the flu, though she was a real trooper and complained little.

Our lodgings were only two blocks from the Roman hippodrome and Hagia Sophia, once the largest Christian church in the world; that was back in A.D. 532 when it was built by the Emperor Justinian. We were just inside the Byzantine fortifications that had remained unassailable until 1453 when Sultan Mehmet II took the city, and it became the capital of the Ottoman Empire. Hagia Sophia saw the addition of four delicate, pencil-thin minarets and its conversion to a mosque.

Istanbul was our first exposure to Islam. Only four months after the World Trade Center disaster it was hard not to feel a little exposed. Everyone with whom we came in contact assured us that the United States was still held in high regard. There was no reluctance by them to make it clear that they did not agree with our policy toward the Palestinians, but they loved democracy, the American people and the American dollars they brought with them.

Istanbul, like Rome, is built on a series of hills, each one replete with massive domed structures accompanied by delicate minarets. Hagia Sophia and at the other end of the hippodrome, the Sultanahmet, are the two most widely visited mosques, although there appeared to be dozens more. They were large, open and welcoming structures that also allow a respite from the city. Religion plays a major role in eastern countries and five times each day the familiar strains of the Muslim call to prayer are broadcast across the city by means of public address systems that have been attached to the minarets with varying degrees of technical skill. Known as the Athan, the chant must be repeated in Arabic and the Salaat ritual followed rigorously. The prayers are simple and the actions an expression of personal humility.

In a feeble attempt to reduce the degree to which we stood out, I suggested that Carla and the girls buy scarves to put over their heads should we go into a mosque or some place where head coverings were required. The scarves themselves are beautiful with striking geometric patterns, not those dreary black ones worn by old ladies. They were, in fact, quite attractive on young Turkish students on their way to university. I don't think the occasion ever arose where it was necessary to wear them, but Carla and the girls had them just in case.

Walking always seems to keep a person's mind occupied, and we saw most of the sights in the old town area — the Topkapi Palace, the Roman Hippodrome and the Museum of Islamic Art. The tumultuous Beyazit Meydani is a modern outdoor bazaar where shoes and jeans, hardware and electronics are displayed on shaky tables or tarps spread on the ground. Backing up against the piers of a massive aqueduct that stood silently in the dirty gray snow was the Museum of Humor and Caricature, operated by an affable Russian expat. The Valens Aqueduct, as it is called, was built by the Emperor Valens in the second half of the fourth century to bring water to the city. Istanbul residents went about their business as though that incredible architectural monument was just another traffic obstruction.

On the other side of the channel, known as the Golden Horn, rose Galata Hill, upon which a lookout tower was erected by Genoese merchants and traders who had congregated north of the city outside its protective walls. The Italian merchants, representative of the Latin culture, were not always trusted and sometimes persecuted by the Greek-speaking Byzantines who considered themselves heirs to the Romans. The Genoese ships and those of the eastern empire, moored in the Golden Horn, were protected by an enormous chain that could be raised across the channel by those in the Galata Tower to deter would-be invaders.

We spent hours along the southern shores of the Golden Horn where an unimaginable maze of open-air vendors spill out from Istanbul's famed Spice Bazaar. This area is truly a visit to a time long past. Everything from videocassettes, socks, hardware, blue jeans and miscellaneous edible offerings are laid out on blankets or tarps that can be scooped up quickly when vendor license inspectors make their rounds. The streets leading back in the direction of Hagia Sophia are a literal sea of humanity.

In a week's time, we had begun to get the lay of the land and could find our way around Istanbul without much difficulty. The shopkeepers had come to recognize our faces and had exhausted their reserves on us. I prided myself at being able to resist the entreaties of many vendors. We simply couldn't lug around souvenirs. To their credit, no race of man is more engaging and persistent than a Turkish rug merchant. You love them, but it is impossible to forget that the neatly dressed and articulate young man who strikes up a conversation as you stand waiting for the traffic light to change is really an extension of the shop, owned by his brother, uncle or close personal friend. At the end of the day, I sometimes found my sense of humor slipping; they are relentless, and they could see us coming a mile away!

The weather had begun to moderate. Except for the streets close to the medieval city walls that received no direct sunlight, the icy slush had all but disappeared. Wet cold feet were just a part of our visit to the City of the World. A day on the streets of Istanbul can be exhausting.

In need of a break from the chaos of the street we found an utterly unprepossessing door at the lower end of a small plaza. The sign matched the name in our tour book, Yerebatan Sarayi, so down we went. The atmosphere was suddenly warm and very close. The moisture-saturated air carried a musty, ancient odor. At the bottom of the stone passage we stood for a moment motionless as our eyes became accustomed to the dim yellowish light. It was strangely quiet except for the sound of water dripping from the ceiling into the water below the walkway. Street level Istanbul was shut out. The pressure of constant social interaction melted away.

Also built around A.D. 532, the Basilica Cistern, as it is called in English, is a huge man-made underground cavern constructed for the sole purpose of holding water. The vaulted ceiling, comprising a series of smooth Roman arches, was supported by regularly spaced columns. Walkways are elevated a few feet above the water surface and permit the visitor to wander thoughtfully through the dark maze. We were all enchanted by this spooky old structure, and we spent the most peaceful hour wandering the waterlogged footpaths. In Byzantine times, the vacuous cavern had been the single most important structure in what was then Constantinople.

As if in direct response to an unspoken inner longing, a couple of metal tables with folding chairs appeared in the hazy light accompanied by the familiar aroma. Drawn to its source I ordered up two cups of espresso. Except for the polite Turkish vendor, there was no one else there. We sat down to take in the utter peacefulness that filled the space.

The girls caught up with us at the table soon enough.

"What on earth is this place?" Lesley asked.

"It is an enormous water tank," I replied, "constructed to supply the inner, fortified city with water."

"This would hold an incredible amount of water. What did they need it for?"

"Istanbul was previously called Constantinople and before that it was Byzantium. It is situated on a hill that looks out over one of the most historical navigation channels in Western history. The river below our hotel is the Bosporus, a narrow channel that connects the Black Sea to the Mediterranean. When invaders laid siege to the city the inhabitants needed food and more importantly a supply of fresh water. That is what this tank was for.

"When they constructed this place," I went on, "the architects used whatever materials were available. If you look around, you will find at least two sculpted heads of the mythical Greek figure Medusa, supporting the columns that hold up the ceiling."

With a renewed sense of purpose, the girls set off to find the pagan artifacts lest they be subjected to another history lesson.

In my opinion there is no city more historic or more romantic than Istanbul. I am not a historian, but it would be hard to suffer through the normal load of high school and college courses and not have a few recollections as to the significance of Byzantium, Constantinople or Istanbul. The markets, the vendors and the throngs of humanity that clog the narrow streets are a world apart from anything we experienced in western Europe. Our time in Istanbul was just a stopover before moving on to Egypt. We were fortunate to have had the opportunity. Our hope is to return some day and become better acquainted with Istanbul as well as explore the rest of Turkey. On our final evening in Istanbul, I remember pushing back from the computer terminal in the local Internet café at the sound of the evening Athan. Preparing for the uncertainty of the next leg of our journey, I took some comfort in the familiar chant.

Egypt

The trip we had set up in Rome for Egypt had fallen through. Rather than trying to wing it in Egypt, we worked with an excellent travel agent in Athens to arrange some activities through their affiliate in Cairo.

Waiting in another line, another immigration agent stood behind another little booth with another rubber stamp. As we approached the yellow line on the floor, behind which all incoming tourists were to remain until summoned forward, I could see an exchange going on between a young, twenty-something man and the Egyptian passport control agent. Things between them did not seem to be going well. The twenty-something had a grin on his face and a somewhat petulant demeanor. I could not hear what was being said, but from what I could gather, twenty-something couldn't seem to keep his mouth shut. Whatever responses he was giving to the agent's questions were interspersed with mildly sarcastic side commentary. I watched the agent's facial expression go from the usual inscrutable administrative glaze to mild annoyance, and as furrows developed in his brow, a look of intense displeasure.

As they clambered up to the line, Lesley and Andrea were tugging at their clothes, fidgeting and bantering back and forth about whose turn it was to carry which daypack. I gave them my fatherly "look." By this time they both knew that passport control and customs agents were not folks to be trifled with. They literally held our futures in their hands. The last thing I heard the agent say to twenty-something in very clear English: "Now you go over there and stand behind that line until I call you again. If you say one more thing, you will find yourself on a plane back to Paris."

The lesson of that little event was a reminder that tourists arriving in a country are would-be guests. A country has no obligation whatsoever to admit any particular guest. Whether or not the person requesting admittance agrees with regulations and policies of the country is entirely irrelevant. Only a few responses are appropriate. The top three on my list are, "Yes, sir," "No, sir" and "Thank you."

You have to put yourself in the agent's shoes. Just how much job satisfaction can a person really derive from sitting in a little plastic booth processing tourist visas all day long?

After collecting our things we made our way into the arrival hall and spotted a neatly dressed, handsome young man, who looked like Omar Sharif. Holding a sign with the name Fisher printed on it, he was obviously our contact, who moved us out and into a van waiting at the curb. There we met our driver and picked up a plainclothes security guard who rode shotgun — more accurately he rode pistol. They suggested the guard was just a routine part of the VIP treatment, which it may very well have been. I wondered if it was probably more of a safeguard. Egypt had suffered a major economic setback in 1997 with the tourist incident at the temple of Hatshepsut. They really could not afford a repeat that would deprive them of any more tourist marks, dollars or pounds. The guard was a pleasant young man, and the bag of truly excellent Turkish dried apricots, which I drew from the food pack, went a long way toward breaking down any cultural barriers.

As pedestrians parted to permit passage of the van, the driver waved, shook hands and responded to good-natured greetings from acquaintances and bystanders. It was almost like they were the ones who had just arrived. There seemed to be an overabundance of licensed guides and people employed in tourist related activities. A common vocational program at the university level is tourism and the study of antiquities. The licensed guides are genuinely knowledgeable and help you get through the throngs of peddlers and not-so-well-studied offerers of assistance.

I quickly went through my complete repertoire of Arabic greetings — about three or four phrases — while the driver and security guard thoughtfully removed the bits of apricot from between their teeth. I was still really struggling with the basics such as counting from one to ten.

Still groggy from the flight, we nodded and smiled while our guide handed out some paperwork and gave us a run down on the things they had planned for us. This was our first experience with a prearranged itinerary. It had been a relief seeing someone standing there with our name on a little piece of cardboard. Not having to wade through the droves of porters, cabbies, guides and hotel agents was nice. At the same time, it was impossible not to feel encapsulated — apart from the life on the street — something to which we had become accustomed.

Our arrangements had been made for only a single day in Cairo upon arrival. We started at the Egyptian Museum and then the pyramids at Giza. The evening plan was a train ride down to Luxor where we would visit the temples of Karnak and on down the Nile by boat to Aswan and the first cataract of the Nile, a rocky place in the riverbed. Finally we would return to Cairo for some free time and then up to Alexandria.

Having a prearranged guide, especially the first day at the pyramids, was probably a good thing. On one's own, the flood of plainclothes con artists at the entry gate, posing as guides, might really have been a challenge to negotiate. As it was, I made the mistake of raising my camera to catch a sun dried native on a camel with one of the pyramids. Soon we were engulfed by the full retinue of fairly articulate support players. The picture with the girls sitting on the camel cost me over twenty dollars, mostly due to my slowness of wit, the swiftness of the onslaught and the fact that I had not yet come up to speed with the new currency. Watching from a few yards away, as a flock of seagulls in sandals descended upon the scent of an open wallet, the security guard from the van stepped forward and offered to get my money back for me. I declined, knowing I had just been harvested and was feeling slightly stupid. They had won, fair and square. I had just let my resolve lapse. It was something we couldn't afford to do very often, but a good lesson, nonetheless.

I took some solace in the story of Mansa Musa, the King of the West African land of Mali. In the year 1324 he arrived in Cairo on his pilgrimage to Mecca with 500 slaves, each bearing five pounds of gold. The procession of slaves was followed by 100 camels, each carrying 300 pounds of gold. Mansa Musa's precious metal was so completely dissipated among the merchants, mendicants and swindlers of Cairo that within a month he was entirely destitute. The proud king was forced to borrow from the same merchants for his passage home.

By coincidence, it turned out that former President Bill Clinton was making a visit to the Giza pyramids the very same day we were there. Access to some areas was restricted. I think he was doing his part to show people how safe it was to travel to Egypt, four months after the World Trade Center terrorist attack of September 11. The irony of all this was that the security arrangements for a visiting foreign dignitary were not on par with those that an anonymous family of four might expect. Security was definitely up. An armed guard was positioned about every hundred yards along what was probably the planned route for his visit. As a result, there were very few tourists, and some areas had been entirely closed. Fortunately for us, Carla had scheduled a couple of days in Cairo at the end of our visit, so we would get another chance to see the pyramids at our own pace. As it was a Friday, the beginning of the Muslim Sabbath, few Egyptian tourists were out and about. This also meant the ratio of guides, purveyors of camel rides and other such services to tourists was very high. We made our first forays into the great pyramids, down to the bottom of one, through the narrow passage to the inner chamber.

Literally every native Egyptian around the pyramids is there for a reason and has carved out a niche that allows him to make some sort of meager income. In the deepest recesses of the great pyramid of Cheops, a man, not too many years older than I was, was giving a brief explanation of the few artifacts remaining in the chamber. Then for the price of a single Egyptian dollar, in his bell-clear voice, he sang out the first phrase of the Muslim call to prayer, Allah u Akbar, which translates into God is Great. His voice was so pure, the sound so perfectly rendered and so perfectly trapped under the 300 feet of limestone blocks, that it continued to echo off the smooth plastered walls for some few seconds. At the end of his mini-tour, despite the fact that I was beginning to feel the pinch of bakshish, I was compelled to ask him to do it again. It actually raised goose bumps on my arms.

From there, we had only a few hours before we were whisked away to catch a train south to Luxor. Arriving at the station about an hour before it departed allowed ample time for some world-class people watching. We spent part of the time trying to come up to speed on the history of Egypt.

The farther we had come south, starting at the Arctic Circle in July, origins of history and culture stepped farther back in time. It is hard to remember that when Alexander the Great arrived in what is called Giza today, the great pyramid of Cheops was already 2,200 years old. Greeks and Romans arrived in the Nile Valley as tourists just like us. Literally hundreds of generations of Egyptian families have made at least some part of their living from tourism. The hospitality industry, like many other things, was invented in Egypt.

When it comes to persistent peddlers, amateur *ad hoc* tour guides, carriage rides, casual passersby whose brothers-in-law have an essential oil shop, papyrus emporium or alabaster factory, there is no equal on earth. It was all invented in Egypt. A young Egyptian I met, who owned a laundry, wondered why many Westerners didn't look up but walked by when someone said hello or wished them a good day. It was difficult to explain to him that as a Westerner, it is impossible to walk more than a hundred feet in any direction in Cairo without being accosted by someone who wants to sell you something. Good natured as it seems, the cost is a constant disruption of a person's thoughts.

From the train station in Luxor we caught a taxi to the riverbank where we boarded a flat-bottomed riverboat that was more of a floating hotel. Most of the other passengers were French speaking. Before setting off up the Nile we spent a day exploring the Valley of the Kings and the temples of Karnak. The morning excursion from Luxor, south to the bridge and over to the archeological sites, was worth as much as the rest of the day for a fleeting glimpse of life in a small Egyptian village. The villages up out of the flood plain reminded me of our years in the desert communities of New Mexico — barren collections of adobe houses, rock, gravel and dust; children passing a soccer ball; goats and dogs foraging for scraps. All were pursuing an existence that had gone on for millennia.

In a utilitarian blend of the modern and the ancient, makeshift donkey carts with rubber tires carried fifty-five gallon polyethylene drums of water back to houses in lieu of modern plumbing. The reliance on the donkey as the primary form of transportation and beast of burden was a striking reminder of the huge gap between the experiences of our day-to-day lives and those of many other people. It would be a mistake to view their lives as impoverished or truly lacking, except for running water. Partly it is our predisposition for viewing the world as a collection of market segments and equating success with physical possessions that sees them as disadvantaged.

On daily shore excursions from the boat we were assigned to a van and an English-speaking guide, Radwahn. An elderly South African couple and, on occasion, two Norwegians shared the guide and van. Facing each other, we struck up conversations and began exchanging bits of information as to our points of origin, occupation and other chitchat as we bounced along. The riverboat staff called us the "independents."

The Temple of Deirel-Bahri, near Karnak, Egypt, and the Valley of the Kings. Architect Senmut built this temple for Queen Hatshepsut. In the foreground, Russ, Andrea and Lesley follow the path where kings, queens and tourists had walked for thousands of years. (Carla)

Conducting our little group through the sheer cliff-like temple gates and mazes of tightly clustered columns, Radwahn did his best to paint an understandable timescape of the complex relationships of dynasties, pharaohs, gods, temples and cults. As we went, the small band of independents looked out for each other. Like most people, I found just trying to grasp the age of the monuments, the technological and tool making skills and the massive social structures that would be needed to coordinate such a gargantuan effort was mind bending.

Each morning I bounded out of bed at five-thirty or six, compelled to witness the sunrise. The dry desert air retained little heat over the course of the night. The temperature was brisk, maybe 50 degrees, and the river was silent except for the gentle throbbing of the engine and the chatter of birds in the clumps of rushes along the banks. Shadows of date palms took form on the sandy bank and immediately began their retreat as the sun returned for another passage, rolled across the sky by the god Khephri in the form of a huge scarab beetle, or at least that is how the ancient Egyptians saw it. Color returned to the rusty hills west of the Nile. These were sights and sounds I just could not imagine missing.

From a practical standpoint it is fascinating to try to figure out how the people of 2,000 B.C. got all that monumental work done. The most impressive aspect of the Egyptian monuments and art works was that much of it was created from pink granite quarried up in Aswan. This durable crystalline rock was the resistant stone that impeded the down cutting of the Nile and created the first cataract. It is a very hard stone with few natural cracks or joints. Four thousand years ago the Egyptians were not only able to quarry this material in huge monolithic blocks but to shape it and carve it in excruciating detail. The famous granite obelisks that eventually found their way to London, Paris and Rome were entirely covered in precise, almost delicate hieroglyphic text. That may not seem too impressive until you realize that these artisans had only crude tools. Metallurgy had progressed only as far as the bronze, 4,500 years ago, not a worthy opponent to the feldspar and quartz of granite.

After four days on the boat, we parted ways with the other passengers. The large group of French tourists had risen and departed early. The rest, including our fellow independents, had dispersed into the fabric of Aswan. The boat was silent. It was interesting how we all became quiet, maybe a little sullen, after the departure of our friends from South Africa. We had grown attached to them. They were easy folks to get along with, and we had genuinely enjoyed their company. Lesley and Andrea felt the loss, maybe more than Carla and I. As time permitted, we had done our best to work in some schooling. The familiar routine of schoolwork helped to get everyone back on track again.

Eager to reclaim our status as truly independent travelers, we set off to discover the people of Aswan beyond the barrier of tourist shops. We experienced a sense of relief as we took a course at a right angle to the river. The invitations and entreaties from shop owners were less vocal and lacked the persistence of those who must capture the fleeting tourist dollars. Eventually we garnered nothing more than a look of casual interest as we walked by. Middle-aged men enjoyed a cup of tea in crowded little shops with hookahs lined up for hire. Chickens, dogs, goats and narrow brown streets disappeared up the hill into a maze of aging structures where people went about their daily lives, as they had since the time before Alexander — ageless, timeless, no prospect of change.

Upon our return from Aswan to Cairo, we spent a day wandering around among the pyramids at Giza. By then the flu had caught up with me, and I staggered along behind the rest of the family. Otherwise, the day was perfect, and the security was more relaxed in the absence of foreign dignitaries. We had become accustomed to seeing the tourist police, those young men dressed in heavy blue uniforms, shouldering ancient carbines and AK-47s that looked like they would pose more danger to the operator than any mildly evasive target.

Cairo is an incredible city to cover on foot. After a dose of school, we set out for some destination on the three-by-five inch map torn from its binding in a travel guide. Once we got away from the large hotels along the river, the intensity of vendors dropped off, and we were more or less free to wander unimpeded.

The Al Azhar Mosque and Islamic University were a good hike across Cairo, but worth every bit of what it took to locate. Construction of the complex began in A.D. 972, only two years after the founding of Cairo as principal city of the Fatimid Caliphate. The Fatimids had returned from their domain in western North Africa to claim a sizable chunk of the Abbasid Caliphate that for over two centuries had stretched from Marrkesh to Merv. Second to none in the world is the adjacent Khan El Khalili Bazaar. We made a memorable foray along the dusty medieval alleys, wandering through the shops of wood workers, tinsmiths, craftsmen, vendors of plumbing supplies, writing tablets and plastic sandals. It made going to an American mall feel utterly insipid.

Our last days in Egypt were spent in Alexandria on the chilly southern shores of the Mediterranean. It was, after all, still January. We had arranged to just wander Alexandria on our own for a few of days. It is not a major international tourist destination, and we were left almost entirely to our own devices. A wonderfully genuine city, we covered vast areas on foot and by taxi. A massive facelift project was going on along the waterfront, and the new, world famous library was almost completed. The apartments and hotels that faced the strand were a little worn and maybe even shabby in some places, but the atmosphere was matter-of-fact reality.

Freed from the confines of packaged travel, we were relieved to be plotting our own course again. We walked the length of Alexandria's open market, picking up fresh fruits and snacks. The market rambles along, a couple of blocks off the strand, for a mile or so. An hour of wandering brought us to the western end of downtown to the working water front area. It was fascinating in that the art of boat building has been a vibrant mini-industry along these shores since the founding of Alexandria. The art of rendering straight planks from rough-cut logs is still practiced by modern boat builders using large frame mounted saws. Trade in the eastern Mediterranean in Roman times was based on bringing timber to Alexandria for boat building and returning to Rome with cargoes of wheat.

Prior to setting out one morning, I asked the hotel clerk to jot down in Arabic the location of the second century A.D. Roman catacombs at Kom el Shougafa and also the alleged location of an alleged Internet café near a shopping center somewhere to the south of our hotel. Summoning a cab, the concierge was very thorough, identifying the driver, taking down his license and cab numbers and giving him a brief lecture, the content of which we could only guess. We piled in and off we went.

The Roman catacombs in Alexandria are every bit as fascinating as those we saw in Rome, maybe even more so. They are out of the way and require some determination to ferret out. Smaller and more personalized than the vast pigeonhole catacombs in Rome, these family burial grounds were excavated from the soft sedimentary rock. Spiraling down some sixty feet into the ground the wide ramp opens into a circular rotunda. Passageways radiated from the center revealing family chambers and small private chapels. Carvings suggest that the family who originally opened the catacombs were practitioners of a religion that combined bits of ancient Egyptian religions along with Roman and perhaps even some Christian influence.

Out doing a little journalizing for the evening news, a young reporter and her television film crew intercepted us as we reemerged into the afternoon light. Holding a microphone to my face, she quizzed me about Alexandria and its famous library. For my part I rambled on, spreading my sparse knowledge of the history of Alexandria across as may words as I could to fill her long pauses. What a find, an American family, actually clueless enough to be wandering the streets alone.

Walking back up the narrow lane toward the point where we had arranged to meet the driver, the flour-like dust in the roadway had been turned into a smooth paste by a passing rain shower. The narrow broken sidewalk, interrupted with short flights of steps, was crowded with dawdling shoppers and vendors expounding on the features and benefits of their wares or just lounging against the doorframe drawing on a stubby cigarette. I watched as a very attractive young lady, perhaps an office worker, dressed in dark slacks and a stylish high collared jacket, negotiated the busy street. I looked down to watch her high heeled, patent leather sandals press through the little windrows of frothy muck, taking care to keep her nail polish from becoming smudged. Life is such a challenge each and every day. People struggle and step patiently through life in circumstances that span the range of human experience. Change takes generations; it was like watching a glacier move toward the sea.

Now flush with cash from the first leg of our journey, the driver had gone off to buy gas. He was waiting for us on our return to the big tree that we had designated as our rendezvous, ready to help us discover the location of the fabled Internet café. Our cabbie was a round-faced, friendly sort. Eyebrows rose in anticipation, he smiled as he deftly touched the bared tips of the two wires dangling from the jagged hole in the steering column where the ignition lock had once been. A little blue spark, a bit of rapid accelerator pumping and the engine sputtered to life. Some drivers admit to speaking a little English, many don't. The driver and I looked at the map. I pointed to where I thought we were and where we thought we wanted to go. I then produced the little paper with the Arabic instructions; lots of nods, grins and enthusiasm ensued. I wasn't sure how much genuine communication was taking place, but we were soon off. Anyone who started his car by touching two wires together was totally acceptable to Lesley and Andrea.

For some distance, we drove through a maze of donkey and camel carts and other beat-up taxis, trucks and buses of all sizes. The driver took us a mile or so south in search of a place to cross a major drainage ditch that had been excavated through the center of it all. As the day was drawing to a close, the vendors from the market place were dumping whatever inventory had exceeded its shelf life into piles along the margins of the canal. This was an effective method of recycling as there was an array of various four-legged ruminants and other hay burners to avail themselves of the free produce. They were not as picky as the people in the market.

This system works pretty well for most things that are in some way edible; even small bits of cardboard are fair play for a small herd of goats. The real problem is the plastic water bottles and plastic shopping bags. Without a doubt plastic is the bane of the Third World, and maybe a good part of the other two worlds as well. As the murky fluid in the canal, which I guessed was primarily water, trickled northward in the direction of the Mediterranean, it carried with it a flotilla of plastic trash.

Pedestrians can cross this canal on small ferry boats that range in size from a rowboat to a small pontoon boat. The distance is about 15 feet, too far to jump and no one seemed too anxious to come into contact with the filtrate in the channel. The banks of the channel were maintained, as any good civil engineer would prescribe, by creating a trapezoidal cross section. The maintenance seemed to be an ongoing process. It was difficult not to notice that the banks were devoid of any rooted vegetation. They were not just made up of soil, but a mélange of indigestible plastic and partially decomposed vegetable matter. It occurred to me that this earthy time capsule probably contained fragments from all ages dating back to the time of Alexander and the very first inhabitants of the Nile Delta. Commuters and shoppers in their polished leather shoes did their best to get across dry-footed, shine intact.

Our search for an Internet café, although there was never really a time that we weren't looking for one, led us to a modern mall. Rather than a sprawling complex surrounded by acres of black top, it was situated in the middle of a busy commercial area and was a narrow affair, probably six stories tall. We spent a little time checking e-mails and sorting out details for our pending arrival in India. Lesley and Andrea checked e-mails and banged out a few brief messages to friends back home. They had received fewer and fewer missives as they gradually fell off the radar screens of the kids back home who were no doubt recovering from the Christmas holidays and coping with the return to school.

Drawn by the odor of things cooking, we rode the seemingly endless continuum of escalators to the food court on the sixth level. It could have been anywhere in the world — middle class Egyptian school girls clustered around tables filled with half-empty Pepsi cups and pita wrappers. They were all neatly dressed with a striking array of brightly colored scarves covering their hair. They laughed and chatted, acting like 15-year-old girls anywhere on the planet. We probably looked a little worse for the wear in comparison, but no one seemed to take notice of our presence. I don't think we ever felt out of place or threatened in Egypt. Maybe we were just too numb or dumb to know what was going on around us, but I prefer to believe that everyone was just going about his or her daily life.

As much as I hate to admit it, the familiar feel of a mall-like food court was a little relief from the new and unusual experience that accompanied each and every meal when we were traveling on our own. We resolutely shunned American franchise restaurants, but the food court atmosphere took some of the uncertainty out of the simple ordering of a meal.

After a couple of days, our tour agent picked us up in Alexandria. For our benefit, I suppose, the driver put on his "American music" tape that, as it turned out, was some pretty hard core RAP. The not-so-subtle sexual innuendos may have been outside the range of their English vocabulary, but it certainly wasn't lost on those of us whose ears are more tuned to that dialect of English.

Finally I broke down and said, "Do you by chance have any popular Egyptian music that we could listen to? It is our last full day in the country."

He gladly slipped in another tape, and we sailed up the Nile Delta through town and village, the driver tapping his fingers on the wheel to the more familiar and more musical rhythm.

We had spent little time preparing for India. We used our last day in Cairo getting the laundry done and doing some Internetting, as we had come to call it. Carla studied the travel books, while the girls did a math lesson, and I worked on updating the budget. The travel books were not particularly kind to Mumbai (Bombay). So, we focused on developing a five-week route through the Indian subcontinent.

Chapter 6 _____

India and Thailand

PASSING THROUGH THE OPAQUE SWINGING doors of the passport control holding room, an arriving passenger's first sight was usually a human wall, expectant family members greeting loved ones. Eyes wide with anticipation and excitement, joyous reunions, clutching for luggage, hugs and exclamations, the clusters of family members were largely unaware of the presence of other human beings. Within minutes this first wave dispersed. What was left, the remaining few were the foreign tourists and an oversupply of second wave participants, consisting of porters, taxi drivers, hotel shills and purveyors of tour packages.

Depending on how much sleep the incoming flight had allowed, we were usually more or less prepared for our arrival. The 2:30 A.M. departure from Cairo was fairly typical of the budget flights that had been arranged for us. We adjusted our watches to Indian time. India has only one time zone, and it is five and a half hours ahead of GMT.

India

On the advice of some experienced friends, we had done very little planning for our stay in India. Taking into account our situation, my sense of humor was in reasonable order as we made our way through the crowd in search of an ATM and a taxi to take us into the center of Mumbai. As a matter of conscious planning, we ordinarily did not have much in the way of spending cash when we arrived in a new country.

No ATM was located at the arrival terminal, but one was alleged to be outside somewhere. I had only a few Egyptian dollars left, but the

"Let's Make a Deal" business attitude of airport vendors can be counted upon to enhance creativity. I negotiated a taxi ride to the city at one of the government sanctioned windows, paid for partly with my few remaining Egyptian dollars and a promise to get some Indian rupees at the first available ATM. The driver, who was ultimately responsible for the final outcome, was visibly anxious about getting the rest of the fare. We stopped at the ATM just outside the terminal and he relaxed when I returned with the remaining amount. Meantime, the four of us were rather groggy, and I don't remember much of the ride into Mumbai — only that it was very crowded, and extremely poor people seemed to outnumber any other demographic segment. It would be fair to say that in the U.S. we do not have people at the same level of poverty that exists in many countries.

True to form, the taxi driver, upon seeing the district in which we had chosen to stay, the Colaba district, and taking account of our paging through a travel book, began to offer his services to find an acceptable hotel. We had, in fact, already made a reservation. When the driver finally located it we found it had already been let. Traffic from the airport had been fairly slow, and we had missed the appointed time slot for claiming the reservation.

The sun was steadily climbing, and the humid atmosphere was filled with a mixture of overripe vegetable matter and diesel exhaust. Carla and I hiked up two flights of narrow steps to a second floor hotel, using the term hotel rather loosely. The not-so-tidy concierge in his not-so-clean tank top and shorts said they had a room, actually more of a stall, actually partitions that did not quite reach the ceiling and were made of something only slightly more substantial than cardboard. We took one look and headed back down the stairs.

After a couple of more stops, we ended up in a reasonable place within two blocks of the India's Gate monument and tourist boat dock. By this time we were all running short on energy, and the abbreviated night's sleep was beginning to take its toll on our decision-making ability. With more thorough research we may have been able to find a place better situated. But since we planned to spend only a couple of days in Mumbai, we hoped to make some travel plans, then set out to see the country.

Lesley and Andrea headed straight for the beds, fully clothed, and were asleep in seconds. While they were napping, Carla and I stepped out to get the lay of the land in the immediate neighborhood. We located an Internet shop for future reference and picked up a couple bottles of water. Clearly we had landed in the heart of the budget tourist district, budget being the key word.

Ordinarily we stayed away from the haunts of foreign tourists, but my resolve began to falter with the aroma of a familiar breakfast. Down the street was Leopold's, a Western tourist icon. We were happy to get the Indian equivalent of an English breakfast and some pretty passable coffee. Dark and cool, ceiling fans slowly stirred the air. The atmosphere was irresistible. At small, round tables couples young and old thumbed through travel books and brochures. Many, like us, were no doubt getting their first exposure to India. Having been on the road for eight months with an estimated 19,700 miles behind us, we began to feel ourselves worthy travelers.

Europe had allowed us to make incremental cultural steps. Istanbul stretched our awareness; market places were more crowded, and the offerings more eastern and exotic. Egypt, while in Muslim North Africa, retained the common thread of history and culture that ran through the countries of the Mediterranean. But India, except for colonial influences, was a world apart.

Travel books were not long on flattery for Mumbai, but we didn't see enough of it to form a valid opinion. In retrospect it was pretty consistent with what one expects from a city of thirteen million inhabitants. We spent a couple of days walking around the Colaba tourist district near the India's Gate monument, making some arrangements and checking e-mail.

Mumbai was, however, a reasonable introduction to the basics of India. Like much of India, Mumbai is a melting pot of cultures and was at first a cluster of seven islands used as a port by Portuguese traders in the early part of the sixteenth century. The name Bombay is an adaptation of Portuguese for "good bay." It has a colorful history and complex social fabric that bears the influences of Hindus, Muslims, Christians and a significant contingent of Zoroastrians. Pushed there by a wave of Islam in the early tenth century the Zoroastrians migrated from their home in Persia. These Persian immigrants came to be known as the Parsi and formed an enterprising middle class of craftsmen, merchants and traders that gave Mumbai much of its vitality.

Sidewalks have an interesting collection of street vendors. My one pair of shoes was showing signs of wear. Some of the stitching was coming undone. Sitting on a knobby root that had erupted through the slabs of cracked concrete was a man with an odd collection of rusty shears, needles, thread and scraps of leather. Wearing what was hardly more than a few rags, his eyes followed mine to the whitish patch on my left shoe, evidence of my sock showing through.

What the heck! I thought; I am determined to make these things last.

I untied the laces and the road worn veteran of seven and a half months of continuous walking fell to the uneven sidewalk. The shoe repairer politely offered a scrap of cardboard for me to rest my foot on while he worked.

Beneath the gnarled reaching arms of an ancient shade tree, we stood and watched as he closed the gap and sewed in a thin piece of leather for reinforcement. In about five minutes he set my shoe down, spread the lace and lifted the tongue. I slid my foot in. Looking up expectantly, our eyes met; I nodded my approval and asked how much. He said ten and held up ten bony fingers for clarification. I made a quick conversion in my head, about twenty-one cents. Feeling quite satisfied with the job, I gave him fifty. He looked down at the coins and appeared absolutely elated. I hated to wreck the local economy by unduly inflating the wage base, but it was certainly worth a buck to me.

One of several dozen street side professionals, his occupation had earned him the title of "mochi." Because he worked with leather, not considered by Hindu custom to be clean, it is likely that he was a man of what was previously the untouchable caste. Many menial tasks can be dealt with along the sidewalk. From the vantage point of our hotel room window, I watched as the various sidewalk entrepreneurs went about their business, one sort of "walla" or another. The Khan-Saf-Walla for example, would, for a small price, remove any excess wax from your ears. Everyone has to make a living and although Carla frequently suggested that I needed to get my ears cleaned out, I was never tempted to pay him a visit.

For people of such bare means and essentially no expectations for improvement, they were always able to somehow muster a smile. Standing on a teeming street corner, we waited for the light to change. The temperature was somewhere north of 95 degrees Fahrenheit. Traffic consisted of a helter-skelter battery of bicycles, taxis, buses and trucks of various descriptions along with an occasional donkey cart to temper the urban milieu. Through it all came a couple of gangly young men pushing a medieval looking handcart with two huge wooden wheels. In the crux was a load of rudely cut poles, still covered with bark and mud.

Barefoot and nearly naked, neither of them was wearing much more than a threadbare loincloth. Guiding their unstable burden through the traffic, one pole slid off the end of the cart about the time they got to the center of the intersection. Traffic hesitated as they recaptured the errant spar and realigned their load. Bringing their palms together in front of their chests, their brilliant white teeth gave evidence of huge smiles. They offered a nod to those who had restrained themselves and off they went, legs and arms in all directions, their bare feet slapping against the hot pavement.

We continued on through the crowd to the tourist boat dock for an escape into the bay. It was on a "luxury" tourist boat out to Elephanta Island (Gharapuri Island) to see the ancient Hindu rock carved temples. I surmised that the word luxury derived from the fact that our boat had plastic chairs as opposed to the bare wooden benches I saw on the others. It was a leisurely cruise on a thirty-foot launch with a sunshade. The waters of the bay were a murky suspension of brown clay but entirely free, I noticed, of trash and debris.

The caves of Elephanta were a dark and cool sanctuary from the city. Hewn from solid rock around A.D. 600, the walls of the caverns harbored relief sculptures of gods and goddesses, and larger than life statues of the Hindu Trimurti — Lord Brahma the Creator, Lord Vishnu the Preserver and Lord Shiva the Destroyer. The elaborate Elephanta sculptures were reminders of the technology available to the artisans of their era.

Elephanta Island was our first occasion to be photographed in India. I have to admit that the first time or two we really didn't get it. In most countries other tourists will hold up a camera with a wistful look on their faces, indicating that they wanted one of us to take a photo of them on holiday with some historical landmark over their shoulder or appearing to sprout from the tops of their heads. We were usually more than willing to cooperate. However, I have to admit my defenses were up from the constant barrage Western tourists received in Egypt. So I was a little reluctant, perhaps a little terse. As it turned out, Indian tourists didn't want pictures of themselves; they wanted photos of us, genuine Western tourists.

Often an individual would have a friend take a picture, while standing there smiling among our family group. Andrea and Lesley found it a bit awkward at first, but soon we all just accepted it. I could never help but walk away wondering how, upon arriving back in their village, they would describe these pictures with an American family. I also wondered if somehow, someday they would end up on my doorstep in Houston, a family of eight or ten, grandma in tow, holding one of those photos.

Before returning to our room in the evening, we wound our way through the crowds and sidewalk stalls and picked up a couple bottles of water and a juice pack or two for the morning. The dusk was at hand, and the sounds of the day had begun to fall away. The shopkeepers spoke in quiet, conversational tones as they brought in their goods and secured their doors. The street vendors were boarding up their stands in the dim yellow glow of a few exposed light bulbs hanging from makeshift extension cords.

I will always remember looking down as we walked by, seeing a young lady seated on the edge of the path in front of a darkened shop. Her bony knees were draped with a thin film of light blue silk, arms folded, head down, the picture of exhaustion. Her vertebrae and shoulder blades jutted out beneath her dark skin that looked hardly more substantial than her sari. At her feet lay a child in the worn, threadbare rags of a street urchin. The child lay there, motionless on the filthy, unyielding concrete. What a terrible place for a child to have to sleep, I thought; the child's body appeared strangely rigid.

Making our way back to our hotel, we stepped around the corner only to be accosted by a ragtag swarm of equally untidy and equally pitiful children, probably less than five years old. Their mothers seated on the ground in the dark chatted casually while the kids pulled at the pant legs of passersby. Tiny silhouettes in the fading light, they thrust their grubby hands upwards, their white teeth against their sooty dark skin. These images persisted in my mind through the night.

A Moment of Weakness

It would be unfair to create the impression that we didn't make any mistakes in our planning and the interactions we had while traveling. During the course of a yearlong, 50,000 mile trip it was reasonable to expect we would make less than perfect decisions. For us, that took place in Mumbai. And let me say, before I go any farther, that our experience had nothing to do with India, its people or the Indian travel industry. It had only to do with poor judgment on our part that could have occurred in any country. The most workable premise when traveling: "If something happens to you, it's your fault." Lack of judgment, lack of observation, lack of awareness of things going on about you, all of these contribute to the situation in which you find yourself.

As the sun rose each day, shops opened up, and the streets were populated with tourists, Indian and foreign. Street vendors, whose capital assets consisted of a wooden crate and some minor tools of the trade, sat along the sidewalk. A familiar sensation of Houston in June, rivulets of sweat streamed down our backs as we strolled through the streets and markets. Lesley and Andrea were always on the lookout for new and unusual clothes. Our plan, such as it was, consisted of heading south along the west coast, first down to Goa. Then we planned to travel farther south to Kerala State to spend a week on a small eco-tourist spice farm Carla had come across on the Internet.

Passing by the desk at our hotel, I asked the lady if she knew of any reliable ticket agents she could recommend. There were dozens of little travel shops lining the streets with people soliciting for tours. Carla's plan had been to walk over to a large hotel and use one of the agents in the lobby. This, by the way, would have been the right thing to do, and I would recommend it. However, being the chatty, verbal type that I am, I thought that the polite lady behind the desk probably knew of someone reputable with whom we could do business without investing in the time and distance to the large hotel.

When I asked her she hesitated for a minute and looked directly into the eyes of the young man standing with her behind the desk. Then she paged through a notebook, picked up the phone and called someone. Hanging up, she said, "He will be here for you shortly."

Great! I thought . . .

A neatly dressed and very polite young man appeared in about ten minutes. We followed him a block or two past the beggars and earwax specialists, bounced over a springy two-by-ten plank across the odor-emitting drain at the edge of the street and entered a small, definitely-in-need-of-a-paint-job office. Furnishings were limited to a desk and three chairs. By this time we had become accustomed to falling-down old buildings and a scarcity of freshly painted surfaces. If we applied standards for what we would expect in the U.S., it would have eliminated entire countries.

There was a conflict that went on in our minds at times like these. We did not want to be too judgmental. Not every place had to look like the cheery travel agents in the U.S or Europe. All we wanted to do was buy some tickets, and he had been recommended by the lady at the desk. Well, maybe not recommended, but it would seem she might have some interest in seeing us treated fairly.

A Mr. Surasa, also neatly dressed and polite, showed up shortly and offered us a cup of tea. He seemed knowledgeable and helpful, and we paid him cash for some tickets down to Goa and Kerala; he gave us receipts, and we agreed to come back in a couple of hours to pick up the tickets. No big deal.

When we returned he had taken the time to put together a complete itinerary for our stay in India after we left Kerala. We didn't have the train tickets yet, but that would all come together soon, and we went over the travel plans he had made. He did not approve of the eco-tourist farm down in Kerala, but we did not let him steer us away from that. Mr. Surasa's itinerary was a nice presentation, item by item, rupee by rupee, and it was all reasonably priced.

Our budget was based on European prices, and a fair profit was included for Mr. Surasa. We signed up and were ready to roll. The next morning was a taste of how it was going to be for the next five weeks.

We had a 7:00 A.M. train for Goa, about two hundred miles south of Mumbai. Up at the crack of dawn, bags packed and standing by the door, we were ready for immediate departure. Mr. Surasa had explicitly said he would send his man around to drive us to the station, then he changed his mind and said he himself would come to get us. As the time drew near, I wandered out into the street. The atmosphere was warm and heavy. A dump truck full of garbage was ripening, and bodies slept here and there. A taxi driver roused himself from the back seat of his cab and asked if we needed a ride. I assured him we were to be taken to the station and that it was all arranged and paid for.

He smiled politely and said, "I do not think he will come."

How could this taxi driver possibly presume to know anything about the arrangements we had made? But by that time we had learned to be polite to everyone. You never know when you may need a bit of help or advice.

Time ticked by and still no Mr. Surasa or his man. At about 15 minutes before the scheduled departure time, we acquiesced to the cab driver, patiently and confidently waiting. We made a dash to the station. I figured it was the best thing we could do at the moment. As it turned out Mr. Surasa was there, finalizing the ticket transactions. We followed along behind him with our luggage as he half jogged along the platform. He quickly escorted us onto the train and gave us a couple of envelopes containing ongoing tickets from Goa to Kerala and then on to Chennai. We shook hands and waved goodbye.

We spent two blissful weeks in Goa and Kerala, but I was having to harass Mr. Surasa via e-mail into finalizing the tentative itinerary he had put together. He finally did so, and we quickly printed a copy to carry with us.

All seemed well until we ended up at the train station in Cochin only to find that the tickets in the envelope, though prepaid, were standby. The Indian train system is extremely well organized and advanced reservations are required on most trains for first and second class berths. A paper printout showing passenger names and seating is always posted on a bulletin board near the ticket window an hour or so prior to the departure of any train. It didn't take long to realize that we didn't have seats as yet. We checked with the very polite young lady at the window, and she indicated she would be more than happy to refund the cost of our second class tickets, but that didn't solve the problem; we needed to be in Chennai the following morning to begin our organized itinerary.

I approached the conductor of the train; he was attending to passengers and helpfully answering questions. I asked if there were any unoccupied second class sleepers on the train. He assured me there were not and that we could not get on the train. However, we could spend the night and try to get on a train the next day but that would have us paying for a hotel room in Cochin and missing a night in Chennai, a paid reservation. It would not have made much difference, if we hadn't already worked out this rather tightly strung-together itinerary.

The conductor had no suggestions. He was polite but not into problem solving. Most of the arriving passengers had gone off with their families, and the departing passengers among whom we hoped to be counted were situating their luggage and calmly taking their preassigned seats. Finally Carla asked if there were first class berths available should we want to upgrade our tickets. It took a few tries to get this across. It probably didn't happen very often. Most Indian and Western budget travelers, which we appeared to be, would just wait until the next day. However, we didn't have any reason to believe the train tomorrow would be any less crowded.

If for no other reason than to simply put this annoyance to an end, the conductor finally admitted that seats were available in first class, and we could upgrade our tickets by paying the difference. So we were now down about 200 U.S. dollars, though our itinerary was intact. And this, it could be rationalized, was not Mr. Surasa's fault; he had done the best he could. Unfortunately he didn't bother to tell us what was going to happen at the station. The remainder of our train tickets were to be delivered to us in Bangalore by the agent who would be meeting us there. This scene was to be repeated in the future.

India — The Land of the Voucher

The one thing I did get out of Mr. Surasa was a signed receipt for the money we had spent and an e-mail document outlining the updated itinerary. It showed the contacts, pickups and hotels that had been arranged on our behalf. It gave Mr. Surasa's office telephone number and his cell phone. In other words, it looked official. In India that is in many cases all that really matters. We had been given some sage advice by Linda, one of the two English ladies who managed the accommodation booking service in Goa. I had commented that our trip was fully planned, but at that time we had no tangible evidence of our 1,200 U.S. dollar commitment except for a couple of handwritten itemized receipts and a print out of an itinerary from Mr. Surasa.

"No problem," Linda exclaimed. "In India, when all else fails, show them a voucher."

"But that's my problem," I said. "I don't have any vouchers."

"Well, just make one up," she said. "It merely has to look official."

She related a story as to how in a similar situation she had sat down at the typewriter and dashed out a letter stating the terms of their agreement with some service provider. To her surprise it was accepted, and everything went off as planned. I took some consolation in the story, but didn't really see how it was going to help me get into a hotel or certainly not on a train.

The rest of the story is that we never got a set of vouchers. We were met at the station in most towns and had a driver who took us to see the appropriate sights, all thanks to Mr. Surasa. But in each case we had to talk our way into the hotel; he had made no contact with them, and we seldom stayed in the place designated on the printed itinerary. The real issue was the train tickets we had paid for in cash, not with a credit card like the rest of the trip.

The only thing we had was a print out of an e-mail I had received after two weeks of harassing him. I presented it at each and every hotel, and as Linda had said, they all took it as a fully negotiable document. The hotels would track down Mr. Surasa, and we always ended up in pretty nice rooms, even by Western standards. The clincher was in Nagpur, where he out and out lied to us, saying that he had purchased tickets and his agent would bring them to the hotel.

Once again with less than ten minutes to get to the station, we ended up boarding the train without tickets. I told the conductor we would board the train and settle up after we were underway. He didn't like that idea and insisted we go down to the other side of the station and purchase tickets. When we came through the doors of the large ticketing hall a horde of customers were at a dozen windows with no sort of organization or queue. Carla and I looked at each other and decided just to go for it. We jogged back down the platform and through the crowd to where Lesley and Andrea were waiting with the luggage. Andrea was biting at her fingernail, while Lesley shifted her weight uneasily from foot to foot.

"Get on the train. It's ready to pull away from the station," I told them.

"Do we have tickets?" Lesley asked, always one for details.

"No, but I'll work it out with the conductor — once we're underway."

"Where are we supposed to sit?" Andrea now joined in.

"Well, just find a seat, and if there aren't any, stand with the luggage between the cars until I get it all sorted out"

We pitched our packs through the open door and climbed aboard, only seconds before the train started to move. Carla and I found a couple of second class seats for a few minutes. The girls, convinced we would be thrown bodily from the train, luggage and all, chose to wait with their packs in the narrow space between the cars with the hot air rushing in and the noise of the steel wheels on the tracks.

Meanwhile, I set out in search of the conductor. He had found his supervisor, and we met midway in the train. I explained what had happened and offered to purchase tickets on the spot, which I did. As circumstances presented themselves, we had become accustomed to dealing with them. We had talked our way from one end of India to the other, waving the itinerary in the faces of hotel clerks, drivers, conductors, you name it. The single copy of the itinerary was getting pretty tired looking after a couple of weeks, but the majority of Internet cafés in India didn't have print capabilities. If they had a printer, the answer, "It is not, at this very moment, working," put a stop to any such radical thoughts. All said and done, we were out about 500 U.S. dollars on the train tickets. I won't go into details about the lack of recourse we had. The fact remained that Mr. Surasa was in Mumbai, and contrary to his heartfelt assurances of meeting us in Delhi to settle things, he did not return calls and in fact made off with part of the ticket money we had paid him. For some strange reason, everything else went pretty much as planned as long as we had our "voucher."

In the overall scheme of things and the size of the total trip budget, 500 U.S. dollars was painful but not a show-stopper. So we learned from the experience and went on. You can't dwell on these things, though they do eat at you when you know you've been cheated. I frequently repeated the Zen refrain: "Walk on."

All that aside, the people we met throughout India were the warmest and most compassionate of human beings. But India is not for the faint of heart. The temperatures, in spite of the fact that it was February, were generally above 90 degrees. The trains were always on time and well kept, although showing signs of intense use.

Goa and the Malabar Coast

A popular beach resort, Goa, a couple hundred miles south of Mumbai on the southwest coast of India was a former Portuguese Treaty port. The Malabar Coast, as it is known, has been at the center of spice trade for 600 years. Traders from Beijing to Lisbon came in search of nutmeg, cardamom and especially black pepper. Pedestrian traffic in the small beach communities is a curious mix of slender, dark skinned Indians and slightly more bulbous and brightly sunburned Europeans escaping the dreary gray skies of February.

Our upstairs flat in a distinctly Mediterranean looking house had a small kitchen. We yearned for nothing more than a home cooked meal. Grocery shopping in the nearby village was a real experience. Produce and seafood were laid out by local ladies in a rather unimpressive market consisting of a concrete floor with elevated decks and a corrugated metal roof, the bare essence of the free market system. As certain activities were repulsive to Hindus, the butcher shop, run by a Muslim, was an insubstantial looking shack around the corner.

Settling in for a week allowed us to get back on a regular home schooling schedule and keep the momentum up. The girls sat at a table on the balcony and worked though their lessons. Creating a welcome distraction, a skinny old man glided effortlessly up the forty-foot coconut trees in the neighboring yard and hacked away at the bunches of coconuts. They crashed to the ground and occasionally through the roof of a neighbor's shed.

As the adventure moved into the ninth month, Lesley and Andrea admitted to feeling a bit less enthusiastic about it all. Changing countries wasn't as exciting as it had been when we started out and the concerns of fitting back in, when they got home, began to find a place in their minds.

Departing Goa by train we headed farther south in the direction of Kerala State, which is pretty far south in India. As is typical of the Indian train system, our names and seat assignments were posted on a roster pinned to a bulletin board near the ticket window. Trains make up such an important part of the Indian transportation network that they run on time. To reduce the time spent in each station, everything is well planned in advance.

The train ride from Goa down to Cochin was uneventful. We boarded in time to order a light lunch and struck up a conversation with a physician and his wife from the port city of Cochin. They were returning home after an extended weekend in Mumbai.

A steady flow of chai wallas waltzed through the swaying cars with large tin pots of more or less hot tea, coffee wallas toting the same battered pots of lukewarm coffee with cream and sugar already mixed and dabba wallas balancing trays of fried snacks and assorted unknown offerings. We began to experiment by starting with the coffee. Indian food spans the range from strict vegetarian meals for the Jains, a mixed bag for the Hindus who hold the middle ground from mild vegetarian to fish, chicken and some mutton, all the way to the Sikhs and Muslims who never miss an opportunity to indulge in a kabob or scrawny rotisserie chicken.

We ordered a couple of lunches, opting for the chicken. Chickens in India are not the plump broilers we're accustomed to; they're more akin to a roadrunner — feathers, beak and an ample pair of legs. Our meals arrived in neat, steaming cardboard boxes with rice and some hot sauce that would rival any salsa found a hundred miles on either side of the Rio

Grande back home. The chicken, consisting of a pelvis with two muscular legs was actually nicely grilled and seasoned with the bright red tondoori powder.

As I dismembered the chicken and mixed the fibrous meat with my rice, cautiously sprinkling on the hot sauce, I noticed a look of apprehension from our physician friend as I plucked the meat from the bones. His eyes became wide, and he began to reel from the spectacle as this culturally insensitive barbarian — me — tore dried flesh from bone. I followed his glance and looked down self-consciously at my greasy, red stained fingers. We were all hungry with no place to hide, so we discretely went about finishing our lunch. Our physician friend and his wife retired for their afternoon siesta, drawing the curtains in front of their berths.

Finishing our meals and feeling somewhat admonished, I carefully packed the paper pouches and napkins, wooden utensils and bones back into the used cardboard box. Gathering up the same from Lesley and Andrea, I entered the space at the end of the cars near the washrooms. Two uniformed attendants in white waistcoats were engaged in an animated discussion of a recent cricket tournament. Balancing my neatly reconstructed boxes of trash, I cast my eyes around for the refuse container. One of the attendants paused, and as I moved toward the little metal flap that covered the dust bin, he said, "Here, I'll take that."

I said, "Well, thank you." and handed him the stack of boxes.

Conversation regarding the cricket match reignited as he applied his shoulder to the door. He held it open with one elbow, and with all of southern India rushing by at forty miles per hour, he hurled the whole lot outside.

I turned to the porter and said mildly, "Ya know, I never would have thought of that." I washed my hands and quietly returned to my seat to reconcile these seemingly disparate bits of cultural wisdom.

Within minutes the chai walla made his last pass, lights were dimmed, shades drawn to exclude the rays of the intense afternoon sun, and the seats were converted to beds. We spent the next hour and a half in our berths paging through travel books and trying to find ourselves on the map, while everyone else settled in for a long afternoon nap.

An hour out of the station, a stage whispered call of "chai" gently brought the burden of consciousness back to the dimly lit corridor lined by heavy dark curtains. The coffee walla, close behind, plied the spaces between groggy passengers, stretching and making their way to the washroom on unsteady legs.

Our destination was a small spice farm/eco farm somewhere in the Cardamom Hills to the east of Cochin. We weren't exactly sure how we were going to get there from the train station but had some rough ideas about buses and names of a town or two in the general vicinity.

Trying to look confident as we gathered our wits in the station, a six-foot and more, handsome young Indian man in a starched khaki uniform and something akin to a Smoky-the-Bear hat asked if we needed help. I immediately showed him a copy of the e-mail we had received with the address and directions. He took out a small piece of paper, wrote a name or two on it, handed it to me and helped me with the pronunciation.

Straightening his well-trimmed black mustache and rising up to his full official height, he began to lay out his plan, while pointing to a haphazard line of buses on the other side of the chaotic parking lot.

Turning to Carla and the girls, he said, "You stay here with your luggage." Now looking down at me, he added, "Do you see those buses out there by the trees?"

"Yes, I do." I answered.

"I want you to walk over there to that white bus and show this piece of paper to the driver; he will probably speak English. Ask him if he goes to Murvatupura and how much he will charge you. If he says no, then try the next one. Only after you have located the correct bus, then you should go directly to the bus and board it."

This seemed like a perfectly logical plan, and I realized, as I worked my way through the maze of porters, taxis and motor rickshaws called tuk-tuks, a plan that was likely to get us where we hoped to go. In fact, the white bus was the correct one. I reported back to the station, where we gathered our belongings and headed toward the bus.

We sat together near the front of the bus. "Only one other passenger so far," I commented. "Maybe not a crowded route." As we waited for the departure with sweat running down our backs, our sole travel companion motioned to me with his thumb, indicating the back of the bus or at least a more rearward position. But when Carla and the girls began to stand, he motioned to them to stay seated.

Ah, I had wandered into the ladies area; in this part of India it was at the front of the bus, opposite to what we had experienced in Egypt and some other locations where women sat on hard seats in the rear with the diesel fumes. Accepting this protocol, I wrestled my oversized pack to the back of the bus near the rear door and attached it to a post to keep it from falling over.

Once we got going it was like Mr. Toad's Wild Ride at Disneyland. The bus would fly through the crowded streets with little or no regard for right of way or lane designation. Our chariot of fire screeched to a halt at irregular intervals, while a young boy would swing a door open and pound on it like a drum. Prospective riders dashed toward the bus and were literally lifted off the ground with his help as the bus accelerated back to full speed, often never coming to a complete stop. This was clearly a commercial venture, and time, as we have all been told, is money.

The young doorman and I talked a little. I am sure we were both speaking the same language, but communication was still minimal. Nevertheless, he assured me he would get us to the right destination. About an hour of swaying back and forth on narrow blacktop roads, winding through the hilly country, I was pressed into the last seat along the back of the bus. We had grown to a standing room only crowd.

We ultimately came to an abrupt halt where I got the high sign from the young doorman. Over the heads of the crowd, I gestured to Carla and the girls at the front of the bus. With little grace, we wrestled our gear through the press of humanity and were extruded out on the gravelly shoulder. Before we had time to turn around, with a wink and a nod, the doorman drummed the all clear on the door and off they went into the late afternoon tropical haze. The fare was about eighty cents each!

Afoot once again, our location seemed to be some distance east of Muvattupuzha and some distance west of Thodapuzha, neither of which we could find on any of the maps in our possession. Somewhere along the way was the tiny village of Kadalikad, home to Haritha Farms, an eco tourist lodge nestled into the lush Cardamom Hills of Kerala State.

Densely vegetated hills surrounding small plots of pineapple and terraced rice fields rose steeply on all sides. There were very few signs of human habitation, a change from Mumbai. A bantam rooster scratching at the ground took one look at us and darted into the pineapple patch. Gathering our wits and belongings, we turned around. Without even time to take a first step, we were greeted by the round, smiling face of Jacob. He had heard the bus coming to a stop and hurried down to greet us. Jacob and his mother would be our hosts for the next seven days.

Accommodations were two nicely appointed brick bungalows. (By the way, bungalow is a word that originates from the city of Bangalore!)

We had no air conditioning, but we did have slat-covered windows, a ceiling fan and mosquito nets over the beds. The shower had fresh water at ambient temperature and, to the relief of the girls, it had a Western toilet. I began to ask about what options might exist for getting some laundry done. Before I could finish, Jacob assured me it was entirely okay to do our laundry in the shower. He went on to say that we could hang our clothesline anywhere it suited us. In this way he could tell us, "No," without having to say it.

All the guests, numbering about seven or eight, including the four of us, ate meals at the common dining area, a naturally ventilated enclosure enveloped in bug-proof netting. We gathered with the other tourists before dinner each evening to compare experiences and make plans for the following day while Jacob's mother and her helper prepared the food. Meals were traditional Kerala fare served on banana leaves, entirely vegetarian and washed down with fresh pineapple juice. Breakfast each morning was an event I looked forward to; Jacob had some home grown coffee that he was proud to share.

A couple of Aussie girls, probably in their early twenties, were staying in one of the cottages. Lesley and Andrea looked at them with admiration, traveling on their own as they were. Only one of the pair showed up for breakfast one morning. We were chatting as the table was still being prepared. Someone asked her where her friend was. Pausing for a few seconds, she looked to Lesley and Andrea and asked casually if they might come up to her cottage. She then admitted that her traveling mate was being held prisoner by a large insect that had landed on her mosquito netting during the night. Neither of them was prepared to go near it, and so her friend was trapped. Houston natives with no great aversion to bugs, the girls set off to help. Lesley plucked a slow moving walkingstick type of critter off the net and set it free outside.

During afternoons we were free to wander the hills and winding country lanes through old rubber plantations. Coconut half-shells were wired to the trunks of rubber trees to collect milky latex that slowly emanated from v-notches cut in the bark. Squatting next to a gnarled phone pole a couple of men in traditional south Indian dhotis were working out the price of a phone call. One of them had set up an *ad hoc* phone connection at the base of the pole. A beat up old phone waited on the ground near the side of the road; it was connected to the lines overhead by a couple of kinky wires with large alligator clips.

Village women walked to and from the river with shapely water jugs balanced on top of their heads, their pastel saris flowed in the sultry breeze. Others carried huge bundles of sticks and twigs, fuel for evening meal. Had we not seen the work they did, we might have been deceived into believing that these ladies were frail by virtue of their size.

Jacob, who among other things was a practicing attorney, took it as a personal mission to ensure that each of his visitors had opportunities to experience any number of unique ceremonies, performances or cultural events that would otherwise go entirely unnoticed by casual travelers. He arranged day trips to tea plantations in the mountains near the town of Munnar and to the elephant-training center operated by the Indian Forest Service. He was especially fond of the traditional Katakali dance performances given in the city of Cochin and also in some of the small villages.

The Hindu devotion we attended spanned a period of three days. We stopped in on two different occasions. During the daylight hours the representation of the deity was carried by senior worshipers around the outside of the temple. The procession was attended by four large elephants adorned with golden head ornaments. Upon the elephants' backs rode three or four younger men who carried various articles of worship to enhance the majesty and aura of ceremony. Several of the more senior individuals went along on foot and rang bells, clashed cymbals and blew continuous tones from trumpets that curved around making almost complete circles that came down near the heads of the musicians. These rather sonorous offerings continued for about an hour at a time. Then the entire entourage moved to the other side of the temple making several complete cycles in a day. While the ceremony was ongoing, the elephants were supplied with large piles of banana leaves and sugar cane to keep them content.

Everyone on the temple grounds was polite and in some ways deferential toward us, greeting us as guests. From time to time, there was a loud explosion orchestrated by a rangy old gentleman who had set up shop under a huge banyan tree. For a few rupees he would fill a small mortar that stood about six inches tall with gunpowder. Steadying it between his bare feet, he carefully tapped in fragments of fired clay brick and brick dust to form a seal on top of the black powder. He then climbed down from the raised area around the base of the tree and carried the mortar about ten yards away. Placing a piece of paper with the offerer's prayer on top of the charge, he then poured a small pile of black powder next to the fuse hole at the base of the mortar. He wasted no time getting clear of the apparatus after he touched his smoldering stick of punk to the powder.

I would be surprised if he had much hearing left. A puff of smoke rose, followed by the report and a shock wave that never failed to make me jump a little, even when I was watching and fully prepared for the explosion. I was just grateful that the elephants did not react the same way I did. It was great fun, and we made several offerings.

We left Kerala for Chennai (Madras), then Bangalore and Mysore. Mr. Surasa had arranged a driver for us in those cities, and it worked out well. Day trips into the countryside took us to eighth century temples and medieval lost cities. Intricate three-dimensional carvings covered every surface in the ancient Hindu and Buddhist shrines; elephants, horses, mythical beasts and flowers in mind boggling repetition, each horizontal band more complicated than the previous was the overall design. It was customary to leave our sandals at the entrance. Out of the reach of the intense rays of the sun, porticoed walkways had been worn smooth by 1,200 years of visiting worshipers. The cool polished granite drew the heat from the soles of our feet. It was a simple pleasure we came to relish.

The city market in Bangalore is incredibly fascinating. A huge central building with an open court in the center of town is filled with flower vendors. Everywhere were great mounds of brilliantly colored roses, marigolds and various types of daisy. Some people were selling bulk blossoms; others were stringing the flowers together into long streaming garlands. The chanting of the vendors and an occasional trumpet blast from a Hindu dressed in a bright orange turban and a gold vest added to the lavish picture. Flowers are big business, and the trade is brisk.

Every bit as fascinating as the ancient Hindu temples and ancient cities were the car trips through the countryside. The rolling semiarid hills gave way to fertile bottomlands with rice paddies and coconut plantations. Young boys managed small herds of skinny black goats along the sides of the road, and every manner of material and commodity moved on carts pulled by giant oxen. These long legged beasts stood six feet at the shoulder with even longer horns. There were essentially no privately owned vehicles, just trucks, buses and an occasional white tourist taxi like the one in which we rode.

Never a Dull Moment

On the broader scene, the Muslims and Hindus were once again arguing over the 1992 destruction of a mosque built by Babur, a sixteenth century Moghul ruler. Archeologists had evidence to support the contention that the mosque was actually built on top of a ninth century Hindu shrine. The site was called Ayodhya, located near the city of Faizabad in the north of India. The Hindu right wing, Vishwa Hindu Parishad (VHP), otherwise known as the World Hindu Council, had also laid claim to the site as the birthplace of Ram, the incarnation of Lord Vishnu; they had seized upon the idea of building a temple where the mosque had been. On February 27, 2002, Muslim fanatics had expressed their displeasure by setting a trainload of returning Hindu pilgrims on fire in the western state of Gujarat; fifty-seven people died. This action sparked a week of intense violence in the Gujarat's principle city of Ahmadabad.

Ayodhya is not too far from Varanssi, the city next on our itinerary. Hindu zealots, kar sevaks, as they were called, began to gather at Ayodhya at a rate of about 1,000 a day by bus and train, until 10,000 had amassed at the site. They were determined to begin raising the temple, despite a government ban on the demonstration. Government forces and police were doing their best to keep the demonstration from taking place. Trains were being searched for anyone fitting the description of a kar sevak. Other trains were being rerouted. Some right-wingers began to talk of Pakistan's involvement, as if either side needed any more problems.

Our itinerary had us going right through the middle of all this. The Hindu fundamentalists had called for a *Bharat bandh* or general strike. It was likely to spread to the neighboring state of Maharashtra and maybe farther; we ended up laying-over for a few unplanned days in the small city of Nagpur, reading the newspapers to see how it was all going to work out. Nagpur was essentially devoid of tourist resources and was just an enjoyable place in which to wander the streets. Except for an occasional persistent gypsy, it was a free and easy place to be. And it was another chance to catch up on school work and recuperate from a debilitating case of intestinal distress that Andrea and I both had picked up somewhere along the way.

Meanwhile, farther north, the Maoists had expanded their campaign in Nepal. Having pretty well wiped out the national police force, they started targeting tourists or at least threatened to. Reluctantly we altered our plans for a week in Katmandu. Until the last possible moment, we had held on to our reservations at what sounded like a great small hotel before we had to face it: we just couldn't risk taking our children into what had turned into a war zone.

The net result of all this was that we spent over five weeks in India and had ample opportunity to see a good cross section of the country. We worked our way up through the center of the country and spent some time seeing the highlights of the Agra-Jaipur-Delhi triangle.

Agra and Jaipur

The eye is drawn to the peak of the arch in the outer gate as it aligns perfectly with the entrance to the great white dome of the Taj Mahal. Passing through the gate the perfect symmetry and order carries forward through the pools and fountains outlined in gleaming white marble to create sense of remote perspective.

The Taj Mahal rises like a budding flower with four elegant minarets completing the serene image of perfect physical harmony. Built in 1631 by the fifth Moghul emperor, Shah Jahan, in memory of his second wife, Mumtaz Mahal, a Muslim Persian princess, there is no other structure so sublime. Don't miss it — but allow enough time to visit the two great red sandstone mosques, walk the grounds and look out upon the broad plane of the Yamuna River.

We had a delightful driver who carried us through the final part of our Indian trek. He drove the dusty highway from Agra to Jaipur with one hand on the horn, dodging overloaded buses, herds of goats, wobbly bicyclers and camel caravans. The country to the west, as we approached the city of Jaipur, was increasingly arid. Camels replaced the steely gray oxen as the most common beast of burden. Brightly colored turbans became the more prevalent headdress, and Punjabi mustaches were still the style.

Seated on a high sandstone ridge, the fortress of Amba Mata, also called the Amber Fort, is a vast and intricate fortified palace a few miles outside of Jaipur. It was first built in the eleventh century and brought to its full grandeur under the Kachhawakas in the sixteenth and seventeenth centuries. Beautiful inlay and mirrored glass cover the walls. The opulence of the time is hard to imagine. From

Amber Fort (Amba Mata, seventeenth century), near Jaipur, India. The only way to travel when visiting the Amber Fort is by elephant. The standard size elephant fits a family of four, plus mahout. (unknown photographer)

the palace walls, fortifications radiate out along every ridge. Crenulated walls and guardhouses stir the imagination as reminders of the fabled era of the Moghul emperors.

In contrast to the weaving course of our bright white Ambassador tourist taxi and the constant play on the horn, the slow lumbering pace of an Indian elephant brings tourists up the steep road to the grand courtyard. Always polite, turbaned mahouts urge the giant beasts up the slope and discharge their cargo of tourists onto a raised platform. Filled with the anticipation of discovery Lesley and Andrea hurried along the narrow passageways and up onto the medieval castle walls.

The final impression we have of India is the bazaar and spice market district near the great Red Fort in old Delhi. The spice market is about as close as one can get to the true feeling of commerce in its most elemental form, as it has been carried out for a thousand years or more. Hundreds of bare-chested porters, leaning on their battered wooden pushcarts, lined the west side of the street, taking refuge in the late afternoon shade. Hundreds more moved sack and box, bail and bucket of every commodity from one place to another. Tiny shops, purveying nuts and dried fruits, were lined up one after another. Casually dressed men sat on pampas grass pads sipping tea, chatting or just staring off into space. No one, except for the porters, seemed to be in a hurry or getting much accomplished. How in the world, I wondered, did they possibly support their families?

No trip around the world would be complete without a visit to the vast steaming Indian subcontinent. India is truly a land of contrasts and contradictions, difficult for most Westerners to fully grasp. After five weeks, we left India with a mental scrapbook of fantastic visual images, odors and sensations, but I am not sure we can claim any deeper understanding, only a collection of observations that we will continue to move around like pieces of a puzzle with hope for a bit of enlightenment.

We left India a little wiser and with a slight sense of relief. Each of us admitted we had a certain fondness for the quick smile and polite, helpful disposition of everyone we met in India. Regarding Mr. Surasa, he earned my grudging respect, if for no other reason than he was an accomplished liar. Besides, I kind of liked him!

Thailand

Sunrise on the fifteenth of March was a narrow streak of red along the dim gray horizon as our plane descended from 30,000 feet into the warm haze that enveloped Bangkok at 6:00 A.M. The landing was routine, and by virtue of the early hour, was not accompanied by the cheery greetings and fanfare that tourists might find later in the day. The first signs of natural light were accompanied by an air temperature right at the dew point — just like home. In some ways, we had an advantage in these warmer regions; we were familiar with the sensation of being damp with perspiration as soon as we stepped out into the humid air.

Bangkok Airport was modern and seemed immaculate after the more cluttered surroundings of India. Everyone we met spoke remarkably good English, and before we knew it, we were in a cab headed for, yes, the budget travelers' district. Obviously, we had all read the same travel books.

The Koa Shan area is a Western tourist enclave, but not the over polished and overpriced Western high-rise district. It is a little grittier, caters to a younger, more lively crowd that is more interested in the experience than impressing each other with how much money they have to spend. The area has some very acceptable hotels and homey little B&Bs.

Andrea and Lesley literally passed out upon seeing their beds. The flight from Delhi had only permitted an hour or so of sleep. We reasoned that the girls would sleep for a couple of hours, so Carla and I immediately went off in search of the Chinese Embassy. We needed to apply for visas, and we figured it might take a few days to get the paperwork processed. Our upcoming visit to China had been entirely planned by an agent back in Houston; all we had to do was get the visas and show up in Beijing on the appointed day.

The ride to the embassy gave us an opportunity to see a bit of Bangkok, its broad clean streets and manicured parks. Bangkok is a modern city loaded with history, Buddhist temples called "wats" and imperial palaces. The architecture is in no way restrained; golden domes topped with needle like spires marked the location of Buddhist shrines. Splashes of azure and wildly decorated dragons and demons with long, pointed teeth guard the entry gates. Mosaics of tiny blue, red and green mirrors outlined in gold covered every surface. Stone and mortar expressions of the vibrant, good natured, always smiling people of Thailand, the wats are truly unique and apart from any Western architectural influence. Without a doubt Thais were the friendliest people we met anywhere. The girls fell in love with Thailand, and it quickly moved to the top of their list.

Our Chinese visa applications in the mill, we relaxed for a couple of days and saw what Bangkok offered. Much of Bangkok is best discovered on foot. During most of our stay, the afternoon temperature hovered around 40 degrees Celsius (or 104 degrees Fahrenheit). To cover some of the greater distances, we tried Bangkok's spotless overhead rail system.

One hot afternoon we wandered quite far south and decided to try catching a long-tail boat back up the river. There is really nothing quite like a long-tail boat. Imagine a gondola from Venice, remove the handsome young gondolier sporting the striped shirt and flat brimmed hat. Replace him with short, polite, smiling Thai; in his hand replace the handcrafted rowing oar with an aluminum extension pipe that has a throttle attached. The extension pipe enables the pilot to pivot what appears to be the motor of a medium sized automobile perched about shoulder-height on a swivel at the rear of the boat. On the other end of this apparatus and directly coupled to the crankshaft is the propeller shaft. The prop is not enclosed and looks like a large and somewhat menacing weed trimmer. The pilot revs the engine similar to what you might hear from an aging '50s-something, potbellied Harley motorcycle sitting at a traffic light. When out in the open water of the river, the pilot twists the throttle grip, the bow rises a foot or two and the humid air begins to rush by. I fell prey to the whole effect, and I could see that Carla and the girls, as their hair streamed behind him, didn't seem to mind the spray in the warm evening air.

For a few baht more, motor on idle, the pilot took us on a sunset tour through the minor canals and byways, where thousands of people live in homes suspended on stilts six feet above the turbid waters of the broad river delta. Kids were swimming, dogs were napping and families sat out on their decks enjoying the evening air. It seemed to me like an acceptable way of life — not unlike southern Louisiana, but a little more crowded and a little more urban.

One of the advantages of being an early riser is that you see the people who actually make it all happen, day after day — the street sweepers, the shop owners and the sidewalk vendors. There was a certain wisdom on the faces of the sweepers as they matter of factly prepared the smooth blacktop surface for another day of anxious tourists, all in search of something meaningful. Morning in Koh Shan was a calmer, gentler affair with the sounds of birds in the trees mingling with the straw broom against pavement herding debris from the night before. Filled with aromas of fried food of every kind, the humid air was heavy with evidence of the lively street life and the scents of dishwashing detergent rising from great battered aluminum pots brimming with serving utensils. Despite the rather temporary appearance of the sidewalk food vendors, a well-scrubbed cleanliness prevailed. I don't know anyone who complained of a food-related illness in Bangkok.

The cluttered, chaotic evening street scene was a maze of makeshift plywood restaurants that lined the sidewalk and offered Pad Thai noodles and fried rice as well as Chinese barbeque, grilled chicken tails on a stick, and crispy-fried giant grasshoppers and beetles. The Koh Shan area had somewhat of a carnival atmosphere. Lots of lanky college age kids with heavy backpacks and looks of cautious anticipation threaded their way through the throng. Crowded Internet shops and bargain travel agents offered bus and train tickets to all parts of southeast Asia.

Bangkok was relaxing. We needed some time to unwind after being on the move almost continuously for almost three weeks in India. For a major city, Bangkok seemed clean and friendly to visitors on foot. Still a morning person, still in search of that first cup of coffee, it didn't take me long to become familiar with the neighborhood. After looking over the previous day's math problems and preparing for the morning lessons, I found a few minutes to add a page or two to my journal. I had gotten very duty-bound to writing and was equally determined to finish the math courses for Lesley and Andrea. They offered only the perfunctory groans and complaints over school. To some degree our collective conscience was comforted by the idea that we were not being entirely irresponsible by seeing to their formal education.

The girls, for their part, seemed to be holding up very well to the constant challenges and uncertainty of travel. They were both going through the changes that are normal for 13- and 14-year-old girls, both physically and psychologically. I have an indelible image of Andrea and Lesley walking a few paces ahead of us with the ankles of their socks showing below the pants that were always too short. As the climate got warmer, they began wearing Capris that didn't appear so short.

There was almost no talk of our home in Houston or their friends, except between the two of them. However, the normal amount of tension between parents and children held in close proximity caught up with us occasionally. So we tried to give them as much time as possible away from our judgmental eyes. The notion of home had contracted to include less of the place and more of the behavioral regularities that a family develops along the way. We had passed through the phase of rediscovering all those little quirks and idiosyncrasies that annoy each other and were committed to trying to enjoy the shared experience. Every so often we found ourselves seated at a table in some obscure little restaurant, finishing up our dinner, talking and laughing about some foolish experience. The days that ended like that became the glue that bound us closer together. We were watching the girls grow up and actually taking the time to enjoy it.

After a few days in Bangkok catching up on home schooling and exploring the main streets, back alleys and canals, we set off for the north. The Super Deluxe VIP Coach held in common most attributes with a regular old Greyhound. The distance was about 360 miles, and the all night sojourn allowed us time to mull over our strategy to arrange a "hill tribe trek" once we arrived in the northern city of Chaing Mai. Carla and I attempted to read and catch a little sleep. Movies ran pretty much all night on the VHS monitor at the front of the bus. With the movie dialog running in the background a couple of young travelers shouted across the aisle, exchanging experiences in French and English.

The coach was darkened except for our overhead reading lights as we motored north. I dug down into the food pack on the floor and found a bag of half-melted ginger candy, a little favorite called, Ting Ting Jahe. I absently plucked bits of wax paper wrapper from the sticky candy, while trying to concentrate on the where-to-stay section of our guide-book. The girls were too wound up to sleep and were avidly taking in the borderline R-rated flick that I tried not to notice to salvage some pre-tense of parental discretion. Carla was intent on learning a few words of Thai. The language tape we had picked up started off by pronouncing all forty-two of the letters in the Thai alphabet. Not an easy chore, since my untuned Western ear could only discern about three different sounds from the whole lot.

I turned to Carla and said "Do these ginger candies have nuts or something in them? I think I just got a piece of shell."

She paused the tape, looked at me doubtfully and shook her head. "I don't think so." Her reply was armed with a mildly derisive chuckle.

As I moved the dense little anomaly around with my tongue, it seemed pretty large for a piece of nut shell, especially since there had never been any nuts in this candy before. As I worked it to the front, I noticed a cool, airy sensation along the right side of my lower jaw — like some-thing that hadn't been exposed for a long time. It proved to be my gold crown. The little pinnacle of tooth that remained beneath was sensitive and grotesque feeling to my tongue. I slowly dissolved the gooey ginger encapsulation from the crown and worked it out into the wax paper wrapper. As I folded the wrapper around it, my mind set off in a new direction. It was the challenge of the day: How to go about getting a crown replaced in Chaing Mai, Thailand.

The light of day began to give definition to the flood of tropical vegetation that threatened to reclaim the temporary presumption of black top. Our Super Deluxe VIP Coach came to a stop in a sort of bus terminal that had been arranged adjacent to a squeaky clean Shell gas station and Handy Food Mart. Several miniature Toyota pickups with plywood camper tops and wood plank benches were positioned around the lot. We would finish the last kilometer or two of the trip in our Super Deluxe VIP pickup. I didn't ask why. Some things are better left to the imagination.

We anchored ourselves on the slick wooden benches by holding onto the ribs of the camper top, while simultaneously trying to stabilize our gear between our feet on the floor. From that vantage point, we had our first glimpses of Chaing Mai.

Winding through the tree lined streets, looking out from the back of the pickup, traffic consisted largely of a swarm of scooters and droning black tuk-tuks that needed only a couple of yellow stripes and a set of plastic wings to complete their insect-like appearance. (The name "tuk-tuk" derives from the sound of the tiny motorcycle motors that propel them.)

Coming to a halt in a tidy brick courtyard, the girls wrestled our gear from the back of the truck while I settled up with the driver and Carla walked over to the open-air reception desk. The Galare Guest House was basically a small two-story motel with an open-air restaurant looking out on the Mae Ping River. Everyone spoke perfect English.

Chaing Mai is a marvelous little city. It has a relatively intact old-town surrounded by a broad moat and gray stonewalls. The old-town district swarmed with Western tourists who took refuge from the sun in Western style restaurants and cafés. We searched newsstands for current issues of English language newspapers. The non-U.S.-based assessment of our country's behavior was refreshing. So much was going on in the world that even the girls anxiously read the articles relating to the post-9/11 developments and the conflict in Afghanistan.

With the promise of a couple of home cooked meals, Carla signed us all up for a Thai cooking class. It was offered in an open air, group kitchen. We each had a small propane cook stove, wok, bowls and utensils. All the other participants were Australian or from the U.S. The instructor was a round-faced young Thai lady with a commanding voice and a lively sense of humor. Our end result was a delicious sampling of Thai cuisine and a cookbook to take home. It was fun and a diversion from regular tourist activities.

We covered much of Chaing Mai on foot. Among the cluttered shops and utilitarian apartment buildings, slender golden spires and sublimely upswept roofs of Buddhist temples rose like oases out of the confusion

Cooking school in Chaing Mai, Thailand. Russ, Andrea and Lesley learn Thai cooking together. (Carla)

of city life. The Thai temples or wats usually enclose a large courtyard surrounded by high walls. Wats are devotional, social, educational and entertainment centers for more than 90 percent of the Thai community. We often found ourselves drawn to the central pagoda or Ubosoth. All visitors are welcomed in a Buddhist Wat. We sat for a while on the cool stone floor before the golden Buddha statue. It was a reprieve, a momentary escape from the stresses of full time travel — a chance to reset our spiritual compasses. Inside the walls of the wat were gardens, small shrines, schools and residences for the young monks and their teachers. For Buddhists, the walls create a zone free from the day-to-day life of suffering and desire, a contrast to the ebb and flow of humanity and the drone of tuk-tuks. Skinny young monks, heads shaved, studied their lessons or played basketball in the yard.

Any idea that Chaing Mai was a provincial outpost in the northern hills could not have been farther from reality. It, too, is a Western tourist Mecca with several high-rise hotels and a full complement of franchise restaurants from McDonalds to Starbucks. We must admit to having had an occasional need for a dose of pizza. We rationalized that pizza had gained much greater international currency than such offerings as burgers that were undeniably U.S. in their origin. Casting a stealthy glance in either direction, we slipped surreptitiously into a Pizza Hut every now and then to break the steady diet of fried rice and Pad Thai noodles.

The night markets in Chaing Mai rivaled anything the Koh Shan district in Bangkok had to offer. There are as many Western faces in the crowd as there are locals, maybe more. The evening market is a brightly lit steady stream of tee shirt and plaster Buddha shops that runs for a few blocks. Some clothing bargains can be had in Thailand, especially of the disposable genre, well suited to young travelers still growing. Lesley scored a pair of black pajama pants with bright orange Thai dragons wrapping around the legs, and Andrea found a pair of Thai fisherman's trousers. The fisherman's trousers are a little more difficult to describe but sufficiently unconventional to be acceptable. Their tastes had begun to take on a distinctly international flair.

The indigenous folks, known as the hill people, live on the border with Myanmar and welcome guest trekkers into their villages; we visited some of the small travel agents in the vicinity of our lodgings. With a bit more caution than we had in Mumbai, however, we settled upon the travel planners who had an office at our hotel.

During the days before our trek, I spent some time getting my tooth fixed. Locating a competent dentist was not a problem. I called over to the U.S. Consulate and got names of a few dentists they considered reliable. The dentist's office near the high-rise district was as modern and clean as any I would find in the U.S. The dentist spoke English with an American accent, and we got along fine. A couple of tuk-tuk excursions, and within a day I had a temporary crown. We planned the permanent crown for my return from our trek in the north.

The trek was the most memorable part of our time in northern Thailand. Our guide and his driver looked after us for a four-day hike through the hilly topography among stands of giant bamboo and tropical hardwoods. The route led us through several "hill tribe" villages that consisted of twenty or so family dwellings all raised on stilts. We ended each day in the home of a hill tribe family. Our guide took care of the communications and helped to prepare an evening meal. Nights were

Near the Myanmar border, northwest of Chaing Mai, Thailand. Lesley and Andrea, flanked by a traveler to the left and our guide to the right, during the four-day trek to visit the hill tribe villages. Our guide's job was to show us the trail from one village to the next, here on the way to a Black Lahu village called Bo Krai. We never knew his name. (Russ)

spent sleeping in elevated cabins made entirely of bamboo in a more-or-less common room separate from the family sleeping room. Chickens, dogs, cats and pigs spent most of their time beneath the house and let out an occasional yip or cluck during the night. The sleeping room, kitchen and a common room all faced onto a roughly triangular elevated deck, the center of family life. Friends and neighbors collected on the deck in the evening sipping tea and talking. Chewing betel nuts is still popular up in the hill tribe regions. Their blackened teeth gave a sort of comical, toothless look when their thoughtful stare yielded to the good-natured smile.

I had picked up a half kilo of Thai coffee while in Bangkok and offered it one evening to a few of the older men as we sat around waiting for dinner. They had heard of coffee but never tried it. I attempted to make it clear by way of gesture that it was genuine Thai coffee; a couple of them decided to take me up on the offer. I took some of the hot water they normally use to prepare tea, added a couple of teaspoons of grounds and let them settle, cowboy style. It was an interesting experience, and they smiled appreciatively. However, no one showed an interest in a second cup. Then they politely poured cups of tea to remove the taste of coffee from their mouths.

After dinner we sat on the veranda, lounging against the walls of our hut. A few ladies from the village began to show up, each carrying plastic bags or tote bins and doing her best to be discrete. There may have been five in all. They entered politely and sat patiently on the bamboo slats until the tribal leader in whose home we were staying gave them the nod. The minor flurry of activity that ensued saw unfurling of blankets and an outpouring of hand crafted items ranging from shoulder bags and water bottle carriers to small items of jewelry. We spent the next hour paying tribute to their skills. Then, with some ceremony, we did our best to purchase at least one item from each. Having made our purchases, we leaned back again and within a minute they were gone. I sat there wondering what was involved in the chief's decision as to who received those concessions.

We had not been able to do any cooking on our own since leaving western India and had resorted to a regular diet of restaurant food. Fortunately, food in Thailand is very economical, nutritious, and it is readily available by virtue of myriad open air or sidewalk stalls. The girls adapted well to the steady diet of Pad Thai noodles, fried rice and side-walk grilled pork chops. Foods they would have been skeptical about at home had become acceptable as their young palates were forced to adapt to new flavors and aromas. The spicy Thai food was of compa-rable intensity to what we had come to accept as standard fare in south-ern India.

Heading back south from Chaing Mai, we stopped along the way at the city of Ayutthaya. Ayutthaya had been built on the model of and named after the site of Ayodhya in India. It had served as the capital of Siam for about 400 years, starting in A.D. 1350. We spent a few days bicycling through the wide imperial streets and the vast national park established to protect the enormous monuments and wats that date from that time. The ruins at Ayutthaya had been designated a UNESCO World Heritage Site. It is one of the most impressive historical sites in Thailand.

Carla and I had resolved to get the girls certified as SCUBA divers before our visit to Australia and the Great Barrier Reef. So we passed through Bangkok again and made our way to the tiny island of Koh Tao in the Gulf of Thailand. Koh Tao was a chaotic little island, the economy of which depended entirely on SCUBA diving and the various functions that support it.

Among the clutter and the mayhem of the small dock, we found our pickup truck shuttle, climbed into the back and set out for the lodgings we had arranged via Internet back in Bangkok. Bouncing down the rutted dirt lane, we came to a stop at a cluster of beautifully crafted cabins nestled among palm and cashew trees that faced out onto the sky blue tropical waters of the coral reef. Lesley and Andrea enjoyed having a cabin separate from ours.

Selecting one of the many dive shops that offered a five-day certification class; we enrolled Lesley and Andrea. While they were in class or out on the boat, Carla and I spent our time diving and snorkeling around the island.

Each morning the girls would set off down the lane for dive class with their books and dive gear. Carla and I would look at each other and reflect on those first days of kindergarten as they disappeared around the corner with their brightly colored backpacks. We had come a long way, and they would be children not much longer.

The occasional splash of water from New Year revelers was a welcome surprise in the sweltering heat back in Bangkok. With the passage of Songkran, a festival of water that marks the arrival of the lunar Thai New Year, we began preparing to move on. Within what seemed the beat of a heart, we were again stuffing our tropical clothes into the bottoms of our packs. I hadn't worn regular shoes in probably six weeks, except maybe for the hill tribe trek. It was early April and Beijing, a little over 2,000 miles to the north, would involve another change in climate. We left Thailand with some feeling of separation and a genuine fondness for everything Thai.

Our last sally into the crowds of Bangkok marked the realization of a goal Andrea had set for herself. It was a search through the maze of sidewalk vendors for one that offered, among other crispy, land-dwelling arthropods — fried scorpions. Scorpions were, at least on that particular night, in short supply. Try as we might, we had to be content with four-inch grasshoppers!

Chapter 7

China and Japan

THE SPONGY THUMP OF THE LANDING GEAR flexing under the weight of the descending aircraft confirmed our arrival on the Chinese mainland, the Peoples Republic of China. We were excited, even though our 1:40 A.M. departure from Bangkok had allowed us only a couple of hours of sleep. Rounding up our travel items, Carla stuffed her book of Chinese phrases into the front pocket of my daypack. She brought her hand out, and in it was my emergency PayDay candy bar, still stashed in its plastic bag and waiting for the day that starvation caught up with us.

I shrugged and said, "Hey, someone might get hungry along the way."

Her response was one that needed no verbal reinforcement. She shook her head, pushed it back into the daypack and headed down the aisle into the jet way.

China

Beijing Airport at 7:30 in the morning was the nicest airport we had been to in a long time. It was extremely clean with English-translated signs all over the place.

The conditioning Carla and I had acquired through the Cold War years, the images of gray-suited Chinese Communists waving little red books, got a quick revision as we were met by a polite young man wearing stylishly faded jeans, a plaid shirt, Nikes and a pair of wrap-around sun glasses. His chosen (Western) name was Jack. As part of the travel and tourism training, all registered guides choose a one or two syllable English name to make it easier on their clients. Jack looked like any young man of Oriental heritage on the streets of Houston or Los Angeles. He spoke English every bit as good as mine and helped us get through the maze of arriving passengers to the van waiting outside. Temperatures lingered in the sixties, and the clear dry air was a pleasant change from the steamy latitudes of the previous night's departure, some 2,000 miles to the south.

Our stay in China had been entirely arranged back in Houston months before departure, roughly a year in advance. We reasoned that the communication barrier would be too big of a leap for us to wing it. Besides, it is necessary to have a travel plan established to get a tourist visa for China. So, as in Egypt, we bit the bullet and worked with a representative of Shanghai Airlines to plan the entire twenty-three days we would spend in China. While most of the time was tightly scripted, Carla had done enough reading to insist on a few free days in Beijing, Xian and Shanghai. These days allowed us to just walk around and fend for ourselves.

The eleventh of April, the day of our arrival in Beijing, marked the completion of ten months of travel. By my best reckoning, we had traveled about 29,700 miles. My shoes, the ones I had worn only on special occasions in India and Thailand, were showing the mileage. I expect, as a group, we were too.

Jack let us spend the day resting up. The girls had a nap, then did some preliminary strolling within a mile or so radius of the hotel. High rise shopping malls and Western franchises were pretty common. No one seemed to take any special notice of a family of Westerners. We stopped at a little fast food restaurant for lunch; if you didn't look too closely, it would have passed for a Kentucky Fried Chicken outlet complete with red and white logo. What was most amusing was the fact that the face of the friendly old gentleman was an Oriental version of Colonel Sanders without the beard. We were so intrigued by the place that we decided to check it out. Employing the point-and-hope method of ordering, we ended up with a delicious assortment of Chinese dumplings and other items; no fried chicken there!

Beijing carried more than a little irony. The chubby, seemingly benevolent face of Chairman Mao still looks out across Tian'anmen Square. His serene gaze is fixed upon a pair of golden arches and an Internet café. Starbucks has outlets throughout the city. Times change, of course. Jack had never read a single passage from Mao's little red book. He recalled his parents telling him they had been required to read aloud from it every morning back in the old days. Otherwise, he just shrugged his shoulders. The whole Cold War mystique had completely passed him by, as it had with Lesley and Andrea. They just thought he was cool.

Beijing, a fast moving, vibrant city, is filled with people going about their lives and adapting to change from inside and without. We felt no restrictions when it came to wandering about on our own. Andrea insisted on rising before dawn and walking the mile or so through the cool air to see the flag raising at Tienamen Gate. As the sun rose to illuminate the massive gray façade of The Great Hall of the People, I realized with some chagrin that we had seen the changing of the guard in most of the great capitals of the world but not Washington, D.C.; we would have to correct that upon our return home.

Included in our itinerary were a few of the "must see" pilgrimage sites. A visit to the Temple of Heaven or Tian Tan in Beijing is a worthwhile commitment of an afternoon. It is a tranquil escape from the sensory overload that goes with any large city. Order, discipline and geometric symmetry are the unifying principles, but they are carried out with a sense of artistic proportion that is uniquely Chinese.

Approaching the circular pagoda where each year on the Winter Solstice the emperors of the Ming Dynasty (A.D. 1360–1640) offered ritual sacrifice to Heaven, we paused to watch a group of middle-aged office workers and professionals standing in evenly spaced rows and columns. They were refining their calligraphy techniques, using long pointed brushes with buckets of water as ink. Their parchments were the porous paving stones of the broad promenade that rose steadily to the Temple of Heaven. Hands clasped behind his back, a wizened master, some years their senior, paced among them applying his critical eye. The students submitted to his terse commentary without expression or response.

The tranquil surroundings and formal gardens had not escaped the flourishing capitalism that, despite fifty years of repression, has filled every available niche of Beijing. Off to one side were the cluttered souvenir shops. Through the middle of it all streamed busloads of anxious comrades from the provinces, all engaged in hushed conversations. To minimize dispersion of the tour groups, each member was given a bright red or yellow "gimme" cap, glowing in stark contrast to grays and navy blues of their bus-wrinkled suits. The "gimme" cap and how to wear it had not reached the high art form among the Chinese that it has enjoyed in Texas. But it was a glimpse of how the Chinese approached tourism. Literally everything is geared to large travel groups — buses, restaurants, hotels and tourist attractions.

As the Temple of Heaven marks the center of the ancient empire, individuals from each tour group come to stand on the marble disk embedded in the paving stones of the rotunda. Elderly ladies wearing dark blue pantsuits and sun-dried old men politely waited their turn for a quick photo. Their deeply lined and tanned faces beamed with delight. The starched bills of the "gimme" caps tilting at all angles created a lighthearted spectacle. The people of China are on the move, and they intend to see their country. I thought of farmers from Nebraska standing in front of the Lincoln Memorial.

Jack agreed to meet us at the main gate. Having exhausted our curiosity, we were whisked off to another tourist destination. However, it seemed that just about every time we were en route to a destination, our path would take us by another craft emporium that guides, like Jack, were more or less required to drag their charges through. Unlike many of our fellow Western tourists, we had no interest in collecting more stuff to carry around for the next two months. We had seen just about every imaginable cultural icon the world's civilizations had developed over the past 4,000 years faithfully reproduced in DayGlo plastic. As a result, the entreaties of the sidewalk vendors rolled off of us.

An excursion to the Great Wall satisfied one of Andrea's stated goals for the trip and completed my list of "must see" pilgrimage sites around the world. Naturally the day's outing would not have been complete without a stop at a state owned jade emporium. As it turned out, we weren't entirely immune, and a pair of small green spheres soon adorned Carla's earlobes. After all, they were easy to carry and green is her favorite color. A cold had taken her down for a couple of days, and she was struggling to keep her spirits up; the earrings brought a smile to her face.

Since everything is negotiable, when buying jade, make your first offer at about 25 percent of the stated price, and you will do all right. Even Lesley and Andrea began to understand the techniques of bartering for things they wanted. The rules are pretty basic, but the ultimate goal is to skillfully exercise "the power of walking away." I had to explain to Andrea that it's not a good tactic to turn to your dad with the sales person looking on and say, "That's the one I really want."

Anticipation is often ninety percent of the joy of acquisition. Lesley and Andrea found the whole process thrilling. Even if you only get a ten to 25 percent discount, you have engaged in the ancient art of bartering.

On one of our free days we strolled through the back streets of Beijing with the purpose of seeing the Hutong district — a glimpse of old Beijing where cobbled, medieval streets were lined with gray stone and stucco houses. Well-used bicycles leaned against the walls in the narrow, dimly lit courtyards. A few potted geraniums reached out for rare bits of sunlight.

Rising from the midst of it all was the ancient landmark and worthwhile stop, the Drum Tower; it was first built in 1272 during the reign of Khublai Khan and was the center of his capital city then called Daidu, or as Marco Polo recounted it in 1298, Khanbalu. The Drum Tower stands on Daidu's central axis which also runs through the Tian'anmen Gate about four miles to the south. On our modern street map, the square-patterned city blocks, broad thoroughfares and massive gates were stirring reminders of The Great Khan's Northern Capital. The nearby Bell Tower was a work of the Ming Dynasty and dated back to about 1420. Both the Drum Tower and Bell Tower afforded excellent views of the Great Khan's capital city and the narrow winding alleys or Hutongs that surrounded the Forbidden City.

Fending for ourselves always made meals an adventure. A bright neon sign formed into the familiar shape of the word "welcome" was enough to draw us into a small but prim little restaurant. As it turned out, the only thing to be found in the entire place in English was the neon sign in the window. Initially we attempted to make some sense of the menu. For a few minutes Carla tried to match the characters on the menu to some categories in our Chinese phrase book. The waitress paused, looked on patiently, then moved on to more fertile ground. The menus were missing any of the handy illustrations you might find in a place frequented by tourists, i.e. picture menus.

Lacking Carla's resolve, I abandoned any pretense of civilized behavior and resorted to the Moo-Snort-Cluck method of ordering. This cut right through any communications barrier and added an element of humor that diffused the tension often associated with ordering food. At the sound of my chicken imitation, which I felt had developed a convincing throaty quality, the waitress' face brightened. Carla augmented my barnyard impressions by pointing to the characters for dumpling and soup in her phrase book and so that's what we had. We never really had any problem ordering as long as we weren't too particular. Chinese is a language that depends strongly on tone and inflection, a hurdle we were never really able to clear. But it was fun to try. You just can't be too self-conscious.

The train trip from Beijing down to Xian was a welcome escape from life on the big city streets. Our compartment was probably the nicest sleeper we had occupied in the entire trip. The whole Chinese rail experience was a notch above just about everything else we had experienced. It certainly topped Amtrak, loyal supporters that we are. In fact, a uniformed attendant stood on the platform and held a card with the car number by each entrance. No dragging our bags up and down the platform, looking for the correct car or someone who might know something. I am sure there are some slightly less polished lines in the Chinese hinterlands, but if they were hoping to make a good impression, it worked. Our round faced young guide, Linda, greeted us in perfect English at the station in Xian and showed us to our hotel.

Xian was the ancient capital of eleven Chinese dynasties and has a relaxed atmosphere when compared to the modern day capital. We were lucky to have had the opportunity to spend a couple of days just walking about and climbing around on the 700-year-old walls that surround the central business district. Linda did, however, escort us to see the Terra Cotta Soldiers and the Huaqin Hot Springs Palace where the Qin Dynasty emperors spent their off hours trying to forget the day to day problems of running an empire.

We were quite a hit with the busloads of school kids out on field trips. Many of them looked to be within a couple of years of Lesley and Andrea's age. Being the only Westerners in sight, we were the recipients of several hundred "hellos" and "good mornings," awash in a river of brightly colored nylon warm up suits and backpacks. Each small group gathered their collective courage, sang out a greeting in English and waved as they passed by. This went on for some ten minutes or so. We felt like visiting dignitaries. Linda said that her daughter in kindergarten was already learning English. It is, she felt, the international language. In twenty years it will be hard to go to any major city in China and not find English spoken by a significant portion of the population.

Home to the great merchants and traders, the Muslim section of Xian held the greatest attraction for us. Residing in its midst is an ancient Daoist temple that was, during the atheistic days of the Cultural

Revolution, converted to a market, just to emphasize the point. It is a fascinating maze of ancient pagoda architecture with shops and stalls shoehorned into every corner — from chickens to costume jewelry to school supplies and hardware. Vendors sat at little plastic tables often playing cards to pass the slow part of the afternoon. While Carla and the girls sorted through the cheap jewelry and school supplies, I began to look for a new journal; my fourth volume would accommodate only a few more days. It is remarkable how scarce decent writing paper is in some parts of the world.

From time to time, we looked back and thought how tame our first market day in the Yorkshire village of Settle was. Whether we knew it or not, the edgy excitement of travel had long ago worn off, and we had become travelers. It was who we were, our way of life.

Lesley and Andrea, however, were beginning to feel the pull of home and were consumed with the notion that everyone there would be expecting a gift of some sort. As keeper of the budget, I counseled them on what was and was not practical. This was a growing source of anxiety for them, not to mention the thoughts of having to go back to school. Would they be able to keep pace with their peers? The girls worried. Struggle as we all might to focus on what was in front of us, we each knew the dream would end some day.

At the outset, a year had seemed a long time. As each month passed and the miles melted away, Carla and I were both conscious that this was a dream; and our girls would be entering a new phase of their lives when we returned home. We had, it seemed, shared the crest, as the wave of their childhood ran up onto the shore. Despite all the pressures of travel and the growing pains of adolescence, we had shared a great adventure, and it wasn't over yet.

Arriving in Chongqing by plane from Xian, it was overcast and a light rain was falling. Again, met by a prearranged guide, we were shuttled down to the banks of the Yangtze River. There we boarded a floating hotel christened the Victoria Blue Whale. Ninety-one meters in length with three levels and a deck, it accommodated 141 passengers and a crew of 115. It was a very upscale river cruiser, and with some degree of embarrassment, we were ushered into two huge suites at the front of the ship. Lesley and Andrea had one, and Carla and I the other. The girls needed their space and time out from under our watchful eyes, but this was a level of opulence we had not envisioned. The Chinese portion of the trip was the most expensive segment. Coupled with the individual-ized shuttles and guides, I began to see why it had cost so much.

As the sun slid behind the rugged hills surrounding Chongqing, we found our way around the boat and onto the upper deck. Carla and I leaned on the rail and tried to put what we had seen of China into some sort of order and reconcile whatever preconceptions we might have had. Liberalization of the Chinese economy was a popular theme in the press. The remarkable courage of the young man standing in front of the tank in Tian'anmen Square was still comfortably lodged among our mental images of China. The path to liberalization in the mid-1990s had seemed anything but clear-cut and certain then.

Yet, here we were, viewing multicolor laser searchlights as they pen-etrated the humid evening air of Chongqing, more than a bit upbeat for this geographically isolated city. With the red, green and blue streaks of neon that highlighted the highways and outlined many of the sky scrap-ers in the central commercial district, the whole place looked as though they were having one major festival.

Carla and I just leaned on the rail and took it all in. We had the boat almost to ourselves the first night. Andrea and Lesley burned off some of their pent up energy doing cartwheels and round-offs on the deck. I turned to Carla and said, "You know, this is not what I expected to see in China. This place is on the brink of a real cultural revolution, and I don't think they will ever be able to put it back in the box again." For me, Tian'anmen Square had not lost its deep philosophical and emo-tional impact, but now I had some fresher images, the opportunity to see what those early Democracy protests had brought about.

We would spend eight nights on board this boat, covering the dis-tance from Chongqing to Shanghai, a straight line of approximately 900 miles. Cruises through the Three Gorges, like this one, would be com-ing to an end in a matter of months; construction of the world's largest dam was nearing completion. The project had generated some criticism outside of China. Undaunted by international publicity, both for and against, the characteristic single-minded devotion to the project was re-flected in the faces of the people, numbering over one and a half million, whose homes and cities would be inundated once the flood gates were closed. All along the hillsides were signs indicating the elevations to which the river would rise in 2003 and the later stage of dam completion.

The silt brown Yangtze River had worn its way down through sev-eral hundred feet of contorted sedimentary rocks. The steep walled canyons are the equal of anything in southern Utah or northern Arizona. Towns all along the river were being evacuated. Buildings and cities were entirely destroyed, taken down to rubble and hauled away in trucks. Some towns looked like pictures of the devastation of Europe during World War II.

People were doing their best to cope, to carry on with their lives as things were being torn down around them, then rebuilt at higher elevation. The first premise of Buddhism: Everything is temporary. It was clear that maintenance had come to a halt. Everyone was trying to salvage things that might have value for their new homes in a designated resettlement community. Men and boys could be seen balancing lumber, bricks, plumbing parts in a wheelbarrow or an enormous aluminum window frame lashed to a couple of worn out bicycles on the steep canyon roads. They reminded me of streams of leaf cutter ants coursing through the underbrush with their tiny green sails. The people didn't seem desperate, just resigned. Having packed up all of our belongings and uprooted our lives, we had an inkling of how it might feel. But ours was by choice, not mandate.

The Yangtze, like any other major river, is used by countless small motorized barges to haul everything from gravel and sugarcane to boat loads of chairs or chickens. The river was a vital transportation network and also the domain of simple river people, constantly learning to coexist. Fishermen in their oversized canoes looked up in casual interest at yet another boatload of tourists. I couldn't begin to imagine what was going through the fisherman's mind as we drifted by. In his world, as he sat arranging his hooks and nets to secure an evening meal for his family, I suspected we were largely irrelevant. I was constantly reminded by such scenes how chance had played its part in our being born in one of the most highly developed countries in the world. We certainly didn't get there by choice or by skill.

During one of our excursions into the hinterlands, Andrea and Lesley returned from the restroom smiling broadly. A group of Chinese-Americans on a two-week tour had, to that point, been spared the experience of Eastern-style toilets. Toilets in most places consist of a hole in the floor with a pair of small nonslip footprints on either side with nothing to rest ones weight upon. Just squat, point and shoot. A spirited discussion was underway in the ladies room when Andrea and Lesley happened upon the scene. The girls, having accomplished their purpose and heading for the door, were enlisted to give some coaching to the group of middle-aged ladies on their first attempts at coping with the Eastern-style facilities. Lesley shyly offered a few pointers and Andrea a couple of suggestions, both based on their hard won experience.

I couldn't pass up the opportunity to remind the girls that back in Greece they had steadfastly resolved that they were not going to use Eastern toilets. At the time, I wondered if they intended to hold it for six months. Three months of travel in Asia had made them seasoned travelers, undaunted by the local variations in plumbing.

On the fourth day we broke out of the narrow canyons and cloud covered peaks into the vast level flood plain of the lowland Yangtze. Happy hour held relatively little interest for us. The girls were doing a round of math homework. Carla and I stood at the railing in the evening sun and filled our lungs with a sweet fragrance carried by the warm April breeze. I thought of honeysuckle, but Carla suggested it was probably jasmine. The river and the mountains and the fields of jasmine gradually melted into the twilight. It was a perfect ending to another perfect day.

A few of us, the foreign independent travelers as they called us on the boat, were grouped together. We shared meals, transport and experiences with Klaus and Renate Roll from Berlin and two retired ladies, Haneloe and Giesela, also from Germany. In no time at all, lasting friendships developed with these adventurous comrades. The rest of the passengers were members of large package tours from France and the U.S., both mostly of retirement age. Our daytime excursions into the mountains were breathtaking. I think we each quietly resolved to return sometime on our own, after we had a chance to gain a little more skill with the language. The bus trips through the towns were every bit as interesting as whatever scenic destination had been arranged for the day by the tour coordinator.

Mountain ranges that bound the Yangtze floodplain are not impressive by their sheer altitude or alpine vistas. Few if any of the peaks rise to much over 6,000 feet. But their spires of barren rock and plunging canyons shrouded in mist were like scenes from a coffee table book on Chinese art. Exotic gabled pagodas sprouted from among the trees in veneration of fierce looking Daoist deities.

Daoism is a complex culmination of philosophical and mystical beliefs that have found political favor over the succeeding millennia, depending on social needs of the time. The tenets of the religion that date back to around 500 B.C. have been passed down in the *Dao De Jing*, a volume of around 50,000 Chinese characters committed to paper by the patriarch and sage Lao Zi. Daoists temples are often crowded with deities who formally number around twenty-three but can include local gods as well. Statues often stood ten feet tall in colorful, flowing robes and wore expressions of malice and terror. They were not a group of benevolent dilettantes but looked more like the contra-positive Seven Dwarfs.

The array of temples, shrines and pagodas can leave the uninitiated in complete bewilderment. It is difficult for a Westerner to gain any sense of Eastern culture without delving at least superficially into the evolution of religious beliefs and the philosophical teachings that have shaped the Chinese spirit. The schools of religious thought, conceived by sages and manipulated over the centuries by the political whims of the passing dynasties have engendered a confusing retinue of deities, rituals and customs. The Way of Daoism, the Enlightenment of Buddhism, the Discipline of Confucianism, even reaching back to the Hindu Way of Eternal Conduct; the common thread is a focus on the here and now, and the accepted way to conduct one's self. This accountability for actions carried out here on earth can be sensed in everything that is Chinese. Humility is something that is still understood and valued.

For our tour group, the river boat tied up for the last time in Nanjing an hour or so outside of Shanghai. Originally settled as far back as 500 B.C. Nanjing was designated as the capital city during at least four of China's dynastic periods. Historic and cultural sites abound within an hours ride of Nanjing and we spent days touring the mausoleum of Dr. Sun Yat-Sen, the Suzhou Lingering Garden and Tiger Hill and somehow found time to take in a performance of a Chinese acrobatics troupe and a visit to a fascinating silk factory. The Yangtze River tour was very professionally conducted. It would have been impossible to see and do as much, traveling on our own.

Outside Nanjing, we disembarked and went our separate ways. Etched in my memory was an American lady traveling with her recently retired husband, probably in their mid-sixties. He had enjoyed a full and satisfying career as a corporate attorney, and we had exchanged hardly more than a few pleasantries over the course of the trip down the Yangtze. After our last evening meal on the boat, she came up and grasped my hand in both of hers. With tears in her eyes she looked at me and asked

"Why didn't we do this when we were your age, when we still had our children with us and our health? " She wished us Godspeed for the remainder of our journey and vanished into the crowd of milling tourists. We never saw her again. We had experienced similar moments along the way but never quite as explicitly as that one.

That familiar feeling — loss of the temporary sense of community that had developed with our fellow travelers — permeated the moment. We had felt it before and had learned to deal with it each time we left the customs and familiar surroundings to enter another leg of the journey. Lesley and Andrea had been attracted to the grandmotherly Giesela and Haneloe. Klaus, Renate, Carla and I had also enjoyed each other's company. We parted ways at the bus station in Shanghai.

Shanghai, China's largest city boasts a population of somewhere between thirteen and seventeen million inhabitants. On the edge of the Yangtze River delta it was first established around A.D. 980 during the Song Dynasty and by way of its location at the mouth of the Yangtze developed into China's most important economic and international trade center. As the world's busiest port, it is in heated competition with Hong Kong as the financial and trade center of China.

Getting around Shanghai was very easy using the ultramodern metro system. Afoot again, we set out from the People's Square station where we looked on as groups of middle-aged ladies practiced a form of exercise involving large fans and elderly men stayed limber with Tai Chi. Searching in vain for some moderately priced clothing stores to find some replacement items for Lesley and Andrea, we spent a day working our way down Nanjing Road to the historic Bund trading district. I did, however, find another sidewalk shoe repairman to do a final rework of my left shoe.

Nineteenth and early twentieth century European architectural styles dating back to Shanghai's days as a British treaty port stand in sharp contrast to the riot of space age and retro-futuristic needles of steel and glass that dominate the skyline of the Pudong district on the opposite bank of the Huangpu River. The pedestrian ambience of the Bund district was altogether absent over in Pudong. It didn't take long to realize that nobody walks in Pudong.

En route from Guilin to our final destination in mainland China, we covered the last thirty miles down the Li River to Yangshuo on a small tourist ferry. Adding local color to the trip — one of the attendants brought out a bottle of "Snake Wine," a large bottle of amber fluid half

Searching for Moon Hill in the countryside near Yangshuo, China. Carla, Lesley and Andrea pause for a (warm) can of soda while on a bike ride. The best way to see China. (Russ)

filled with alcohol-preserved snakes. The same two girls who had to be coerced to put yogurt on their cereal back in Norway insisted that Carla and I each have a shot, so they could sample it too. A group of American tourists looked on with amazement. It didn't taste like chicken. It tasted like snakes!

Entirely on our own for three days in Yangshuo, we ventured on foot and by bicycle out into the surrealistic countryside. Yangshuo is the setting for the thousands of Chinese paintings depicting mountain cottages, precariously fastened to sheer rocky pinnacles covered with lush subtropical greenery. I had long wondered if that style of painting was the product of some strange, exaggerated land of Chinese mythology. In fact, the radical landscapes, limestone spires and sinkholes are the surface expression of a network of subterranean caverns. In the case of Yangshuo, the caverns, which eventually collapsed leaving only a few supporting pillars, were on such a grand scale that it was hard to imagine.

Since our jogging schedule had been difficult to maintain over the past three weeks, bicycles were a great release. We set out down the road from Yangshuo through the flat-bottomed valleys surrounded by limestone spires that looked like something out of a Dr. Seuss book. A few miles from town we were finally away from the constant presence of fellow human beings. The serenity of the pastoral setting and the vast open countryside seemed at odds with my notion of the world's most populous country. Pumping along on our rented 5-speeds, we traveled by postcard panoramas of chaotic peaks reflected in the glassy surfaces of freshly planted rice paddies. Rice farming is still a largely manual occupation. Entire families with pants rolled to their knees bend over for hours each day, placing the young rice shoots into the soft mud of the flooded paddy.

Stopping at a small town for a can of soda, market-day was in full swing. Entertainment was free. We watched as our fellow human beings coped with the challenges of daily life.

A remarkable bit of mechanization typical of rural China is a form of a motorized three-wheeled plough tractor that seems to have evolved into an all purpose pseudo-pickup truck and general transportation. It is noteworthy for the huge, single-cylinder gasoline-powered motor that looks like an oversized Briggs & Stratton lawnmower motor. An imposing two-foot diameter flywheel is cantilevered out over the single front wheel and looks sort of like a motorized warthog, the mechanical incarnation of raw power.

Standing at the curb and sipping our warm sodas, we looked on as a farmer made several runs at a gravel ramp from the main market street up onto the paved highway in his utilitarian tractor rig. Pulling a beat-up little trailer of crushed rock, he had clearly reached the capacity of his little mechanical mule to surmount the six-foot grade. Dogged determination finally paid off as he made progressively longer running starts down the main drag, engine pumping little black puffs of soot that hung in the still humid air. No one seemed to take any special notice. Evidently they had all faced similar tests.

Out in the countryside we pulled off to rest and have a drink of water. Lesley and Andrea found a cave to explore, while Carla and I made plans for Japan. In less than a week we would be in the Empire of the Rising Sun and had no real plans beyond the first few days in Tokyo.

Changing countries had become routine for us. Each time we cast aside the maps, tour books and language texts to make room for the next influx of literature. It was this perpetual challenge of having to read ahead that kept us constantly stimulated. Carla had really taken to learning the Chinese characters, and she was feeling more comfortable with the language. Many Japanese characters are derived from Chinese, and we reasoned that plenty of English was spoken in Japan.

Lesley and Andrea had become well-seasoned travelers and even more seasoned at eating unusual foods. The barbecued chicken feet for breakfast in China made the prospect of eating sushi in Japan a non-event.

Japan

Based on time and budget constraints, we planned to spend only two weeks in Japan. The travel books talk about the hustle and crush of the Japanese train system; we approached it with some caution. Even under the most stressful conditions, the Japanese were so civil that it was really quite easy to get around. The train ride from Narita Airport to our lodgings in the Yanaka district was quick and painless. In China we had been encouraged by other travelers to purchase seven-day Japan Rail Passes when we stopped over in Hong Kong; this was a good piece of advice, since such passes are only available outside Japan and through Japanese travel agents and airline offices.

We had booked into a ryoken, a traditional Japanese guesthouse. The ryoken experience provided an introduction to Japanese customs such as afternoon tea, bathing and, not to be overlooked, slipper protocol. The Sawanoya Ryoken was a very casual little family guesthouse somewhere between a B&B and a hostel. The owner and his son went out of their way to make Westerners feel at ease, including a personal performance of the "lion dance." The feeling of community with the other guests was something we always looked forward to. Listening to other travelers recount their experiences, we tried to gather a sense of just how to go about seeing Japan.

It didn't take us long to master the Tokyo underground rail system. Some travel publishers put out these things called *City Packs*, or something similar. It is an abbreviated travel guide with short descriptions of the many places of interest with a detailed city map. We found them for many of the larger cities we stopped in, and the one for Tokyo was especially useful. We covered large areas of the city, including the famous Ginza commercial district out to the Maritime Museum near the port, and, of course, we had to pass through the SONY building. There the computer and electronics buff can while away hours sampling the latest electronic gadgets soon to appear in the stores.

I was somewhat out of it for a couple of days. From China I had brought with me intestinal symptoms that earmarked a case of *giardia*, a vicious bug that tends to hang around too long. I never had to buy souvenirs; I always seemed to come away with such truly personalized mementos. No telling where I picked it up, but by the time we reached Tokyo it was in its last stages. I suffered through, but as Carla and the girls would be quick to point out, not in silence.

The Sawanoya Ryoken was in an excellent location. It was within walking distance of the Ueno Japan Rail Station and the Nezu underground stop. The area is perfect for exploring on foot. The peaceful atmosphere of the giant Ueno Park with its manicured lawns and gardens to the west of the Ueno Station offered an escape from the crowds streaming through the dizzying array of market stalls that stretch to the east. Every imaginable bit of clothing and paraphernalia was on display in brightly lit stalls, interspersed with noodle houses and coffee shops. Fitted in among the commercial clutter were dozens of prim little Buddhist shrines like first aid stations offering a breath of spiritual oxygen before plunging back into the melee. A person could get turned around but never really lost.

Catching a train into Tokyo one afternoon, we stopped in to absorb a tourist-sized dose of Kabuki, the classical Japanese theatre. The origins of Kabuki can be traced back to seventeenth century Kyoto where it was mostly dance and performed by women. It has evolved over the past 400 years into highly stylized performances, including some dance but mostly melodramatic folk tales and mythology. After the removal of women from the art form, male actors took on women's roles and developed a strained kind of falsetto, while those in male roles spoke deeply from their throats. Kabuki heroes often display super human strength and emphasize their prowess by exaggerated movements and crossed eyes glaring at the audience. It is acceptable, if done correctly, for members of the audience to call out during the performance in support of a character or a particular actor. Musical accompaniments are made on traditional instruments like the three stringed shamisen and the taiko drum. A performance can last several hours. Kabuke Lite, as we called it, was scaled back for the uninitiated. After an hour or so, I remained uninitiated. "Definitely," I commented, "an acquired taste." Carla loved it and could have stayed all day.

As far as acquired tastes go, while looking for a place to eat, we ducked into a little lunch-counter-style, quick noodle shop near Ueno Station. Ordering up four something or others by pointing to the pictures on the laminated plastic menu, someone dropped a quarter into the jukebox, and we hummed along to R&R oldies from the 1980s. I looked across at Lesley and Andrea; they were chatting idly while playing with their chopsticks. I pointed out that all the strips of fish, artfully arranged on the bowls of noodles in the pictures, were probably raw. They just looked up briefly and said "Yeah, so?" and went back to their conversation. What had I expected? After all, we were in Tokyo.

Sensory overload from city streets reached saturation after a few days. We longed for the countryside and some fresh air. With the ultimate target of Kansai Airport near Osaka ten days off, we headed out into the hinterlands.

A view of Mt. Fujiama will have to be the highlight of our next trip to Japan because the two days we spent trying to get a glimpse of the eminent snowcapped volcano found it enshrouded in drizzly fog. So, after a day soaking in a hot springs *onsen*, we headed into the Japanese Alps, as they call them, with a stop at Matsumoto. There we paused for a few days to absorb a little more Japanese culture. The lady who ran the hotel was slightly on the obsessive-compulsive end of the scale, even by Japanese standards. At our first meeting she patiently admonished Andrea, who was hopping around at the threshold on one foot, trying to unlace the other shoe, while struggling to figure out which pair of sandals to put on, before stepping into the house, not to mention attempting to balance her backpack in the meantime. The wheels on the backpack needed to be cleaned, Andrea was advised, and any signs of dust removed from the outside of the pack before entering.

The rooms were traditional Japanese style, and we slept on the floor on pads laid out on tatami mats made of rice straw. They were perfectly comfortable, especially as compared to some of the less firm beds we had experienced along the way.

Mrs. Tidytown, as Andrea had christened her, (a reference picked up back in Wales), saw to it that our slippers — which remained outside the doors of our rooms — were arranged properly — at a precise ninety degrees to the wall. It drove her crazy to see them out of order and not properly paired. She very kindly brought us tea each afternoon with a special plate of biscuits, a peace offering, I thought.

The first night we were a little short of ideas on where to eat dinner; in our wanderings, we drifted back to the train station, a place where we derived some sense of comfort. English language signs were fairly scarce away from the major cities, but train stations can usually be counted on for less provincial orientation. So with nothing on our minds but a decent meal, we stepped into small restaurant with a French name; it was owned by a Turkish man who served almost exclusively Indian food. I washed my Reshmi Murgh down with a Guinness. Who says the Japanese are not multi-cultural?

The castle at Matsumoto is really quite beautiful and worth a visit. It is a five-story wooden structure supported by massive rough-hewn timbers. An immaculately kept courtyard and mote surround the castle. The Japanese skill for woodworking is always a pleasure to observe. The tour through the castle can be a challenge, since visitors are required to remove their shoes. Unlike the customs in some countries, where the shoes are left outside in a rack, in Matsumoto they supply handy plastic bags, equipped with a drawstring, so that shoes can be carried along. That seemed like a reasonable idea until you try to climb the staircases at about thirty degrees from the vertical, while juggling a shoe bag and a camera — in your stocking feet on polished wooden surfaces.

The rail passes allowed us unlimited access to trains. Some great hikes, framed by spectacular mountain vistas, were to be had a short ride up the tracks. Walking the country lanes to the foot of the mountains, we passed through the small plots of rice, most of them less than an acre, farmed by families with neat little motorized ploughs and buggies to carry things about. This was quite different from China where the water buffalo still enjoyed a secure future.

Memorable among the days in Japan was a walk from the village of Magome across a ridgeline to Tsumago, another small town. Magome is an old Post Road Village from the Edo period (1603–1868) and consists of a string of beautiful little shops along a narrow ridge with a flagstone lane right up through the center. Even the tourist shops are a study in the Japanese philosophy of careful understatement. Naturally the town is a stop for Japanese tourists, but they walk through the shops, pick up a few souvenirs, then get back on the tour bus. Even trinket vendors, who overrun a person in some countries, were so polite in Japan I

Matsumoto Castle, Matsumoto, Japan. The impressive five-storey Matsumoto Castle, surrounded by a broad moat and stone walls, was built first in 1504 and, after several seiges, brought to completion in 1590. (Russ)

wondered how they made a living. The hike through the hills above the town was only five miles but a real pleasure. Andrea and Lesley reverted to their less complicated selves and recaptured a certain natural beauty that only time in the outdoors brings to the surface.

Along the way we stopped for a lunch of dried fish and some strange gelatinized, green tea flavored confections. Carla and I listened to the nearby creek, while the girls did a little exploring in the woods. Lesley, in one of her less prudent moments, leapt from a tree that lay across the creek about eight or ten feet down to the steep leaf-covered bank. Unwilling to admit that she had twisted her ankle badly, she attempted to soldier on and made it most of the way down to Tsumago. Her color began to fade with the onset of a minor case of shock. Carla had her lay down on the trail and recuperate while Andrea and I walked the last half-mile into the village in search of a taxi.

I thought that if this is the worst injury we have on the whole trip, when the rest of the world appeared to be coming unglued, we had much to be thankful for. We found a taxi to carry us back to the train station; we were soon relaxing on the train, until jostled back to consciousness by the strangely euphonious recording of "Mat-su-mo-tooh, Mat-su-mo-toooh, Mat-su-mo-toooh," comical, but decidedly lighthearted by Japan Rail standards.

Continuing our migrations around to the other side of the mountains, we checked into the town of Takayama. The hostel we had booked was attached to the Tenshoji Shinto Temple. It was a peaceful temple, nestled high among the tall pine trees. Outside, in a great log framework, hung a huge brass bell with a six-foot log suspended in a rope sling. Pulling on a tasseled rope at ground level caused the log to pull back, then ram into the side of the bell. The temptation was too much. We tried our hand at ringing the bell and found it to be great fun.

The hostel was an enjoyable experience and another lesson in slipper protocol. Street shoes are left in the rack near the front door and exchanged for semirigid plastic sandals worn around the hostel but left neatly outside the door of the sleeping room. Heading down the hall to the restroom, one dons general-purpose indoor slippers until arriving at the bathroom door, at which point one trades in general purpose slippers for some hard rubber slippers more suited to water and tile surfaces in the bath area. There were several comical occasions where we hobbled around on one foot, while trying to figure out the appropriate set of slippers. I never fully warmed to the idea of putting on a pair of slippers that everyone and his brother had worn before me.

Access to laundry facilities was something we had lacked since we left Bangkok, and it was a real pleasure to not have to contend with doing wash in the shower. There had been little time and essentially no facilities for doing laundry in China, especially on a tour; hand washing of a day's worth of clothes had become a ritual. Returning home with two weeks of dirty laundry, as many short-term travelers might do, was not an option for us.

Taking a bath was another story altogether. It was a three or four step affair. And, yes, I did share a bathtub with another man, a young German, who was very up on proper Japanese bathtub etiquette. He wore his little hand towel on his head when fully immersed in the hot communal tub.

In Japan Andrea and I began getting back on a regular schedule of early morning runs. It had been more difficult to keep in shape in China where our itinerary was mostly full of planned activities. I needed physical activity to keep my disposition in order; Andrea wanted to get back in shape for soccer before we arrived home. Passing quietly through the deserted streets shortly after sunrise, we reestablished a bond that we have developed over the years of shared running.

After a run and a shower, an ample Japanese breakfast, consisting of miso soup, boiled eggs, some interesting little accompaniments and plenty of green tea got us off to a good start. I was carrying a mixture of Thai coffee and a brew I had picked up in a grocery store somewhere. Usually a microwave generated hot water, and I could prepare a reliable cup of cowboy coffee. After a good run and a cup of cowboy coffee, I was usually ready for just about anything.

We found eating in Japan very easy. Most restaurants have detailed pictures on the menu that take much of the uncertainty out of ordering. Some restaurants even have complete dishes arranged in the window, showing exactly what's on the menu. On occasion we invited the waitress out to the sidewalk to show her exactly what we had in mind. Takayama had a reputation for a unique type of miso soup with heavy homemade noodles. Noodle shops were quick, easy and inexpensive places to get a meal that would hold us for hours. Menus were limited and ordering was easy

Mornings were still the time of math classes. Carla had finished the English curriculum, but I still had a few sections to go in math. I just couldn't allow myself to let off on the lessons. Lesley seemed to have a real understanding of geometry and was benefiting from her previous year's algebra. I owed it to the girls to make sure they returned with the best I had to offer. One important lesson they came away with: I didn't teach them math, they learned it. I only guided them and helped when they had difficulties.

The countryside around Takayama was gentle rolling hills; we passed a few afternoons just walking the country lanes. The hostel had bicycles for rent, and we set out one morning after math class for an outdoor folk museum, located a couple of miles outside of town. The day was gray and a little misty. Peddling up the steep hills to the museum, we found it almost empty, except for a single busload of Japanese tourists. The museum consisted of a dozen or so traditional rural dwellings from different periods and locations around the island nation; they were clustered together among tall pines and millponds. Some of them bore a strikingly similarity to the massive all-under-one-roof dwellings in the Black Forest back in Germany.

In a matter of only a couple of days, we were back on a train for Kyoto, our last major stop in Japan. Andrea was taking a Self-Test and Lesley was completing exercises in a workbook. A succession of three trains took us from Takayama to Kyoto without a hitch. Train schedules are accurate to within about 30 seconds; most everything is easily marked, and for the first time in Japan we were on a train that had more passengers than seats. Before we knew it, we were pulling our bags along the platform in Kyoto.

The main train station in Kyoto takes a page from the film, *Star Wars*. This huge complex rises ten stories and stretches a thousand feet across the center of the city. It is a train station, hotel, shopping mall and an entertainment center that dominates the skyline for several blocks as you approach on foot. It is an alluring, vibrant place. The sharp rectilinear lines are in stark contrast to the massive columns, timbers and exaggerated upturned roofs of the sprawling Higashi Honganji, Nishi-Honganji and other Buddhist temples and shrines dotted around the city. Temples that date back hundreds of years to the time when Kyoto was the political and cultural center of Japan are major complexes, each occupying several city blocks. Their simple pagoda structures had a certain draw. They seemed to welcome travelers, offering refuge — a place of escape from the hyperactivity of the city.

Andrea, Lesley and I rose early and completed our morning run through Kyoto, jogging the circuit around the huge stone walls surrounding one temple complex. The air was a comfortable sixty degrees; we shared each other's company communicating only through our rhythmic breathing and the sound of our shoe soles on the damp pavement.

Our jogging routes had carried us from the rugged hills of Killarney and the Yorkshire dales, through the streets of Moscow, Prague and Paris, around the Coliseum in Rome and the Parthenon in Athens. There is hardly a more visceral way to connect with a city. Now Kyoto was another in our collection. The ponderous gates of the temple were just opening as we passed. The first of the morning pilgrims waited with Japanese composure.

The religious side of Japanese life is everywhere apparent but in no way strident or ostentatious. On a walk up a lonely mountain path we often came across simple shrines. They were usually attended, we surmised, by forest gnomes, because they were fastidiously kept but with no signs of human disturbance. The relationship of Shinto, the state sponsored religion until the Japanese constitution of 1947, and Buddhism is not readily appreciated by the casual Western traveler. A visit to a Shinto shrine or temple felt similar to Buddhist traditions that are widely accepted in Japan. Offerings to deities or Kami of the traditional Japanese folk religions are often made by tossing a few coins or small packets of rice near an object that symbolizes the Kami. The supplicant follows the act of offering by ringing a large bell, then two bows, two claps of the hands and a one final bow.

We figured out the city bus system and the underground in Kyoto pretty quickly and made several forays out into the surrounding communities for hikes through the hills. On one of our outings, we were fortunate enough to catch a river festival in the Arashiyama section of town near the Togetsu Bridge. The festival of elaborate barges, propelled by sturdy oarsmen, culminated in the laying of fans on the water. Those who understood the ceremony had rented rowboats and positioned themselves to retrieve the fans.

Along the banks was a crowd of Japanese onlookers, sporting every conceivable type of high tech camera, all of them on tripods with huge telephoto lenses. The Japanese penchant for the latest in optical gadgetry was in no way understated. Fidgeting with the complicated equipment and jostling for optimal position on the riverbank, the whirring of videos and slamming of hundreds of shutters drove the birds from the trees.

Feeling like characters in a Japanese film version of *Honey I Shrunk the Americans*, we continued on along the banks of the river through the bamboo forest of Sagano. It was remarkable. Lesley and Andrea walked ahead, while Carla and I were reduced to speaking in quiet, almost reverent tones. The towering green stalks, some eight inches in diameter, swayed listlessly in the humid breeze thirty feet above our heads and creating a cathedral-like ambiance; it was impossible not to stop in awe every few paces to try to regain a sense perspective in the filtered green light. The experience was infinitely Japanese.

On the May 21, 2002, we departed the Empire of the Rising Sun with enduring memories of crowded, fast-paced cities, alpine vistas, tranquil Buddhist shrines, and the warm and welcoming smiles of the Japanese people.

Chapter 8 _____

Australia and Rarotonga

IT WAS A BIG LEAP FROM JAPAN'S KANSAI AIRPORT to Australia's northeastern coastal city of Cairns in the diverse state of Queensland. Measured along a great circle, it was about 3,600 miles almost due south. Eleven months into our trip, we had realized the goal of crossing the equator.

Australia

Glad to be on the ground at Cairns, (pronounced cans, more-or-less), we headed over to the airport car rental desk, anxious to pick up our rental car. As we gathered up our gear, the man at the desk wished us the best and followed with, "And remember, stay out of the water, whatever you do."

This was a bit odd, I thought; we had come to northeastern Australia with precisely that in mind — going into the water, that is. "What do you mean?" I asked.

"Jellyfish," he answered.

"Well, we will just have to figure that one out when we get there," I replied, and off we went.

Foremost on our minds was the reunion awaiting us up the coast a few miles with my brother Mike from San Diego, his wife Liz and their two boys. They had decided to spend a couple of weeks in Australia, taking in the sights and sharing some time with us. Mike's young sons, Robert and Will, were excited about seeing our girls, and we were all looking forward to some familiar faces.

At the beach side motel in Palm Cove, Queensland, we found them enjoying a dip in the pool. Not really knowing what to expect from a family traveling for eleven months, Liz said, "You all look remarkably good." This was certainly welcome news to us. We had no idea how we appeared to others after these months of travel.

In celebration of the day, I broke out my well-traveled Venetian espresso maker and brewed cups of the real thing for our guests, while flying foxes, a type of enormous bat, foraged in the trees overhead and a kookaburra sent out a riotous call to a mate in the nearby hills. Then we settled in for a session of catching up on the news at home.

The shock of the World Trade Center disaster had begun to subside, but we anxiously listened to everything they had to tell us. Since Mike and his family had come to Australia on vacation, looking for a change of scene, we resolved to put it all aside and enjoy the time together. When it came to natural distractions, Far North Queensland was in every way obliging.

In spite of the fact that it was technically winter in the Southern Hemisphere, the weather was still warm and balmy. At Cairns we were only about 17 degrees south of the equator. With regard to climate, 30 degrees latitude is a useful reference. It is the latitude of Houston and also of Cairo, Egypt. Around 70–80 percent of Australia is nearer the Equator than 30 degrees latitude, making the climate more comparable to North Africa than to North America.

I asked the clerk at the motel desk about this "swimming thing." He explained that weather conditions in the early months of 2002 had not caused the seasonal die-off of the Box Jelly Fish, also known as stingers; they are common in the near shore waters of North Queensland. Fortunately these sometimes-fatal stingers are mostly a shallow water phenomenon and not present out on the Great Barrier Reef, our planned diving destination.

At the beach our kids eyed a small area enclosed by a net that was supposed to keep the stingers and sharks out, but it just didn't look all that convincing. The wind was up, and the net didn't appear to be holding up well in the surf. Reluctantly they turned to search for shells and climb trees, with the beach soon forgotten.

Aborigine culture is experiencing a growing appreciation, and we passed a day at the Tjapukai Village Aboriginal Cultural Center. Without a doubt, it was worth a day's commitment. There is a primal urge that makes some of us want to try our hand at launching a spear or throwing a boomerang. Our attempts were at least entertaining, and we found that greater age does not equate to greater skill. Since it was off-season,

Tjapukai Village Aboriginal Cultural Center near Cairns, Australia. Lesley, Uncle Mike and Cousin Will get boomerang-throwing lessons from an Aboriginal guide. Everyone duck! (Carla)

the park was lightly attended, and the guides and demonstrators were pleased to spend extra time with the kids. Trying to get a respectable sound from a didgeridoo is something I will have to work out during our next trip to Australia!

The range of mountains that runs more-or-less north-south through eastern Queensland is densely forested on the seaward side. Annual rainfall in Cairns is close to sixty inches, about fifty of which comes in the months from January to March. This intense rainfall over the past several million years has carved deep canyons where tropical vegetation finds a protected nursery. A sky-cable tramway took us soaring over the valley from coastal plain to the mountaintop and the backwoods town of Kuranda. But the kids agreed that the highlight was a day spent hiking and picnicking at Granite Gorge. Up and away from the coast, Granite Gorge was hotter and drier, and the crystal spring-fed pools were a natural swimming hole. We scrambled around the rocks, while families of miniature kangaroos called rock wallabies looked on warily.

Going Under in the Land Down Under

The city of Cairns originated in the latter part of the nineteenth century as a supply point for mining interests farther inland and began to flourish with the introduction of sugar cane in the twentieth century. The vibrant tourist Mecca that Cairns has become owes its success to Jacques Cousteau, the inventor of the self-contained underwater breathing apparatus (SCUBA) and also to its proximity to the world's largest living coral reef. Cairns is a jumping off point for numerous dive operators who shuttle divers out to larger dive boats that remain on the Great Barrier Reef. The larger boats can accommodate dozens of divers for stays of two or three days, or longer if you like.

The dive training the girls had received on the island of Koh Tao had been in preparation for our excursion out onto the Great Barrier Reef. We arranged for a two-day excursion to one of the reef dive boats. The water was perfectly clear, and the temperature comfortable, although a thin wet suit helped to extend the dives by warding off hypothermia that can set in even at 80 degrees Fahrenheit.

Mike's boys were a bit young for SCUBA, so they spent two unforgettable days discovering the warm blue water of the shallows around Green Island, a tiny coral cay surrounded by world class snorkeling. In fact, it has come to be known as the world's most eco-sensitive resort destination and is the only five star resort on the Great Barrier Reef.

The whole reason for being on a dive boat is to dive, then nap and eat enough so that you can dive again. It was a rewarding experience for Carla and me to watch as Andrea and Lesley confidently glided through the pristine water, exploring nooks and grottos for the likes of candy-striped shrimp, brightly colored surgeon fish and giant cod. Sometimes our field of view was entirely filled with swarms of darting sprites in rainbow colors. Before ascending the mooring line, we stopped for a photo op with a giant clam that measured nearly three feet across. Its iridescent pink and violet gills ruffled in the gentle surge. I think it smiled for the picture.

The ultimate experience was the night dive to Thetford Reef with only our underwater flashlights and a compass to guide the way. The four of us stayed closely packed together, like a small school of fish, afraid of losing each other on this distant side of the globe in a place most people only read about in magazines. There's nothing more "other worldly" than a night dive. The reef is entirely different in darkness; it is possible to glide next to a sleeping fish or see the luminous body of a squid gliding overhead. It is truly unforgettable. Carla's gift for navigation served us well and brought us back to the mooring line safely.

Regaining our land legs, we loaded our stuff into a tiny Toyota-mounted camper or caravan and headed north to the small village of Daintree.

Hiking around Cape Tribulation and Daintree Rainforest Environmental Centre is on well-marked trails that are sometimes elevated boardwalks to keep from disturbing the delicate vegetation of the forest floor. Protected from the intense sun by the tropical canopy, we paused to contemplate the empty caissons of the giant strangler fig that stand as reminders of the bygone tree that once provided support for the tenacious, reaching vines. What appeared to be a tree was just a network of crisscrossing vines sent down to the ground by the fig as it eventually engulfed and killed the tree.

An ecological island, the Daintree Rain Forest has been isolated for an estimated 135 million years and gone its separate evolutionary way. Prehistoric life forms were in abundance. Springing from the spongy damp forest floor along the trail were ten-foot-tall fern fronds unwinding like giant green millipedes. The warm rainforest air was filled with the odors of millions of years of accumulated vegetation, decay and re-growth. Every surface was covered with something moist and green. The area is home to over 3,000 plant species and 100 animal species. Local naturalists claim thirteen animal species are found only in the Far North Queensland forests. The elevated decks of the forest observation tower brought us face to face with rainbow colored birds and the reaching vines of the canopy. I think each of us felt smaller looking out from that vantage point in awe at this unique part of our world

Most notable among the indigenous fauna is the 18–20 foot long, man-eating estuarine crocodile. Unlike the comparatively shy alligator of the U.S. Gulf Coast, this Australian cousin is not a creature to be ignored. Our early morning boat ride through the backwater channels of the Daintree River estuary held the potential of encountering these ancient reptiles as they lay waiting for the warming rays of the sun. No one was tempted to drag a hand in the water!

Farther north, the Cape York Peninsula remains a wild and untamed corner of the world. With no paved roads, we prudently stayed on the tarmac or sealed roads as they are called in Australia, turned around and headed south to Cairns.

05/31/02 — Russ

We said our family goodbyes on the main street of Cairns. The boys, Robert and Will, were tired after a long day and a big dinner. They crawled into the back seat of their car and told us a sleepy farewell. Lesley and Andrea will miss the company. Back to the RV Park.

Heading South

Back on our routine, we were still plugging away at math. With only a few sections remaining, it looked like we would finish before arriving in Sydney, 1,300 miles to the south.

The Great Dividing Range runs pretty much north-south along the east coast of Australia and jogs inland only as far as about 300 miles. It essentially divides the narrow coastal strip, maybe 50 miles wide from the remaining 2,500 miles of savannah and arid outback that stretches endlessly off to the west. Ecologically the change is striking. As we crossed the ridge, it didn't take long to get a feeling for the term "outback." To the east things are green; to the west they are mostly tan to brown.

Small rural communities, founded by prospectors in search of gold and other minerals, have settled into a sleepy existence supporting the regional sheep and cattle stations (ranches). We were reminded of the cultural interface between English settlers and the indigenous people as we drove along the two-lane blacktop through towns with proper English names like Abingden Downs and Charters Towers, alternating with Goonyella and Boonderoo.

The uplands to the west and south of Cairns are reminiscent of the high plains of Texas or Wyoming. Reddish soils gave indication of volcanic origin as we headed into a sparsely forested region, aptly named the Forty Mile Scrub National Park. Rising above broad amber meadows, a few symmetrical promontories concealed depressions that in recent geological past (a couple hundred thousand years), yielded several cubic miles of runny black volcanic lava. This lava, similar to that of the Hawaiian Islands, tends to crust over on the top as it fills local depressions and fans out over the countryside. The surface crust becomes solid rock and flow channels become fully enclosed conduits for the outpouring of lava. In some cases the crust is sufficiently insulating that even as the volcanic source becomes depleted the lava in the conduits continues to flow. When it is all over and the lava drains out, the conduits are left empty and can run out a mile just beneath the surface of the land. The Undara Volcanic National Park is one of the best-preserved and accessible collections of lava tubes.

Bouncing along the dusty dirt tracks at Undara through grasslands dotted with clumps of spindly trees, we shared a tour van with some folks from Southern Australia and a couple from England. English spoken with three different accents made our conversation entertaining. With a light cloud of dust the van came to a halt, and we clambered up the gentle slopes of low lying volcanic vents. The cool dark tubes go entirely unnoticed from the road. However, plunging into the darkness with our eyes stretching wide to gather any available light, we entered an underground network of caverns ten to 15 feet across. Frozen for the rest of eternity, the smooth inner walls of the lava tubes looked as if it had been only a few years since the runny black lava had emptied out onto the prairie. A few remaining drips, stretching down from the ceiling, had cooled and solidified, forming something akin to stalactites. Hikes through the lava tubes engendered a cool almost prehistoric feeling.

Back on the surface, the squeaky suspension of our van startled an occasional kangaroo or wallabee or brightly colored tropical bird. Completely inured to the huge flocks of pink and white cockatoos that we would only see in a zoo, the Aussies didn't even turn their heads, accustomed as they were to this startling abundance of wildlife.

In the evening we sat around a campfire with fellow travelers and exchanged stories and jokes. In the reaching shadows at the edge of our circle of light, walaroos and bettongs, cousins to the kangaroo, picked about quietly. Lesley and Andrea were captivated by our furry visitors that stole pieces of Fruit Loops cereal that had been dropped nearby.

Australians, as a group, are the closest people you will find to Texans. Friendly and affable, it was never difficult to strike up a conversation. Dress is casual and unpretentious in clothes that fit the climate. Northeastern Australia was the only place on the planet that someone actually said they liked to hear the way we spoke English. Texans were not commonplace in towns along the dusty western slope of the Dividing Range. A stopover point along the way, Charters Towers, was a spic and span little community of red brick buildings and porticoed sidewalks with the history of a gold rush in its background.

We rolled along through dozens of tiny towns that looked like communities we might pass through on our regular trips through the western U.S. It was a delightful trip along what the map showed as a "Developmental Highway." Hundreds of miles of golden meadow, lacking any evidence of human habitation, streamed by peacefully. The otherwise unbroken land surface was regularly punctuated with six foot tall termite nests. The random shaped mounds were constructed from red clay soil and baked in the sun to a consistency of hard stucco; they looked like giant jack-o-lanterns sitting out in a sea of waving grass. Lesley and Andrea couldn't resist climbing one in an impromptu game of King of the Mountain.

A Developmental Highway, we found, was not a superhighway in the building. It was a single lane of blacktop that cut through the dense highland forest and prairies. The road had a fairly well developed crown that sloped to the shoulders for good drainage. Shoulders were stabilized by coarsely crushed rock. The significance of all these civil engineering details proved important to us as we found ourselves in an impromptu game of chicken with a "highway train" of freshly cut timber, headed in the oncoming direction. These highway trains are double and triple trailer rigs, moving at a rate just above what good judgment would allow. It was very clear to us who would do the yielding — the chicken!

These encounters meant lurching the top heavy little camper over to the sloping shoulder, while dodging bits of rock turned up by a passing monster. With not so much as a single tap of the horn, they vanished in the rear view mirror as quickly as they appeared, leaving swirling eddies of dust in the cool upland air.

Another curious thing was the massive front grillwork that many of the otherwise normal looking family sedans or station wagons sported. This, we came to realize, was a defense against the occasional kangaroo that happened to find himself in another one of those unfortunate games of chicken. Wallabees, kangaroos and every other variety of marsupials had adapted to the environment.

After several days of leisurely travel, we pulled into the tiny town of Sapphire to the Blue Gem Caravan Park. The sign above the communal

TV welcomed travelers; "The Blue Gem, Where There Are No Strangers, Only Friends You Haven't Met Yet." The television and outdoor barbeque grill were situated in the open shelter where the residents and travelers gathered in the evening for a beer and a televised rugby game.

Most everyone was there to spend a few days "fossicking" — digging around in the stream bed with shovel and sieves looking for sapphires, little greenish yellow chips of rock large enough to be cut and mounted by Barry of Barry's Rock and Jewelry, of course. The weather was perfect, and we passed a couple of days sifting through the dirt and coming away with some shinny bits of sapphire to show for our work. I think Carla would have had a couple set if we hadn't run out of time and needed to continue on south.

In my memory, our time in Sapphire was some of the most enjoyable. But the pressure of being crammed into a tiny RV, after traveling together for 358 days, finally boiled over between Andrea and me. There were some harsh words and a shove. I guess it was too much to ask to have no real conflicts with the constant pressures of travel, but I finally cracked under the strain and lost my temper. I suppose I was beginning to feel the pressures of returning to our conventional life, and there was no way to deny it. Nevertheless, we had a couple days of cool conversations.

06/11/02 — Russ

There is frost on the grass, and the sun is steadily burning its way through the gray shroud of fog that formed just before sunrise. I sit here at this old picnic table at the roadside rest we chose for a campsite last night and watch Lesley and Andrea poke at the fire. They are a little disappointed that I got up first and started it, but I didn't want to wait for them to get out of bed before I got warm.

This is day 365 for us. I can't think of a better way to start it off. I realize now how much I really enjoy the time we spend camping. There is nothing like staring into a fire before going to bed; and nothing like getting up in the cold fog in the morning for the first cup of coffee and a warm fire.

We have covered a lot of ground in the last year, and I don't know how it has affected us all, just that it has. Carla and I have watched the girls grow up on this trip. There is still a bit of child left in both of them, but they are more adult, perhaps wiser than they were when we left.

We are an interesting little tribe of individuals, all struggling to find our place on the planet. It is just that now our range of familiar, comfortable places is much larger.

I woke up startled a couple of days ago, realizing Lesley is soon to be 15 years old. Everyone always told me the time would go quickly, and in some ways it has. I feel lucky that when the opportunity to do something truly life changing presented itself that we took it. This year together has been a unique and I hope permanently bonding experience, especially for Lesley and Andrea.

The girls sit there silently, staring into the coals, warming themselves. I can't help but wonder what is going through their minds. I hope they have a million campfires to stare into and never lose the desire to do so.

We stopped for a couple of nights in the Bunya Mountains National Park, 140 miles northwest of Brisbane. It seemed a bit off the beaten path, since the lead in from the north was very steep and quite narrow. I was surprised the little Toyota had the power to make the climb. In total darkness, a light rain began to fall as we parked our miniature caravan in a vacant field.

The next morning we found it difficult to open the door of the camper; a horde of outdoor enthusiasts had filled every available square foot of space. Australians have a great love of the outdoors. An escape from the sultry lowlands along the coast, the Bunya Mountains is a favorite weekend destination.

Another of Australia's ecological islands, the Bunyas are home to an ancient species of pine tree, the Bunya pine (*Araucaria bidwillii*). They grow well over a hundred feet tall, the tallest measuring 169 feet, and have a very primordial appearance. On other continents, they seem to have gone out of existence, and there does not appear to be any fossil evidence of Bunya pine in recent geological sedimentary rocks. There were, however, abundant Araucaria species in the periods before 65 million years ago in rocks found in South America. As a result, these little colonies are unique, and the Bunya is sometimes referred to as the dinosaur tree. Every three years the trees produce huge pine cones that contain starchy pine nuts, each two to three inches in length. Aboriginal tribes subsisted on these nuts for thousands of years. The Bunya harvest was a time of social gathering and great celebration among the indigenous tribes of the region. Harvesting rights to a particular tree were passed down through generations. Foothold notches used to assist in scaling the huge trees were still plain to see. During our short stay, we had our fair share of Bunya nut muffins and cookies, or rather biscuits, in the local shops.

Descending the winding road on the west side of the Bunyas, the utter vastness that is Australia stretched out before us. Looking out across the undulating pasture of the Darling Downs, one could almost sense the curvature of the earth. It felt as though we could see all the way across the continent to Cape Inscription 2,400 miles away.

Driven on by the passage of time, we continued our trek south through Brisbane and on to Sydney. With only a week left of a year long journey, we were lucky enough to have the opportunity to renew a friendship with Bev and Peter Leszinsky, an Australian couple we had known back in Texas. They welcomed us into their home for a couple of days, while we made final arrangements to return the RV and prepare for the long trip home. Their two daughters, Anya and Mia, had been in an Indian Princess tribe with our girls for several years at our neighborhood YMCA.

It was coming on to winter in Sydney, and we enjoyed the cool weather, while making a circuit of the famous Sidney Opera house in the arching shadow of the harbor bridge. The coast around Sydney could be likened to the upper northwest of the U.S. Rugged green hills conceal dozens of small inlets and bays. To the west, the Blue Mountains, a stack of sedimentary rocks dissected by step canyons, rise to an elevation of 3,600 feet. Anxious to send us away with an appreciation of the natural beauty, Bev and Peter led us on a truly exquisite excursion out across the Blue Mountains and through the broad limestone tablelands to Jenolan Caves, near the town of Katoomba. The caves were truly world class, as were our friends. After a day of hiking we did our best to solve the world's problems over a glass of Australian wine.

In the midst of all the preparations and socializing, we arranged a visit with a fairly distant branch of the family. I had been told since childhood that some of those who left County Tipperary, Ireland, had migrated to the U.S. while others struck out for Australia. I was determined to make contact.

With a few fragments of information from the folks back in Ireland, we were able to contact Berenice and Mike Smith. I had sent them a letter from somewhere along the way explaining who we were and that we would be coming through Sydney sometime around June 2002. I would not have been too surprised if they had chosen not to respond to this unknown bunch of itinerants, but as the time drew near we traded e-mails and arranged a brief meeting. In true Australian style, they welcomed us; we spent our last evening in Australia getting to know each other and trying to figure if we were really in any way related. They have a charming daughter, Nerida, and two handsome young sons, Adam and Simon, who did their best to make conversation with very reticent Lesley and Andrea. It all made for a common thread, admittedly tenuous, and some good conversation. I firmly believe that taking those little risks is what makes life interesting.

We spent our last night in Australia in a cozy RV park about a block off of Botany Bay. Rising on the morning of the seventeenth of July, we made our last checks for lost socks stuck under the seat cushions and found our way through the warehouse district where we returned our little camper to its rightful owner. It had been a marvelous three weeks and 1,300 miles down Australia's eastern coast.

A couple of delays for mechanical reasons and various details had us making an unplanned overnight stop in Aukland, New Zealand. Undaunted by a drizzly morning we dashed into town for a quick plate of fish and chips at the local seaman's center. With scarcely enough time to eat, we finished our lunch and set out for a brief walking tour around Aukland's port.

The drizzle turned into a downpour; we jumped into a cab that had stopped at a light. The polite young cabbie appeared to be of Middle Eastern origin, dressed in a pressed and laundered blue blazer; white shirt and tie. He welcomed us in, pointed his cab in the direction of the airport and promptly installed his favorite RAP cassette, presumably for the benefit of Lesley and Andrea. Climbing out into the clearing air, we settled up and left "RAP" behind us.

Rarotonga, The Cook Islands

Trying to forestall the inevitable as long as possible, the opportunity presented itself to make one last stop on the flight back to the U.S. The tiny island of Rarotonga is one of about fifteen islands in a group known as the Cook Islands. They are located just east of the International Dateline and are scattered across an area of over 1,500 square miles of the South Pacific. The total land area of the entire group could be put into a square ten miles by ten miles.

The Cook Islands are a semi-independent autonomous country divided into the southern group that includes the most populated island Rarotonga and its neighbors Mangaia, Atiu and Aitutaki. The northern group comprises such memorable designations as Rakahanga, Manihiki and Pukapuka. First exposed to Westerners in 1595 when Alvaro de Mendana stopped at Pukapuka for provisions, the islands are not overrun with tourists and have retained their essentially Maori culture.

We had been lucky enough to find a little cottage via the Internet where we could cook our last few meals, sit on the porch, drink coffee and feed the dozens of chicken that ran freely among the tilting palms and hibiscus bushes. Carla and I had agreed not to get overly anxious about tourist attractions and to just relax. Nevertheless, inveterate tourist that I am, the first morning on the island I found myself making reservations to visit the local Maori Cultural Center for their demonstrations. Carla coaxed us into the local museum, and we did finally attend an "Island Night" at one of the local hotels.

Rarotonga and its sister islands are the closest thing to a tropical paradise that anyone can hope to find. It was the perfect place in which to calm our minds before returning to our civilization. The main island, Rarotonga, the largest of the group, is about 20 miles in circumference, surrounded by intensely turquoise water. Deep shades of green cover all but the craggy summit of the mountainous core of the island. There is a paved road all the way around the island and every hour two small buses set out in opposite directions. Riders just flag them down.

Afoot again, we made the hike over the top of the island past Needle Peak. That little venture almost finished off my leather shoes. After a couple of impromptu fixes in India and China, it looked like they were actually going to make the full trip — much to the credit of the Bass Shoe Company.

Rarotonga, The Cook Islands. The final day of a year-long dream, counting up shells and stowing away memories. (Carla)

I will always remember the afternoon of our last day, drifting along the deserted beach, picking up shells, all in quiet reflection — and asking myself countless questions.

We had come a long, long way since Tipperary.

What had we done? Where had we been? Had we truly paid attention to every minute? How had we changed? What would we do when we got back?

Uncertainty was something we had come to accept as a central theme of our daily lives. I had no earthly idea how I was going to make a living, only the confidence that after making it once around the globe, I would just have to figure it out. My feeling, prior to our departure, had been:

I could conceive of no greater gift to give to my children.

The second part of that feeling is that the value of a gift is in some measure related to the level of risk or sacrifice accepted by the giver.

06/21/02 — Russ

Today we will pack our things for one of the last times, actually the last time on what would be considered "the trip." I must admit at times I have to struggle with a little surge of emotion as I look back over the past twelve months. The daily effort, the edge we have developed, constantly making decisions, actively guiding the course of each day. In some ways it was like a dream. I can see us in so many different situations — in trains and buses, apartments or cottages, on hikes in the jungle or a crowded market surrounded by exotic fruits and vegetables. We haven't done it all, and there is plenty left to see and do. But we have opened the door and expanded our awareness of the world.

I am truly thankful that we recognized the opportunity when it presented itself — that we had the courage and resolve to take advantage of it.

Re-entry, LAX

I THINK EACH OF US WAS SURPRISED TO gauge his or her own individual reaction as we arrived back in the U.S., passing through passport control and picking up our gear for the last time. We had really become travelers, and Los Angeles felt like just another stop. If our actions were any reflection of what we missed most, we all headed for a plate of Mexican food at the cantina in the airport.

The girls were anxious to get back to our street — the old familiar places — but at the same time apprehensive about seeing the friends they had left behind. There was also a feeling of not wanting to reach out too quickly and break the spell that had bound us together for 376 days and carried us over 50,000 miles. We had learned the utter pleasure of togetherness.

Home Again

In Houston we moved back into the same motel we had stayed in before our departure, until we could gather the keys to storage facilities, get the car started and have the utilities turned back on in our house. What lay ahead was moving back into the house, getting unpacked, replacing a refrigerator and a microwave, and beginning to start over from where we had left off.

Without fanfare or ceremony I carried my one pair of walking shoes into the garage at home and listened as they landed heavily at the bottom of the empty trash container. They had served me well, but it was time for them to go. Still — all was not lost.

Safely stashed at the bottom of my daypack was our emergency provision. The PayDay candy bar was intact; it would be held in ready reserve — until the spirit moved us to do it again.

Planning the World Trek

Looking back, nothing was more important to the overall success of our trip than planning. Carla did the majority of the planning, and it is her voice you will hear in this section of the book.

The most common question we are asked, "How did you ever plan such a trip?" can be answered in a few words: planning began before the decision to take the trip was finalized and continued until the last suitcase was unpacked for the last stop — home.

Another version is, "How long did it take to plan for a one year trip?" Easy answer — one year plus many prior years of dreaming. After the big decision, I stopped working and devoted endless hours to Internet surfing, phone calls and travel guide reading. No hardship there, as these are some of my favorite pastimes. Most surprising was how many facets were involved.

What resources were needed? It all started with a good library and an Internet connection for surfing the web. International friends who travel abroad offered advice freely. A travel agent/friend also accepted endless questions, while a trustworthy ticket consolidator picked up tasks we could not do ourselves. Lastly we allowed plenty of time for dreaming.

Building on the experience of travel authors and friends allowed us to move from the starting point sooner. I address here the various categories of tasks and helpful information for tackling a trip such as ours.

The Time Line

A good project manager knows the first step in any major undertaking is making a time line of essential tasks. We chose Microsoft Project to set up critical path charts. That is where it got technical. We soon realized how many major and minor tasks were involved in trip planning and preparing to leave our home for a year. Certain tasks had to be done sequentially for the proper outcome at the right time. It was vital not to forget anything. An example simplified task list is shown to the right to give an idea of what needed to be considered. Tasks were assigned to each person, both to share the experience and to insure that all work was tracked by a responsible party.

Research

This is an exciting part of the planning process. All you need is a computer, a relatively high-speed connection and a reliable printer with several ink cartridges. Did I forget to mention, it takes time – lots of time!

HINTS

- Do a search on "around the world travel."

- Look for travel forums on locations you might want to visit.

- Join discussion groups.

- Read, ask questions, collect opinions.

- Surf the web and learn.

Where Do We Go?

The first logical step was to select countries we wanted to visit. But with four minds eagerly working in different directions and myriad possibilities, this became quite a task. On a large *National Geographic* world map we each placed dots on our favorite countries. Then, back to

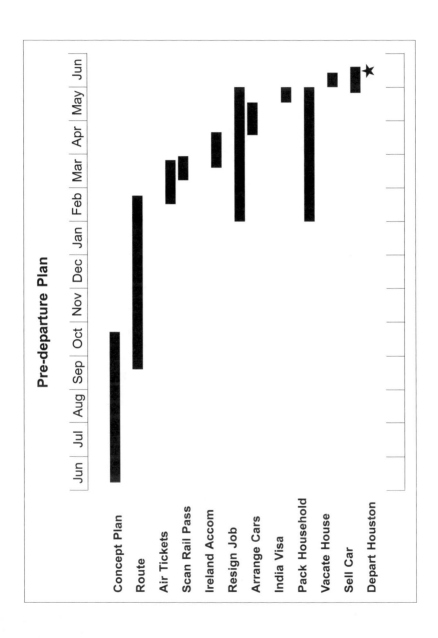

kindergarten — we started connecting the dots. Patterns began to emerge; the path led to some favorite spot one of us had always wanted to visit.

According to some schools of travel, we could have seen 365 countries in 365 days. I shudder to think about that! We would have been truly homeless! Instead, our weekly family meeting produced a plan to stay in most large countries for one month and less in smaller, closely spaced European countries. That way we could devote one week to each of several areas within a particular country. This list kept changing until at least halfway through the planning year. It is impossible to see everything. So you just have to accept that and try not to run yourselves ragged.

In the first few countries we attempted to choose these weekly locations but left later countries for future decisions. The real goal was to investigate each country well enough to identify a mix of historic, scenic, rural and metropolitan areas that would give us a good feel for the culture. Travel books from the library were useful, but our best resource was the Internet. Each country and region had tourist bureau websites with varying amounts of detailed information. See the facing page for our preliminary time line for the first half of the trip and page 234 for the time line for the second half of the trip.

How to Get There

Many people have heard about "around-the-world" tickets offered by some airlines that formed alliances with other international airlines. For certain people these are very attractive for both cost and ease of use. Airlines offer a variety of set itineraries to the most popular destinations, including Circle-the-Globe or Circle-the-Pacific tickets. Of course, we never seemed to do things the easy way, and those tickets just didn't fit our plans. Two restrictions knocked these tickets from consideration: In most cases you can't change hemispheres, plus you can't backtrack. In addition, there were major segments where we wanted to take ground and sea transportation.

Of course, transportation on a trip like ours was a major expense, and we made every effort to keep costs down. The best option for our style of travel was to use a ticket consolidator who purchases batches of airline tickets at discount prices primarily from international airlines. Consolidators offer no frills, so don't expect to get much travel advice,

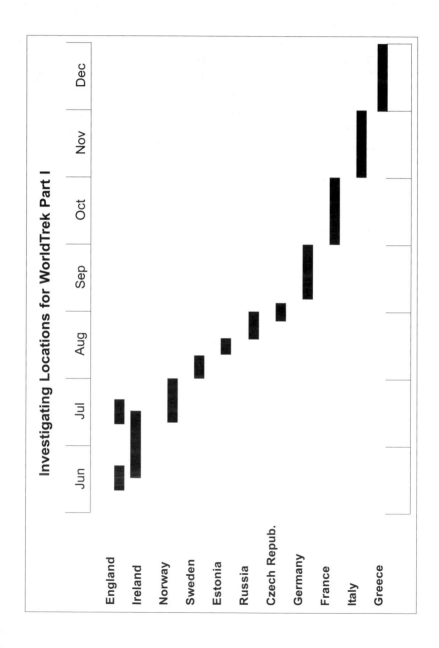

continued on the next page

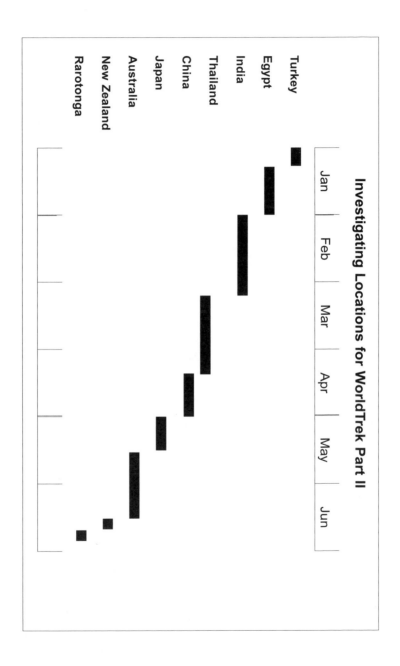

but the price is right! An excellent resource for learning about cheap airfare is the book, *The Practical Nomad: How to Travel Around the World* by Edward Hasbrouck (Avalon Travel Publishing); it contains not only recommendations but also gives an excellent understanding of the process. (See the Resources section of this appendix.)

We were only able to purchase tickets for the first six months of travel before leaving the U.S. Consolidator's discount tickets are generally not available any farther in advance than that. Not a problem — we hadn't tied down any lodging plans past the first three months either. I spent so much time on the Internet with the ticket consolidator that our daughters began to think that "Jack the Airbroker" was part of the family.

Transportation was definitely a significant part of our adventure, since it varied so much around the world. The longest hops we made by plane, using international airlines wherever possible. Yes, even airlines offered their own cultures and challenges, such as deciphering signs and schedules on Russia's Aeroflot or Air China, sampling the exquisite airline food aboard Air France or listening to stewardess' announcements on Air Egypt.

Ground Transportation

No mode of transportation is off limits to the world traveler; we took it as a challenge to try each one. To cover significant distances without flying there were four options: car, train, bus and ferry. Desirability of each depends on who you are and where you are. Trains and buses topped our desirable list with the objective to meet and interact with as many people as possible. But for economy of travel with four people in Europe, we couldn't beat a leased car.

Several car companies offer short-term leases on cars with options to pick up and drop in different cities or countries. We primarily considered Renault and Peugeot, choosing the latter both for price and locations (see Resource section). A car must be reserved and contract signed before leaving the U.S., which meant giving definite dates for our rental period, which turned out to be a little over eleven weeks. This was a much cheaper option than renting a car, even with weekly discount rates. A Eurail Pass would have been great fun, but for four people the leased car price won. Although we were isolated from everyone else by our family "box," it allowed us to explore many less developed areas in Europe, such as France's Gorges du Tarn, than would have been possible using public transportation. As in all decisions the advantages must be weighed against the disadvantages. One significant factor in choosing a car was volume of trunk space. Four mediums to large backpacks plus groceries and miscellaneous items meant that closing the trunk lid was often a two-person affair. I'm sure we looked like a comic team to bystanders!

Trains are an excellent mode of transport. Rail passes are more economical when traveling in Britain, Scandinavia, Europe or Japan than buying several individual tickets, especially since we planned to move around a bit. A BritRail, ScanRail, Eurail or Japan Rail Pass allowed us to hop on a train without any reservations and was the ultimate in spontaneous travel. For lowest prices, purchase these passes before leaving the U.S.. In fact, some passes such as BritRail and Japan cannot be purchased once you arrive in that country. Be aware, though;, many travel agents don't have much experience with obtaining these rail passes, and you may need to guide them through the process. Or just purchase them online. I recommend using Standard rather than first class seating to save a bundle and have the opportunity to talk with other travelers. A FlexiPass let us ride trains for a set number of days (four, eight or fifteen days) in two months for a more leisurely style, whereas the pass that covered consecutive days of travel required travel every day for your ticket period of four, eight, fifteen, twenty-two or thirty days which was too much moving around for us.

Flying into London Heathrow or Gatewick Airports, it was worthwhile to purchase an additional Airport Express Pass to avoid the high cost of taxi travel to downtown London. The trains leave from the airport terminal and are used by many passengers with their luggage, so we weren't the only ones dragging our suitcases onto the train. A London Visitor Travel Card was also good, since we were spending several days in the city, and the London Pass for admission to a menu of tourist attractions may also be worthwhile. Just make sure it includes the things you want to see. Cost of all these passes mounts up quickly; we made some hard choices on what we really wanted to visit.

In all countries, travel by first class sleeper trains may give you a slightly better night's rest, but you are insulated from other people on the train. We were advised to take first class in China, but I would like to return and try second class. A second class A/C Sleeper in India was both comfortable and an experience not to be missed; it came with a continuous supply of food from vendors wandering the aisles. Don't expect much from the restrooms, though. When we didn't have a rail pass, purchasing onward bound train tickets at the station as soon as we arrived at a location insured that seats/beds were available when we wanted to continue traveling.

Bus travel could also be arranged on the spot in most cases. This was a good budget travel option with great opportunities for people watching, elbow rubbing (and sometimes more, as in Rome) and eaves-dropping. My dad taught me that you will make many instant friends by something as simple as sharing a pack of gum on a bus! Quality ranges from basic school bus-style seats to VIP reclining, padded-seat buses, but all are carefree. As always, it was prudent to watch the luggage being unloaded at intermediate stops to make sure our bags weren't removed by mistake.

Ferries were a relaxing way to travel across water. We used them between England and Norway; Finland and Estonia; Italy and Greece. For various crossings we purchased tickets while in the U.S. via Inter-net, at overseas travel agents and at ferry counters abroad. During peak travel times (i.e. the summer) it was best to make reservations as early as possible, since we wanted a cabin for overnight crossings. Frequent pro-motional programs reduced the cost significantly. In most cases these were large vessels with comfortable seating, dining and duty free shop-ping areas. Some were down right deluxe!

Of course, the best transportation was by shoe. Our philosophy was that the only way to really experience any location was by walking. We did this for mile after mile after mile — so much so that, upon returning, our daughter's schools awarded them physical education (PE) credit for the trip!

A good pair of walking shoes was essential, especially a pair that was broken in before starting those long walks. My favorites were basic shoes from Rockport with a chrome-tanned leather that can go through rain and snow, and still come out looking good. We discouraged the athletic shoe look, since it was informal and typically identified the wearer as an American. (We were hoping to blend in and avoid the overly casual appearance that typifies many U.S. tourists.) Comfort was really num-ber one; the best sights were to be found by walking the back streets in St. Petersburg, Paris, Beijing or any other locale.

Where to Stay

Well, it depends. Or should I say, "It depends on your travel style, budget and expectations." Wherever we have traveled, the night's accommodations were considered a place to rest between adventure days. I could sleep in a Five Star hotel or a One Star motor inn, nestled in a hammock or on the ground. It just didn't matter so long as the sheets were clean and a bathroom was nearby.

Hostels — contrary to the old image — are not just for backpacking college students anymore. Of course, some of the people, a few years back, were those students, but the facilities have changed as the backpackers aged. Hostels now actively recruit families with designated family rooms and group prices. As a family of four we sometimes rented a private family room that often had a private bath. With two sets of bunk beds, the adults got a lower berth, especially if we pulled rank. This was not a problem in Japan, since a ryokan (a small, traditional-style Japanese hotel) had rooms with tatami mats where everyone slept on the floor. For community bathrooms a long nightshirt or robe was handy for those middle of the night dashes, although waiting lines were never a problem. My favorite hostel was an old converted hotel in Balestrand, Norway. The rooms were comfortable with two people each. The bathrooms had heated floors, very welcome on chilly July mornings. Other memorable hostels were the Daoist temple in Japan and a timbered house in Germany. With advance reservations we could have stayed in Scottish castles or even on a boat in Oslo, Norway.

To take advantage of the reduced member prices, it was necessary to join our country's chapter of the International Youth Hostel Federation. In the U.S. this is Hostelling International. Membership is free for children younger than 18. There is an annual fee for adults and seniors. We received a membership card, recognized at IY Hostels around the world with access to a great Internet reservation system we used at many Internet cafés. We also took advantage of their free e-mail system, called EKit, designed for use anywhere; this included calling cards for international calls at the least expensive rates I found. We had difficulty using these cards in many locations, though. The best method we found for making calls was to purchase a local phone card we could use at any location in that country at a low cost. There are also international cell phones at more reasonable purchase prices now; these may offer a better option.

Many great private hostels with budget prices are listed on other websites. To check their quality we joined some of the travel forums and ask if anyone else had stayed there. This was especially helpful when we were looking at the Hostel Asia in Moscow, where the IY Hostel had a poor reputation among backpackers. Several of the websites listed in the Resources section have links where reliable information on hostels or other backpacker favorites may be found.

A note about sleeping accommodations outside the U.S. — rooms generally have beds for only two or three people. As a family of four, we were often required to rent two rooms, the privacy of which was much appreciated by our teenage daughters. In fact, the girls almost felt like royalty when given their own large suite at no extra cost on the top floor of a Cairo hotel. Egypt's tourism had been devastated by post 9/11 travel fears and may have accounted for this largesse. Separate bedrooms kept family harmony as we, the parents, did not have to witness firsthand our daughters' incredible exploding suitcases that immediately filled any and all available space.

Budget accommodations abound around the world. "Self-catering" is a common term for rentals used by Europeans; that and "vacation rentals" are helpful terms to use for Internet searching. Some agencies will send catalogues of rentals with detailed descriptions and reservation forms. Most are able to make and change reservations online. One difficulty we encountered was rental confirmations sent to our U.S. home address, even after we were traveling. Difficulties can't always be avoided, but sometimes companies will fax the paperwork to a postal station or hotel for you.

Reservations

With all of the hundreds of reservations we made over the Internet, only one didn't work out. We had trouble finding Internet cafés in western Germany and didn't get a booking confirmation for a Paris apartment in time. Other than that, reservations through a variety of companies and individuals worked flawlessly. We used a separate credit card for these online payments rather than our ATM card. Our reason for doing this? If the number of the card was stolen, no one could empty the checking account connected to our ATM/VISA card.

Prevention — Stay Healthy!

Foreign travel frequently necessitates reviewing your medical history followed by a pre-trip visit to an international vaccination specialist. To prepare for this visit, we had three tasks:

1. List our destination countries plus the order we would visit them and anticipated length of stay.

2. Review of medical records for each person in our family, listing past vaccinations and boosters with dates.

3. Collect data from the Center for Disease Control (CDC) website, National Center for Infectious Diseases – Travelers Health pages. There are destinations guides by country or region that list current disease problems and recommended vaccinations. Be sure to maintain a cool head and don't let this scare you, because the descriptions are quite complete.

When visiting a doctor it is best to bring along as much knowledge and specific information as possible. We prepared a list of recommended shots for each country, and those suggesting preventative medicines such as for malaria. This detailed list we gave to the doctor and told him what we thought was needed. He made a couple of suggestions but basically agreed. I don't think he would have devoted the time to working it so completely or would have truly realized the extent of our proposed travels otherwise.

The one book that accompanied us the entire journey was *Staying Healthy in Asia, Africa, and Latin America* by Dirk G. Schroeder (Moon Travel Handbooks). Part first aid guide, part illness diagnosis and treatment, this book gave us a reasonable idea of what was going on before we had to communicate with a doctor or pharmacist. I highly recommend reading this or a similar book prior to departing and during your trip.

Center for Disease Control also sells the *CDC Yellow Book: Health Information for International Travel*. It is updated every two years and may also be available in your library.

Since one of our quartet takes prescription medicines, additional planning was also required. It was necessary to obtain a supply of the medication that would last the length of the trip plus an additional two weeks or more, so that we were not scrambling to get a refill immediately upon returning. We purchased a thirteen-month supply, since our trip was scheduled for one year. The major disadvantage was that most prescription programs would only pay for a ninety-day supply at their reduced rate. We had to find the correct person to authorize filling the prescription for this longer time period. It cost more but just became part of the budget.

Rather than carrying several bottles with us and risking that they would be seized at some dark border crossing where we were mistaken for drug smugglers, we placed a four-month supply in two of the boxes to be sent en route. This worked well, though there was the risk that the packages might not arrive.

Travel and Medical Insurance

Have you ever made reservations for a trip where the travel agent recommended you purchase trip insurance? How can you possibly cover travel for an entire year? Even the consolidators at Airbrokers and AirTreks will suggest companies for travel cancellation and medical insurance; however, they were not pushing it like some travel agents do.

Medical insurance was a serious consideration on the trip. No one anticipates or wishes to become ill or injured while traveling, but sometimes it happens. Although medical help is available anywhere in the world, a good insurance plan makes obtaining treatment much easier and less costly. Many U.S. insurance policies will cover you outside of the U.S. while on vacation; however, it is wise to check restrictions. It may be necessary to call for treatment pre-approval, even from a place like Bangkok.

One of the side effects of Russ quitting his job was potential loss of medical insurance. We solved this by applying for coverage under a law known as COBRA (Consolidated Omnibus Budget Reconciliation Act of 1985) which requires that most employers sponsoring group health plans offer a temporary extension of health coverage at group rates in cases such as loss of job. Although only good for the short term, it covered us on our yearlong trip. This continuation of coverage had to be requested in writing from our former employer. This coverage may last from eighteen months to three years, depending on why the health care insurance was terminated. It is advisable to maintain all the same health coverage you would have at home.

Our insurance company was also associated with the Assist America travel assistances program. If we traveled 100 miles or more from home or to a foreign country (yup, that's us!), then we had access to emergency medical assistance. They offered an international network of 10,250 physicians and relationships with more than 8,600 hospitals and clinics. Included were medical consultation and evaluation, medical referrals, hospital admission guarantee, critical care monitoring and, if medically necessary, evacuation by some expeditious form of transportation to the nearest facility offering appropriate treatment. They would arrange and pay for repatriation, if medically necessary, including care of minor children left stranded by a parent's emergency.

Before purchasing travel insurance, it was important to thoroughly quiz our own insurance company to see what less known benefits they provided. It saved us from paying for coverage we already had. This was especially true for the medical repatriation, as that seems to be a common carrot from the travel folks. Not all travel agents are familiar with this, so it pays to investigate on your own.

Many companies, including AAA, offer trip cancellation travel insurance. We chose a relatively low level of coverage for cancellation of one or two segments of air travel. Since they didn't require that we specify which tickets we were covering or which travel dates, we just considered each new segment to be the one covered. It worked for the insurance company, it worked for us and it kept costs down. Trying to insure the entire year's worth of travel would have been expensive and unnecessary.

Home Obligations — Bills, Repairs, Furniture

Leaving the country brought new questions as homeowners, such as deciding if the house would stay vacant, be rented or sold. Would our furniture remain or be moved out? We decided to rent the house for the year and store all of our belongings. A rental agent was vital; we needed someone to handle any problems that might arise in our absence. Even so, it necessitated changing utility billing, setting up a post office box for mail, changing numerous addresses and lots of other details.

Then there was the actual packing and moving of everything we owned. It was an opportunity to sort through 15 years of living in the same house. All were moved to a storage facility down the road, piece by piece. My biggest concern was for the piano. When the last box was stored we were ready to leave.

Wills and Other Things You'd Rather Not Think About

Okay, something must be said about the subject of wills. There is the remote possibility that Big Foot will stomp through your camp at midnight, carry you and your significant other to the high Andes, leaving your children to fend for themselves.

Think about updating your will or having one drawn up before leaving the country on an extended trip. That way your children and/or possessions won't be sitting in a basket on Aunt Shari's doorstep hoping for adoption in case you don't return. A guardian was appointed for our children, spelling out how they will be supported with monies from the estate and when the inheritance comes into their control. It was worth securing the services of an attorney to do this correctly, and it gave us peace of mind.

All documents such as a will and investment/financial records should be checked to make sure addresses are correct and that someone you trust has the key to your safe deposit box. We were able to leave knowing that for once in our lives all of our affairs were in order.

Driving Abroad

At some point we planned to lease or rent vehicles, so it was necessary to have international drivers' licenses. These are easily obtained at the local AAA office, whether you are a card carrying AAA member or not. Bring a passport photo with you. This was the easiest part of our pre-trip arrangements. It also gave us an additional ID that was recognized in most countries. Of course, there are some countries where we decided that driving was best left to the locals, for instance—India and Egypt. AAA can also take passport photos and exchange some currencies on the spot to give you cash for starting out. This really wasn't necessary, though, since ATM machines are found almost everywhere.

Planning on the Fly

Two things made on-the-fly planning possible: local tourist offices and Internet cafés found in most towns or cities around the world. These, plus a good idea of what we wished to do, made on the road reservations workable, if not easy.

Even in most small towns local tourist offices maintain listings of cottages and flats available for short-term rental. They were always helpful in arranging on-the-spot rentals by the week or more, since this seemed to be a very common way of taking a holiday, especially in Europe. We simply walked in, found the person with an accommodations list, stated our requirements for sleeping arrangements and location, then gave them our acceptable price range. They generally called owners on the spot and made arrangements to view the house/cottage/flat/room. Rentals ranged from basic to deluxe with varied locations from downtown to country estates. Occasionally a very reasonable locator's fee was charged. In some towns these arrangements could be made ahead by Internet or phone by contacting the tourist office directly. We didn't find this necessary, though.

In as many locations as possible we rented accommodations for a week at a time. Although we were vagabonds upon entering a town, we never failed to find a treasure of accommodations at a reasonable price. This gave us a feeling of stability, allowed economizing by cooking our own meals and gave a point from which to see the sights. After one week we always sensed it was time to move on. I still get that feeling of restlessness and yearn for the excitement of reaching a new destination.

Within a short time we established a routine for entering a new week in a new town:

1. Find a grocery store and buy supplies for two days of meals. (We often arrived on the weekend and found markets were closed on Sunday.)

2. Locate the tourist office for accommodations, maps and information on local sites.

3. Find a rail or bus station and buy advance tickets for departure.

4. Identify the closest Internet café and its hours.

5. Look for a place to do laundry.

The Internet

Concerned about the quality or location of hostels and other places you find on the Internet? We found the chat rooms and bulletin boards of travel publications such as *Lonely Planet*, *Let's Go* and *Rough Guides* to be helpful. Their experience-based and frank assessments of cleanliness, friendliness and ease of finding the place were valuable and accurate. We posted questions on where to go for must-see destinations, best times of year to see the local festivals and hidden treasures not found in books. Of course, it was necessary to take some of the advice received with a grain of salt. One person's taste may not be another's.

On the road the Internet was our lifeline for making and confirming reservations. Internet cafés were much more prevalent in other countries than in the U.S. The charge may be by the minute or by the hour. Often the location had a dozen or more computers in a room with people busily typing away. In Germany we ran into coin-operated computers at hostels where it was necessary to continually put in coins while surfing. If you ran out of time, then you were disconnected from your website and had to start the connection all over. Some countries, such as Germany, also had slightly different keyboards that made typing a much slower operation.

Clothing

Do you remember those mix-and-match articles about getting twenty looks out of five pieces of clothing? Choices require careful consideration when you are attempting to fit a year's worth of apparel into one suitcase. For that reason one of my new favorite stores is the Travel Smith catalog, along with other brands, like REI, made specifically for travelers.

Several qualities were important in our clothing. Synthetics dry quickly, resist stains well and don't sag after long train rides. They don't require ironing and usually pack into much less space than their natural fiber counterparts. High tech synthetics are especially durable and look good, too. There were many periods where our laundry was washed in the bathroom sink and dried on our traveling clothes line. Denim was definitely out!

Layering was also important to adjust to varying climates. A rain-coat works well in snowy conditions with sufficient layers underneath. Silk-weight underwear transforms many clothes for inclement weather. Styles were conservative to go from casual to more formal situations such as the opera, while respecting local culture and not advertising "tourist" immediately.

Packing

What would you need on a one-year trip? How many climates, how many seasons, what social situations and customs will you encounter? As you can guess, the possibilities are almost endless. So how do you pack for an entire year of travel?

We started by considering how much and what type of luggage to take. From previous experiences on trains and buses, we knew there would be times when mobility and weight would become really impor-tant. A new breed of wheeled luggage that converts to a backpack ap-pealed to us right away. With wheels, it could be pulled most of the time, but also worn like a backpack when you found, as we did in Sweden, that the hostel was up a steep, damp gravel road from the train station. This luggage comes in various sizes from small to humongous. REI and Eagle Creek bags were the best for us, but many other good brands are available. It was also important that all zippered openings have locks to prevent curious hands from investigating luggage contents. Locks on all four of our bags were set to the same combination, making customs and airport checks easier. Once available space was known, it was time to critically assess the growing piles of clothing and other necessities.

We are dedicated list makers in our family. It seems the best ideas occur in the shower, at three o'clock in the morning or while driving in heavy traffic; a list to jot down thoughts is essential. For this reason our packing lists were begun early in the planning stage; this allowed for adjustments as we learned more about our destinations. Any items, not to be used before the trip, were placed in a "travel" box. Finally, the task of eliminating nonessential items was begun and continued until the last zipper was zipped prior to departure.

Languages

Good phrase books for each language are a necessity. We had purchased several of these before leaving but not enough. At times it was difficult to find the English to another language conversion, although some were available from Lonely Planet. Unavailable in other countries were the cassette tapes or CDs to let us practice speaking with the correct pronunciation. Next time we will purchase all of these at home and have them shipped to us en route. Here are a few terms essential in every country.

1. Thank you, hello, good day

2. Numbers 1–20

3. What, who and how

4. Prepositions: over, under, upon, behind, in front of, to the left, to the right, straight ahead

5. Food and drink

6. Travel terms: luggage, train station, bus stop, ticket

7. Telling time and more prepositions

8. Common verbs and nouns

9. Where, when and how much

Home School

What kid doesn't dream of being on vacation year-round? No classes, no homework, just play all day every day. (You can add in a couple of adults I know, too!) We put it plainly to the girls — study on the trip or fall back a year from their friends—which made the decision easy. At the dinner table we confronted each other, their fears and our determination to make it work. This generated many concerns, including:

· Subjects to teach

· Requirements to satisfy the school district upon returning

- Books, workbooks, supplies to take
- Motivation
- Tests
- Documentation needed

First step was contacting the school district to get a Scope and Sequence curriculum for each class. Math and English were taught adhering to these guidelines. World geography and history came from reading and discussing prominent authors in each country. Creative writing was a daily journal of thoughts and experiences. We experimented with teaching science, but finally abandoned it.

Home-schooling programs are well developed to make what at first seems an enormous task into a manageable one. The local home school association gave us a list of companies offering instruction materials. Key was finding ones that didn't require sending tests somewhere else to be graded.

The best advice came from our friend Cindy who had successfully home-schooled her son and daughter in their teenage years. Cindy stated, "*The Shurley Method* is the best I have ever seen for teaching English, bar none!"

We ordered online. When the materials finally arrived there were ten workbooks each for Geometry and Pre-algebra courses plus two of the *Shurley Method*'s inch-and-a-half-thick study books and a two-inch Teacher's Manual. This two-subject mountain soared higher than a stack of clothes for a year and weighed more than the rest of the suitcase. It was obvious that carrying a year's worth of courses was impossible unless we sacrificed all of our clothing.

The last couple of nights in town found us ripping heavy, hard covers off of books. (I felt a twinge of lawlessness in doing that.) English books were unbound and torn into trimester-sized sections, the latter two placed in boxes to be shipped when needed. Math workbooks were also divided, leaving a heavy, though more manageable stack of materials to carry. These travel boxes opened up possibilities to ship other items needed enroute such as guidebooks and language tapes. At any given time I would guess that fully one-fourth of the volume and weight in our luggage was paper!

Can you imagine having to spend the morning in your hotel room studying pronouns when the streets of Bangkok are beckoning? Many times each of us felt like throwing away the books . . . but we didn't.

Don't tell the girls, but we snuck in some practical learning as well. One night each week they were required to cook dinner; this included shopping at the local market, talking with shopkeepers and using that country's currency. Tricky, weren't we? In the labyrinthine city of Venice they were challenged to navigate the streets using maps and compass. Decisions and travel plans were round-table as much as possible.

The final step was the most uncertain. Returning home, we contacted the schools our daughters hoped to attend, trying our best to explain their education in the past year. We collected all the information on course plans and to what degree we felt goals had been accomplished, then put it in outline form. This summary was the document that enabled each girl to get credit for all the hard work and tears of trying to study while trekking the world for a year. In the end they received credit for English, Math, World History/Geography, Creative Writing, and PE (no couch potatoes here, we never stopped walking and hiking). Success!

Resources

Always borrow or buy the most recent editions of the following books from your local library or bookseller. If your local library does not have the most recent edition of a book, ask if they can borrow it from another library using the Inter-Library Loan system. Know too that the following books may be available in a variety of formats, including hardcover, softcover, ebook, audiobook and more.

Books on Airline Tickets and Planning Information

Take Your Kids to Europe: How to Travel Safely (and Sanely) in Europe with Your Children by Cynthia W. Harriman (Global Pequot Press)

The Practical Nomad: How to Travel Around the World by Edward Hasbrouck (Avalon Travel Publishing, Inc.)

Staying Healthy in Asia, Africa, and Latin America by Dirk G. Schroeder (Moon Travel Handbooks)

Books on Home Schooling

The Shurley Method Series by Brenda Shurley (Shurley Instructional Materials)

Books on Languages

Eyewitness Travel Phrase Books (Dorling Kindersley)

Lonely Planet Phrasebooks (Lonely Planet Publications)

10 Minutes a Day phrasebooks (Bilingual Books)

Magazine on International Travel

ITN: International Travel News (Martin Publications, Inc.). A monthly that provides information on many less-tourist-visited places with advertisements by smaller specialty tour operators. Website (www.intltravelnews.com) offers past articles, travel specials on custom tours and links to excellent information sites. Telephone: (916) 457-3643.

Around-the-World Air Ticket Websites

These tickets are often sold by consolidators and discount airfare companies with experience in multi-stop, extended complex itineraries. Many sites are good for initial explorations before picking up the phone to talk with a live person.

Air Brokers International, Inc. (www.airbrokers.com) Extensive tips and planning pages have information on travel documents, travel insurance www.insure.com, hotels, Rail Europe (with link to European private hostels) and Auto Europe.

Airtreks (www.airtreks.com) Look at the Trip Planner, an "imagine" section with experiences of other travelers, sample trips and tips.

JustFares.com (www.justfares.com) Ticketing site includes a travel planner, currency converter, hostel listing, example itineraries

Rail Travel Websites

BritRail (www.britrail.com) Website offers maps, schedules, trip planning, ticket purchasing, discount attraction cards and links to other British tourism information. Family and individual Travelcards for London transportation are also available.

Eurail (www.eurail.com) offers many choices in European countries, travel periods and ticketing methods. Purchase tickets online with free worldwide delivery.

ScanRail (www.scanrail.com) Scandinavian trains through Norway, Sweden, Denmark and Finland can be booked from the U.S., click "English" to change language. Purchasing their pass also gives discounts of up to 50 percent on buses and ferries, a significant savings.

Ferry Websites

Color Line (www.colorline.com) Ships traveling between Germany, Denmark, Sweden, and Norway.

(www.Ferries.gr) A large database of Greek ferry companies. Connections and schedules between Greece, Italy, Cyprus, Israel, Egypt, Turkey, Albania and all Greek Islands.

Fjord Line (www.fjordline.co.uk) Connects England, Norway and Denmark.

Silja Line (www.silja.us) Travels the Baltic Sea between Sweden, Finland, Russia, Estonia, and Germany.

Stena Line (www.stenaline.com) Service to Ireland to England, Scandinavia and north European routes.

Viking Line (www.vikingline.fi) Visits Sweden, Finland and Estonia.

Car Leasing Website

Auto France (www.autofrance.net) Peugeot car leasing at reasonable rates.

Accommodations

Gastgeber.net (www.gastgeber.net) A German-language site with some very good cottages all over Europe.

Gîtes de France (www.gites-de-france.fr) Offers a wide range of wonderful, inexpensive houses, flats, rural rentals and B&Bs across France. Make reservations online or by telephoning: 011-33-1-49-70-75-92 or faxing: 011-33-1-49-70-75-80. Be prepared to speak in French if you call — an English-speaking operator may not be available.

Hostels (www.iyhf.org and www.hiayh.org) Websites for the International Youth Hostel Federation and U.S. Hostelling International with links to hostel locations, descriptions and reservations.

Interhome (www.interhome.co.uk) Cottages, villas and other accommodations in Europe.

Shamrock Cottages (www.shamrockcottages.co.uk) Lovely cottages in Ireland to rent at reasonable rates.

Travel Guide Websites

Lonely Planet (www.lonelyplanet.com) Comprehensive travel website with excerpts from their guides. I especially like the "Thorn Tree" forums for opinionated advice and lively discussions. Includes finding a hostel accommodations page, travel advisories (although I prefer the U.S. State Department), even a personal trip journal website that allows you to order a CD after you get home but has a monthly fee charged for full service.

Rough Guides Travel (www.roughguides.com) Online excerpts from their travel guides, but without the accommodations sections (you have to buy the books). Also, journals submitted by fellow travelers, a traveler's health section and Travel Talk Forum that has a Round-the-World page.

Travel Planning Software

Rough Guides intouch Online (www.roughguidesintouch.com) Offers software and a website you can connect with anywhere in the world from Internet cafés or your own computer. Planning section plus online diary that friends can also access while you are on the road.

U.S. Government Websites

Center for Disease Control, Travelers Health (www.cdc.gov/travel) Lists regional and country disease outbreaks with preventative measures. Good information on malaria medicine and chloroquine resistance.

U.S. Department of State, Bureau of Consular Affairs (http://travel.state.gov) Issues travel warnings, public announcements and Consular Information Sheets for countries around the world. News Flash area has most recent warnings to monitor changing political climates. Also www.state.gov/travel/ has broad information covering many reasons for living abroad – travel, work, study, etc. It is worth checking these sites periodically as you prepare for your trip. Also has sections on passports and visas, country background notes and foreign consular offices (can access this abroad via Internet cafés when needed). www.travel.state.gov/foreignentryreqs.html lists visa and passport requirements by country.

Travel Advice Websites

BootsnAll Travel (www.bootsnall.com) Includes an exceptional variety of travel info on destinations, tickets, budget hotels, private hostels, vacation rentals, travel blogs and links to other sites. This site takes you to the brink of "tmi" (too much information).

One Bag (www.onebag.com) Excellent lists and insight on packing light.

Tourism Offices Worldwide Directory (www.towd.com) Search for destinations including U.S., many with websites. A good point to begin gathering information on various countries.

Fun Sites

TheTravelRag.com (www.thetravelrag.com) Interesting site with reader contributions. Wonderful photo section will get you excited about many new destinations.

Travel Adventures (www.traveladventures.org) Photographs, articles on destinations, plus travel forums.

WorldTrek Websites

www.WorldTrekOnline.com

www.TurnstoneTravel.com

Trip Budget

Why a Budget?

Next to finding the time, finding the money is the other big factor in planning a long term trip. Within the limits of reasonable family finances, for us at least, there were obvious financial constraints. The occasional loss of financial presence of mind would have to be few and far between, if we intended to meet our travel goals.

We didn't embark on a yearlong adventure because we wanted to save money. However, knowing how we were doing financially as we went along did give us a feeling of control. One of the underlying ideas of the trip experience was to maintain some semblance of a structured life, while the physical surroundings were constantly changing.

The operative word was discipline. That sounds harsh but discipline in a positive sense meant sticking to our objectives. Those included enjoying sights we'd never seen before, learning languages, carrying out a fulfilling home schooling program, staying physically fit, interacting with people and, of course, making it all the way around the world in a year.

Discipline also meant incorporating certain activities into our daily routine and doing them unfailingly. Choosing a place to stay, shopping for groceries, doing laundry all involve purchases, recording each purchase and regularly tallying them up gave organization to our daily lives, vital to the emotional and intellectual success of the whole adventure.

When we first talked about the budget with Lesley and Andrea, they were excited to be included in the discussion. To our surprise, they wanted to have an understanding of it all. At first they felt apprehensive about what it would mean to live on a budget. On the other side it helped them understand the trip was not just a random leap and that their parents had not entirely lost their minds.

Budget Background

Travel was always required as part of my job, and I had some ideas about what it cost to travel in the U.S. Over a four year period I had developed some averages by inputting general category totals into a spread sheet before turning in a biweekly expense report. Dividing the annual totals by the number of nights spent away from home gave me some average values for travel in the U.S. Those averages were the basis for our budget.

If you are an accountant or a detail-minded person, you may have budget categories of your own, but we distilled it down to six: Food, Accommodations, Surface Travel, Admissions, Miscellaneous, and Air Fares.

The sixth category, Air Fares, we kept separately. Carla purchased airline tickets in three big chunks, usually a month or more in advance of actually receiving the tickets. The tickets for the flight from Cairo to Mumbai in February, for example, were purchased in October when we were in France. That cost had nothing to do with the cost of traveling in France. We wanted to see the smooth flow of costs as we went along and air ticket purchases were somewhat lumpy.

We felt the travel costs within the U.S. would be a little on the high side of the world average. The items over which we had the most control were the cost of food, the level of accommodations we were prepared to accept and the means of surface travel. I put down some average values for Meals, Accommodations, Overland Travel, Air Travel, Admissions and Miscellaneous, added them all up for 365 days, and that was the budget.

The original budget was put into a spreadsheet, before we left home, and sent to our travel e-mail address; I wanted it handy so I could refer to it along the way. There were a couple of times I looked at it, but the average daily amount for each category was really all we needed to remember. After all, a budget is just a guideline, not the law. Little adjustments can be made. Some days you may spend less; some days you spend more. As long as it's not too outrageous in one direction, you'll be fine.

The budget categories were not rigid. We just tried to be consistent. It is not likely that you will want to go through the same painstaking detail that we did, but perhaps our experience will give you the kind of guidance that was not available when we were planning our trip. Of course, if you tend to be a "details" type of person, enjoy the challenge.

The Journal

The idea of keeping a cost journal was borrowed from the accounting profession, and it made the whole thing work. We truly had the desire to know what our trip cost and received a sense of pleasure from keeping track of how we were doing. The only way to do it was write everything down, pretty much the moment it happened. My journal was a four and a half inch by two and a half inch lined notebook with about forty pages and flexible paper cover. I kept the journal, along with copies of our passports, in my shirt pocket. Over the period of a year, I went through four notebooks.

When the girls purchased an ice cream snack, I'd just say, "What did you pay?" They would tell me, and I would write it down in terms of local currency. As we bought clothes, ate a meal, paid a toll, tipped a driver, it all went into the journal. The process became second nature. Every day I started by writing the date and our location in my notebook, then began putting down expenses as they happened.

Every few days I transferred the cost from my pocket journal to one of five sheets of notebook paper I kept in a zipper-sealed plastic bag, a general ledger in accounting terms. Each sheet represented a cost category, Food, Room, Travel, Admissions and Miscellaneous. At that point local currency was converted to U.S. dollars as I made the transfer. Each day I wrote down the amount and the running total for the category. That small effort allowed me to see how we were doing between any two dates.

Periodically I would make copies of my ledger sheets and send them home; thus, I had a cheap backup. With regard to a laptop computer, my advice is not to carry anything you are not prepared to lose. Besides, a computer would have been worthless in many places. So, we didn't carry one. I did, though, carry an inexpensive pocket calculator to help me with the totals.

Food

This budget category encompassed everything that entered our mouths: soft drinks, mints, gum, snacks, alcohol and, of course, groceries and restaurant meals (excluding medicine). While Food is where we achieved the greatest savings over our budgeted amount, it is not the place to skimp. Good, balanced nutrition comes first, then finances.

All four of us enjoy cooking. Working together in the kitchen is relaxing, and helps to create the important concept of home. The biggest adventure each week, when we arrived at a new location, was to find the grocery store and shop. New vegetables, cheeses, meats, breads, local wines and beer — we would walk the aisles, trying to figure out what things were and how we could put together meals. Buying and preparing food turned out to be one of our favorite sources of entertainment plus an enormous cost savings. Of course, we had to occasionally sample local specialties at restaurants as well.

The budget number for food was $72 per day for the four of us. In the major cities we spent every bit of our daily food budget just about every day — sometimes more. Breakfasts were frequently included in our room cost. I would make a judgment call as to the quantity of food offered then subtract it from Room cost and add it to the Food account. The gross average for food for the entire trip was $47.50 per day. That was a savings of $24.50 per day or $9,212.00 for the duration of the trip. When I use the term gross average, there are no qualifiers.

Room

Room means the place we slept, and what we paid for it. For a least the first half of the trip, we tried to stay in the same place for seven nights. That became less practical toward the end of the trip but had four beneficial results. The first benefit was we could rent cottages, apartments, or small houses. Even if we rented rooms in a pension or small hotel we could often negotiate a weekly rate at a meaningful discount. The second and largest benefit was the lower cost of food purchased at a grocery store and prepared in our kitchen rather than eating in restaurants. This also insured that I could find a good cup of coffee first thing in the morning.

The third benefit — home schooling — was facilitated by having enough room to spread out each morning and do lessons. Thus, Lesley and Andrea frequently had their own room.

The last and maybe most compelling reason to slow down and look for a cottage was the opportunity to interact with people. Staying put for a week is almost long enough to get comfortable. People going about their daily activities begin to recognize your face and some take time to pass a few words. The best places to visit, sights to see and local delicacies often come from recommendations of natives. You can remove yourself from the isolation of a car, walk into town and get to know a little about the place.

Our budget number for Room was $50 per night for the four of us. When we were in places like Moscow, Paris, Venice and Rome, we expected to pay more than we would in a small village in France or the southwest coast of Ireland. In the big cities we frequently paid $100 or more per night. The country stays sometimes were as low as $35 per night. The gross average for the trip was $58 per night. This number includes the cost of some pretty extravagant places in China that have a substantial markup for foreign tourists.

Travel

The Surface Travel category is a bit of a conglomeration. It includes all modes of travel except for items that involved some element of transportation but were purely for the purpose of visiting a particular site. Examples of excluded costs would be a tram ride up to the top of a mountain or boat ride up a small tributary to see a unique waterfall. It was a subjective call, but you have to draw the line somewhere. These other incidental transportation costs I included in Admissions.

I put airline tickets in a separate category, Air Transport. Many people seize upon the cost of airline tickets. It seems logical to expect they are the biggest part of transportation. The interesting result was that air travel was slightly less than the total for Surface Transportation.

The Surface Travel budget was based on paying $50 per day for a rental car and $10 per day for gas. That was $60 per day, every day, as the benchmark. In reality it covered ferryboat, cruise ship, bus, rail passes, rental cars, subways, taxis, rickshaws and "tuk-tuks." All these things got thrown into the Surface Travel category. The gross average was

$50.50 per day, so we were $9.50 USD under budget for the duration of 376 days. That amounted to a savings of $3,572.00 USD for that category.

Admissions

As originally conceived, Admissions were to be the cost of entering a museum, roadside attraction or some sort of educational event. However, we used it for everything that was site specific and educational or entertainment oriented. It ranged from tickets to a Gilbert and Sullivan operetta to donations at a Hindu shrine. That made it easy to determine where those costs went.

Most gratuities ended up in Admissions. A tip to a taxi driver would fall under Surface Transportation, but the more-or-less constant stream of tips to the sometimes marginally involved — self-appointed guides and hosts — ended up in Admissions.

I had hoped we would not pass each and every day in a museum but I allocated about $16 five days a week or $11.43 per day. Our actual Admissions cost worked out to be $15.40 per day, on average. Since these items were truly educational, going over budget wasn't viewed as a problem.

Miscellaneous

The Miscellaneous category picked up everything else. Put more succinctly, it was everything we bought along the way that we didn't eat. Included in this category were items like replacement clothing, soap, toothpaste and toilet articles, postage and shipping, school supplies, visa and departure fees. This was a catchall category, but these items had to go somewhere!

Bakshish, Tips and Gratuities

The best I can gather is that the term "bakshish" originated somewhere in the Eastern Mediterranean, in the Byzantine Empire. The word has taken root in many cultures. In the U.S. we call it a tip or gratuity.

Here again the difference between being on vacation and being on a long trip becomes quite apparent. Bakshish can mount up very quickly on a long trip. My only advice is to be very prudent and use your best judgment.

Currency

The issue of currency and exchange was pretty chaotic ranging from 0.7 British pounds per U.S. dollar to 1,374,000 Turkish lire per U.S. dollar. Even with the introduction of the Euro in the EU countries there still remain substantial cost differences for the same item between countries in part based on availability of goods but also due to local taxes, the Value Added Tax (VAT). To make the whole thing more tractable, I converted everything to U.S. dollars at the exchange rate we experienced at the time we were in each country.

Air Travel

The total cost of air travel for the entire trip was $17,944.64. Most of this cost was in the big leaps between Moscow to Prague, New Delhi to Bangkok and on to Beijing. There is really no other way to cover vast distances around the Pacific than to fly, unless you have a lot more time than we did.

The Bottom Line

The all-inclusive cost of traveling for the period of a year for four people was $187 per day. There are a few reliable generalizations you can make from what we learned. Clearly, packaged travel is more expensive than arranging it yourself. Ireland was the most economical place to travel for us, at a $104 per day. The majority of the time in Ireland we spent in cottages cooking our own food. On the other end of the scale were the cost of traveling in Egypt at $232 per day and China at $334 per day, where we were required to purchase prearranged packages prior to our arrival in the country. I would say that if you shopped pretty hard you could travel in China more cheaply than we did.

India would probably have cost less if we had done more booking on our own. Even with three weeks of more or less arranged touring in India, it is still a bargain. Thailand is just a great place to go and moderately priced.

If you simply multiply our average daily cost of $187 by the days you expect to travel, you will see what it might cost for a family of four to travel at the level we chose. Think about the descriptions of some of the places we stayed and the kind of food we ate. You can then adjust upward or downward what you think your budget might look like.

It would be entirely incorrect to take our numbers and divide them in half for two people traveling. There are some definite advantages traveling as a group of four and also as a family. The number of people has the biggest impact on cost. It does not, for example, cost proportionately more to rent a car for four people compared to two. Many cottages or vacation flats rent by the week and don't charge for additional people. Food preparation just gets cheaper as you add people and spread the cost of material across more participants.

Being a family has its ups and downs, but there is a level of familiarity that is difficult to develop with traveling companions. That might result in additional room costs, especially after several months. A family also has a preestablished hierarchy, and the decision making process is not 100 percent democratic.

Carla and I set the tenor and pace of travel and also looked after group finances. Not all travelers will be willing to submit to the rigors of a budget. As for the rest, go, enjoy, and come back happy with what you've accomplished.

Our WorldTrek is a priceless chapter in our lives.

Index

About the Authors

Russell Fisher grew up in Canton, Ohio and remembers falling victim to the allure of distant horizons during a fourth grade geography class. He moved west after high school, and a six year adventure in Socorro, New Mexico, earned him bachelor's and master's degrees in Geology from New Mexico Tech — plus his traveling companion Carla, stalwart navigator and love of his life. Between family adventures Russ manages construction and business development projects, works weekends with Habitat for Humanity and tutors students in math.

Carla Fisher was born in Gunnison, Colorado. She inherited a love of travel and the outdoors from her parents, a U.S. Forest Service accountant and a farm girl from Montrose, Colorado, and the family explored the U.S. from border to border and coast to coast. After she finished high school in Albuquerque, New Mexico, Carla earned a bachelor's degree in Biology from New Mexico Tech and a master's degree in Fisheries Science from University of Arizona. Since returning from the WorldTrek, Carla arranges travel excursions through Turnstone Travel (www.TurnstoneTravel.com) and tutors Sudanese students in math and English.

Russ and Carla were married in Ciudad Juarez, Mexico, and eventually settled in The Woodlands, Texas. They raised two daughters, Lesley and Andrea, who were exposed at early ages to the thrills and challenges of travel, domestic and international. After the WorldTrek, Lesley finished high school then enrolled in engineering at University of Missouri-Rolla, where she also volunteered for service in the U.S. Army ROTC. Andrea donates a portion of her free time to Habitat for Humanity and, with a bent for things practical, plans to pursue a career in engineering.

Having completed one passage around the planet, the Fishers wait with anticipation for the next WorldTrek opportunity — to take to the road on a moment's notice, equipped with a love of adventure *and the PayDay candy bar, in case someone should get hungry along the way.*

The Fishers can be reached through their website:

www.WorldTrekOnline.com

Reader's Planning Pages

Reader's Planning Pages

Reader's Planning Pages

Reader's Planning Pages

Reader's Planning Pages

Reader's Planning Pages

Reader's Planning Pages